ROMAN DEATH

Roman Death

The Dying and the Dead in
Ancient Rome

Valerie M. Hope

continuum

Continuum UK, The Tower Building, 11 York Road, London SE1 7NX
Continuum US, 80 Maiden Lane, Suite 704, New York, NY 10038

www.continuumbooks.com

First published 2009

British Library Cataloguing-in-Publication Data
A catalogue record for this book is available from the British Library.

ISBN 978 1 84725 038 4

Typeset by Pindar NZ, Auckland, New Zealand
Printed and bound by MPG Books Ltd, Cornwall, Great Britain

Contents

For Oliver, Matthew and Jacob

Illustrations

17   Tombstone of Lucius Vettius Alexander (ex-slave), Vettia
        Polla (free-born), Vettia Eleutheris (ex-slave) and Vettia
        Hospita (ex-slave).

Acknowledgements

I would like to thank the staff at Continuum, especially Michael Greenwood, for their help during this project. Thanks are also due to my colleagues at the Department of Classical Studies at the Open University, and above all to my family: my parents John and Margaret Hope, my husband Art and children Oliver, Matthew and Jacob, without whose support and patience writing this book would have been impossible.

Abbreviations used in Notes

AE   *L' Année Épigraphique* (Paris 1888–)

CIG *Corpus Inscriptionum Graecarum* (Berlin 1828–77)

CIL *Corpus Inscriptionum Latinarum* (Berlin 1863–)

ILS *Inscriptiones Latinae Selectae* (H. Dessau (ed.): Berlin 1892–1916)

RIB *Roman Inscriptions of Britain* (R.G. Collingwood and Wright, R. (eds.): Oxford 1965 and 1995)

Note inscriptions are from Rome (largely found in *CIL* volume 6) unless otherwise stated in the text or notes.

Introduction

*Regulus has lost his son, the one evil he did not deserve . . . Now that his
son is dead he mourns insanely. The boy used to own a number of Gallic
ponies for riding and driving, also dogs of all sizes, and nightingales,
parrots, and blackbirds; Regulus had them all killed around the pyre.
That was not grief but a show of grief.*

*Regulus decided to mourn his son, so he mourns like no one else. He
decided to commission as many statues and portraits of the boy as could
be made, and all the workshops are busy portraying him in colour, in
wax, bronze, silver, gold, ivory and marble. He even collected a large
audience recently to hear him read a book of his son's life: the life of a
mere boy! Nevertheless he read it, and has had many copies made to send
throughout Italy and the provinces. He has written a public letter to the
town councils asking them to elect one of their number with the best voice
to give a reading of the work.*[1]

In his letters on the death of the son of Marcus Aquilius Regulus, a fellow
but rival senator and orator, Pliny the Younger employed a judgemental
tone. There was something showy, false and even inappropriate in Regulus'
behaviour. In Pliny's opinion this was not how a Roman gentleman should
behave. The death of the young man became a means for the bereaved
father to play out his grief in public and for others, such as Pliny, to
observe, comment and provide counter-perspectives. Throughout his
letters Pliny the Younger provides many fascinating insights into the
social and political world of Rome at the end of the first century AD,
including how people died, the impact of their deaths and how they were
mourned for, commemorated and missed. These aspects of Roman death
were clearly worthy of observation and comment. Pliny's letters included
accounts of deaths through disease and suicide, of deaths that were bravely

met and of how people prepared for death by writing wills and ordering monuments. The letters included obituary notices that praised the dead and commented on the grief of the survivors. Some letters noted people's belief in ghosts and spirits, and the memory strategies – statues, tombs, bequests, speeches and memoirs – that sought to keep the names of the dead alive.

The letters touched upon the lives of members of Pliny's social sphere, largely his male aristocratic colleagues, but also their wives and children and some of the slaves and freed slaves who were essential to the running of their lives. The letters were a showcase for Pliny; they were not casual correspondence but carefully written vignettes about his life, which allowed him to show humanity and observe it, or the lack of it, in others. We can note, for example, that Regulus may have received the rough side of Pliny's literary tongue, but his friend Fundanus, similarly bereft at the loss of a child, received sympathy and understanding (*see* p. 51).

How people died and how they were buried, commemorated, mourned and remembered were all central aspects of life in Rome and its empire; they demanded scrutiny, comment and ultimately judgement. To say that death was an important and unavoidable element of life in ancient Rome, as Pliny's letters illustrate, may be to state the obvious. Mortality rates were in all probability high (*see* p. 43), and death was ever present and to some extent an accepted feature of daily life. Nevertheless, death still represented the ultimate challenge, which for the stability of families and society needed to be confronted, mediated and controlled. To investigate death and funerary customs in any time period or culture is to explore the mechanisms a society employs to explain, cope with and regroup itself in the face of life's greatest obstacle, and thereby such an investigation goes to the very heart of societal identity and self-definition. Human life is centred on the human body and on controlling the body of the self and others; bodies and body parts are filled with cultural symbolism. Death transforms the body, challenging the identity and personhood of the individual and their status among the living. Funerary, mourning and commemorative rituals allow the survivors to negotiate a pathway through death, to remove the body from this world and then reintegrate the identity and memory of the dead into the world of the living. The intention of this book is to look at these processes in the Roman world. How did people prepare for death spiritually, practically and emotionally? How did rituals guide people's behaviour? Were the dead imbued with a new but separate life? How were the living supposed to mourn for the dead and remember and commemorate them? This book is unusual in seeking to encompass all these themes and in addressing Roman death as a subject. Much has been written about the varied aspects of funerary customs – about, for example, tombs, monuments, and funerals – but rarely is death, from pre-death planning to the grave or from the deathbed to the afterlife, viewed as an integrated topic. Doing so allows for the gauging of the impact of death on Roman life while throwing new light on Rome and its society.[2]

This book is intended to provide an account of Roman death rituals and funerary customs that will appeal to a wide spectrum of readers. Ancient sources are given in translation, and some basic information and reminders about the extent, in terms of chronology and geography, of the Roman Empire are provided in this introduction (see also the appendices). At times it has been necessary to use broad brushstrokes in order to cover a lot of ground, in terms of sources and information, in a small space, but the intention has remained to provide a survey that places renewed emphasis on the importance of death, dying and the dead in ancient Rome.

THE ROMAN ERA

The chronological scope of this book is broadly the first century BC to the second century AD. These three centuries are rich in evidence of all types and represent the height of the expansion and maintenance of Roman power. However, Rome, the city and its empire, lasted for many centuries, and chronological boundaries cannot always be strictly enforced in any study. The best surviving description of an élite Roman funeral, for example, dates to the second century BC, and sometimes late sources, including Christian authors, provide valuable insights into the 'old customs'. Besides which, Rome was a city very much aware of its past, drawing strength and essential aspects of its identity from tradition and ancestral customs. This is not to say that things were unchanging, although appeals 'to get back to basics' and to traditional virtue suggest the continuing importance of legitimizing the present through the past.

Rome evolved from a small town to become the leading city of a vast empire, and its appearance, organization and population also evolved. Some of the most striking and dramatic changes were shifts in governmental structures, most notably from the élite rule of the Senate, with its two annually elected leading consuls that controlled Rome for the final centuries BC, to the rule of one man, the emperor, from 31 BC. The former system and period is termed the Republic, whereas the rule of the emperors is entitled the Empire, Principate or Imperial era. The flux, infighting and ultimately adaptation to the new system that characterized much of the first century BC and the early to mid first century AD should not be underestimated. People, especially the senatorial élite, had to renegotiate their social and political roles, often in precarious and dangerous times. The second century AD represented a period of greater acceptance of the Imperial system of government and to some extent greater stability. Thereafter the empire and its governmental structures entered a period of protracted decline.

This is not the place to give a detailed chronological narrative of the Roman era, but it may be useful to provide a thumbnail sketch from the perspective of some of the characters who appear in this book. It should be noted that such a sketch prioritizes the city of Rome and leading political characters and authors, but at this stage it will serve to highlight, in a basic fashion, how political systems and society shifted, while introducing some key themes and names related to the study of Roman death.

The politician, orator and writer Cicero provides a useful starting point. Cicero's life (106–43 BC) spanned the end of the Republic, the system that he staunchly served and defended. Cicero was consul in 63 BC, and he witnessed the power struggle between Pompey and Julius Caesar, the assassination of the latter, the rise of Octavian and the power-sharing of Mark Antony, Lepidus and Octavian (the second triumvirate). Cicero fell victim to Antony in 43 BC. Cicero's surviving works are rich and varied. He was a prolific writer who provides us with many valuable insights into death and funerary customs, including laws and honours concerning burial, philosophical musings on how to confront death and grief, and the touching letters written at the death of his own daughter, Tullia. In Cicero we have a statesman, philosopher and family man who was conscious of the traditional political and philosophical ideals, such as self-sacrifice for the state and the need to put public duty before private sentiment, but who was none the less put to the test by both personal and political trials.

In 31 BC, after the defeat of Mark Antony at the Battle of Actium, Octavian (later to take the name Augustus) became in effect the first emperor of Rome. Uniting the city and empire after years of civil conflict was no easy matter, and literature and architecture (including a vast Imperial mausoleum – see Figure 13) that promoted the new regime were integral to forging a revived, but traditionally based, image for emperor and city. Augustus claimed to have restored the Republic, and Republican traditions, values and memories loomed large in what was in fact a new Imperial age. Poets such as Horace, Virgil, Ovid and Propertius received patronage from Augustus and his circle, and they often praised the new regime in their works, if not completely forgetting the destruction of civil war and toying with more subversive subject matter such as love. These poets, especially Virgil in his great epic *The Aeneid*, often looked to the past, to ancestors and to the dead to justify the creation of the new present.

By the mid first century AD, the Julio-Claudian dynasty, the descendants of Augustus and his wife Livia, was on the point of collapse. Nero was the last Julio-Claudian emperor (AD 54–68), and the early years of his reign, when he was under the guidance of Seneca the Younger, were regarded as good. Seneca the Younger (c. 4 BC–AD 65) was an important statesman, but he was also a Stoic philosopher, with the two roles often seeming ill matched. Seneca is an essential source for the customs and expectations that surrounded death and dying at this period. In his writings Seneca explored ways to die calmly and bravely, how to accept human mortality and how to cope with grief. Seneca's unwavering perspective often reflected hard-line philosophy, and we cannot take his views as being necessarily representative of the wider populace, but his life and works illustrate how the élite were negotiating a role in the Imperial system, and trying to hold onto the traditional virtues of freedom, dignity and respect in an increasingly tyrannical regime of one-man rule. Seneca was ultimately implicated in a conspiracy against Nero and sentenced to death by enforced suicide in AD 65. Another probable victim of Nero's was the author Petronius, best known for his satirical novel *The Satyricon*. One of the central characters in this work is the crass and ostentatious freed slave Trimalchio, who verges on having an obsession with death and all things funereal. At an extravagant dinner party Trimalchio reads his will aloud, plans his tomb and even enacts his own funeral. Petronius was playing with the human challenge of squaring life and death, framed by debates current in his own day about who deserved to be remembered after death and how individuals should be mourned and commemorated. Trimalchio is a fictional character, a parody, but Petronius was perhaps also highlighting a real feature of the Imperial system, which allowed men such as Trimalchio, including former slaves, to get on and to get rich, while still denying them the advantages of high titles and élite status.

Following the civil wars of AD 69, Rome came to be dominated, in the latter part of the first century AD, by the Flavian dynasty. The poet Statius wrote under the final emperor of the dynasty, Domitian. For our purposes the poetry of Statius stands out for its expressions of grief, loss and heartfelt lament (*see* p. 147–8). The work of Statius seems to represent a greater sense of emotional freedom, a challenging of élite formal 'stiff upper lip' ideals, that would have been frowned upon by the likes of Seneca the Younger. The authors Tacitus and Pliny the Younger also lived through the regime of Domitian and prospered, although they would subsequently blacken the name of the damned emperor. Tacitus and Pliny the Younger wrote mainly during the reign of Emperor Trajan, who was perceived as a good and reliable emperor, famed for extending the empire and ruling benignly. Under Trajan, a historian such as Tacitus could look back on earlier emperors and expose them as little more than tyrants or puppets. Tacitus (c. AD 56–118) had a distinguished public career, serving as suffect consul in AD 97. In his works literary death scenes become particularly evocative: how many people were killed or forced to suicide under an emperor was telling, as was how individuals met their death. Pliny the Younger (c. AD 61–112), who was consul in AD 100 and ended his career serving the emperor in Bithynia, provides insights into the values and principles that were honoured, or supposed to be honoured, by the élite of this period, including those surrounding death, dying and the bereaved (*see* p. 1–2).

The second century AD, under the emperors Hadrian, Antoninus Pius and Marcus Aurelius, was seen as a time of relative stability. The boundaries between Rome, Italy and Empire were becoming increasingly fluid. Plutarch (c. AD 50–120), a prolific writer in Greek, lived at the cusp of this age, producing philosophical discussions and also a series of biographies, that consisted of parallel lives of Greek and Roman statesmen. In biography the death scene has elevated status, the final moments of a life providing its crowning or failing finale. Plutarch provides fascinating insights into the importance of how a 'Roman' died and how the memory of that death was propagated. Another interesting character, about whose life we know little, was Lucian (born c. AD 120). Lucian originated from Samosata (Syria) and was a prolific writer in Greek. He wrote rhetorical works fusing comedy and philosophy, often with a satirical bent. Lucian is a potent reminder of the cosmopolitan nature of the empire. He may never have visited Rome and we cannot know for sure who read his works, although their survival is an indication of his popularity. Lucian provides an often irreverent and challenging look at the traditions, including funerary traditions, that underpinned the Graeco-Roman world of the second century AD.

A basic overview, with a few of the names that will star in this book, serves to highlight the length and breadth of the period under consideration; how death, dying and the dead were essential subject matter in varied literary genres; and how the authors' agendas, including how they described death and death rituals, were shaped by the political and social contexts in which they wrote. One of the challenges of investigating funerary customs across this period is that of identifying and understanding change. Evidence for some customs, funerals or will-making for example, either clusters into certain periods or is stretched across several centuries. There is a real danger of piecing together the evidence to create a picture that lacks any sense of chronological specificity. We cannot assume that a funeral held in the first century BC would be identical to one held in the second century AD or that mourners always behaved the same regardless of era. Unfortunately, the often-patchy nature of the evidence means that some generalizations are inevitable or at least cannot be completely avoided. However, it is possible to identify some chronological changes which suggest that how people were expected to die, how they were buried and how they were commemorated did shift in subtle ways that can often be related to changes in the political and social systems.

ROME AND EMPIRE

If the Roman era was vast in terms of time, it was also vast in terms of space. The empire stretched from north Africa to north Britain, embracing people of varied cultures, religions and languages. A process of so-called 'Romanization' is often explored by modern investigators. To what extent was the empire homogenized? Were 'little Romes' founded across the empire, with people dressing in togas, speaking Latin and going to the forum? The reality, where it can be investigated, was often a more subtle process of cultural fusion and dialogue. It is not the place of this volume to explore these issues in detail, although it is worth noting the role that funeral and burial customs often play in illuminating the interaction between Roman and indigenous cultures and identities.[3]

The focus of this volume is largely Italy and the city of Rome. However, as with chronological parameters, it is hard to draw definitive boundaries. Authors, for example Lucian (see above), were not always from Rome; epitaphs and monuments that provide fascinating insights survive from across the empire. Rome was part of the empire, and the empire in all its varied forms often came to Rome and vice versa. Note, for example, how in promoting the memory of his son, a lad who had probably rarely left the city, Regulus sent copies of the boy's eulogy to towns in Italy and the provinces. Rome was the centre of the known universe, and it is on Rome that much of the available evidence (especially literary) is focused, but Rome was underpinned by the empire.

One fundamental relationship was that between Rome and Greece. In many respects, despite its supremacy, Rome lived in the shadow of Greece and its former glories. Rome may have become the territorial master of Greece, but the intellectual, artistic and cultural legacy of the Greeks was a potent and continuing presence. Roman or Latin philosophy, architecture, art and literature all had Greek antecedents. The main philosophical schools of the Epicureans and Stoics (*see* p. 19–21) originated in Greece; literature such as poetic laments and philosophical consolations, even if composed in Latin, often adapted Greek models (*see* Chapter 5); beliefs in the afterlife built on Greek traditions (*see* Chapter 6). Often we need to speak not of Roman culture but of Graeco-Roman culture, an amalgam of influences in which it can be difficult to isolate the different strands. However, this is not to say that there was no such thing as a Roman identity. In particular, the élite of the late Republic and early Imperial period distinguished between Greece and Rome, maintaining the superiority of the latter. Many aspects of Greek life and culture may have been admired, or even aspired to, and this was especially so in the second century AD when there was a renaissance of some aspects of Greek culture (the Second Sophistic), but what was adopted was made to fit the Roman vision. In studying funerary and commemorative rituals, it can sometimes be difficult, and even needless, to separate the Greek from the Roman, but we still need to remember that how one died, was buried and commemorated could be part and parcel of self-definition. Where rituals and customs actually originated could matter less than the belief that one was following the traditions – traditions that were firmly believed to be rooted in Rome's past.

SOCIETY AND SOURCES

Roman society was patriarchal and hierarchical. During the late Republic, power was concentrated in the hands of senatorial families; these were the *nobiles*, or society's élite. Under the Imperial system the Senate retained its importance. It furnished the emperor with advisers, governors and army commanders. These senators, numbering at most 600 men, were a small minority (even if one includes their families) of Rome's population, let alone that of the empire. The equestrian order (*equites*), for membership of which certain property qualifications had to be met, was a larger group, the administrative roles of whom increased under the emperors. Some equestrians were as wealthy and influential as senators. The wider population, sometimes termed the urban plebs or masses, was made up of Roman citizens, non-citizen provincials, ex-slaves (who became citizens if formally manumitted) and slaves. There was a clear status hierarchy, with the emperor at the top of the pile, the lower orders fanning out beneath and slaves at the bottom. However, this hierarchy was not unchangeable. Families died out, the ranks of senators had to be replenished, new equestrians were made, slaves were freed and non-citizens were given citizenship. People's status and fortunes could change. Cicero, for example, was the first member of his family to make it to the Senate. There were some glass ceilings that could not be broken; an ex-slave, even one as wealthy as the fictional Trimalchio, could not become a senator or equestrian, but his children or grandchildren, if free-born citizens (and extremely fortunate and well-connected!), might make such strides.[4]

The major access point to Roman society, especially its higher echelons, is the surviving literature written during this period. All types of literary evidence can illuminate attitudes toward death and funerary customs.

Legal texts record the laws and regulations associated with the transmission of property and the respectful burial of the dead. Biography and history recall the deaths of the great and good, and the impact of deaths upon the bereaved. Philosophy examines the ideals associated with facing death and how to accept the mortality of the self and others. Poetry (in all its guises – epic, satire, lament, elegy), whether dealing with mythical or non-mythical subjects, opens up the world of sorrow, loss, acceptance and afterlife beliefs. Death and its impact was everywhere, and it inevitably pervaded all types of literature.

The surviving literature of the Roman period, however, has serious limitations: it tends to present a view of the world centred on the city of Rome and it was also the product of, and mainly intended for the consumption of, a small, male, educated, élite minority. Women, children, the poor and those of limited education might read or be read to, but they were not authors. Writers were men, mainly of high status (senators or wealthy equestrians) or supported by those of high status. The perspectives these writers present cannot be seen as representative of society at large. We struggle to hear the voice of the majority. In terms of the available literary evidence for death, burial and commemoration, we are then presented largely with male élite ideals about how to die well and mourn well and about the importance of memory. It can be difficult to move beyond these perspectives and to understand how the wider population regarded their mortality, how they expressed their grief and whether they believed in the afterlife. It is not that authors reveal nothing about other social groups, but they are often dismissive of the beliefs and practices of others, contrasting them with traditional élite ideals (see Chapter Five, for example, on the ideals and stereotypes associated with mourning). To broaden the perspective and challenge the élite male bias, we need to look beyond literature.

Literature is complemented by other sources. Funerals and the commemoration of the dead have left many material residues. Epitaphs inscribed onto stone survive in their thousands, and funerary monuments, sculpted and decorated, that marked graves or held human remains are frequent discoveries across the empire. Skeletal remains and the graves themselves also hold clues to the people and their beliefs and customs. All this evidence was produced by, or preserves traces of, a wide social range of people. The élite or privileged voice may remain the loudest, but we can at least try to restore, in part, the voice of the silent majority. Where possible in this book, an integrated approach is taken to the evidence. Previous scholarship has often focused on specific authors, genres or types of evidence. Here, to illuminate the varied aspects of Roman death, the full range of literary genres, as well as visual, material and epigraphic evidence is used.

LIFE AND DEATH

This book is nominally about the dead, but in reality it is very much about the living. It is living people who write wills, build tombs, organize funerals and remember the dead. To study death, or more accurately a society's death beliefs, customs and rituals, is to illuminate the living society. It is a frequent irony that we can often learn more about a society through its dead than through its living; or at least that skeletal remains, graves, tombs and cemeteries are often better preserved than other aspects of life.

The evidence for Roman death and burial is substantial, although it is far from being the only available evidence for Roman society. It is thus not possible to engage with everything that is relevant to the chosen topic in a single book. Note, for example, that thousands upon thousands of graves have been excavated and that epitaphs also survive in vast quantities. It is therefore understandable that the subject has previously often remained bound by disciplines. Archaeologists dig up graves, epigraphists study inscriptions, art historians focus on funerary sculpture, textual specialists dissect poetry and so on. Recent decades have seen a more contextualized approach to the evidence and, as a result, increasing understanding of the Roman traditions surrounding death. However, much of this research still focuses, for practical reasons, on single features of Roman death, such as the funeral, consolation literature or funerary monuments. This book seeks to integrate not just different types of evidence but also the varied facets of the process of death and dying – to trace all aspects of the journey(s) followed by the dying, the dead and the bereaved.[5]

The book is organized into six chapters that approximate to the course of the process of dying, disposal and acceptance. Chapter One considers how people planned for their death philosophically and practically. Chapter Two analyses life expectancy, the ways in which people died and how they were expected to die. Chapter Three considers the evidence for Roman funerals and how the corpse was prepared, conveyed to the cemetery and then disposed of. Chapter Four discusses afterlife beliefs – what people expected for themselves and their loved ones after death. Chapter Five looks at the survivors and how the bereaved expressed and coped with their loss. Finally, Chapter Six evaluates the place of the cemetery in Roman life, the interaction between the living and the dead and the importance of memory. At times, for the sake of brevity and clarity, it has not been possible to provide detailed analysis of all features of Roman life. For example, to fully understand Stoic and Epicurean teachings about death (*see* p. 19–21) would involve further engagement with the wider tenets of these philosophies, and this is something that is just not possible in the context of this book. I have provided, however, where possible, detailed notes and a substantial bibliography, allowing those who are interested to pursue specific strands further. Another caveat is that, as noted above, the focus in this volume is largely the city of Rome. I have chosen not to engage extensively with the mainly archaeological evidence for death and burial surviving from the Roman provinces. Much remains to be written, in an accessible form, on death rituals in the provinces, but it is unfortunately beyond the scope of this book.

Despite sometimes employing broad brushstrokes to tell the 'story' of Roman death, the intention remains to highlight the significance of death, dying and the dead in ancient Rome. As the letters of Pliny the Younger make clear, how people died and how they were buried and commemorated mattered; these things were noted, commented upon and analysed. Roman authors realized that death was revealing, both about individuals and about society overall. The same holds true for the modern historian; the remains of death rituals are a fundamental, rich and exciting source that has the potential to reveal much about the original society's organization, social structures and beliefs and how these were affected by factors such as chronology and political change. What has survived of the Roman way of death is not just dictated by chance, but instead reflects the careful decisions of the living to 'inscribe' or 'memorialize' their values onto the dead. Death is always interwoven with life and can become a tool manipulated to reflect and reinforce what is important to the living.

Across the chapters of this book certain themes emerge as being particularly important in both the ancient and modern evaluation and commentary on Roman death; these include gender, memory and self-identity. At the outset I would like to highlight two themes. One is the balance between continuity and change. Whether speaking of funerals, mourning practices or afterlife beliefs, ancient commentators often dwelled upon the importance of tradition – of doing things as the ancestors had done and of maintaining Roman customs and identity as enshrined in Roman funerary practices. As we shall see, the real antiquity and origins of many rituals and beliefs were open for debate, but the perception of their 'Roman-ness' remained key. Simultaneously, there was an awareness of change – that people did not mourn quite as they used to or that funerary monuments may have had their day. For us it is fascinating to quantify and to trace changes in epitaph production, for example (*see* p. 171), and to seek to understand what caused this in terms of social, political or economic factors, but the very fact that the ancients themselves also commented upon change, if not seeking to quantify it, and noted it in many aspects of their funerary customs is just as striking. A second theme is the extent of the interaction between the living and the dead. The living were supposed to be active in their remembrance of the dead, visiting graves, observing festivals and honouring the dead. Memory strategies, the content of wills, tomb design, afterlife beliefs and cemetery location all aimed to tie the living to the dead. This is worth stressing because it may seem strange or distant to a modern observer who is used to the rapid reduction of the dead to a handful of ashes, for whom remembrance is largely private and personal and 'moving on' is the best way to compartmentalize the dead. For the Romans, interaction with the dead characterized not just death and funerary rituals but also many aspects of daily life.

INVESTIGATING ROMAN DEATH

This introduction has sought briefly to identify the importance of investigating Roman death and also to point out the inherent challenges. Piecing together the evidence from across the social, chronological and geographic range can be like assembling a jigsaw puzzle. And taking a piece from here and a piece from there, a few lines from this poet, an epitaph from this province, a grave from that date, can be problematic. It is all too easy to lose chronological, geographic and social specificity and thereby create a sort of composite Roman who never could have existed in space or time. It is important to be aware always of the nature of the evidence and the chronological, geographic and status perspectives that it represents. It is all too easy to speak of 'Roman' customs or 'Roman' rituals without careful consideration as to what type of 'Roman' we are speaking of and when that 'Roman' lived. However, we should not throw the proverbial baby out with the bath water, and sometimes we have to take the risk and assemble the jigsaw, even while questioning the value of each piece.

Issues of methodology are particularly potent in the study of a subject such as Roman death. Attitudes toward death and funerary customs were a central aspect of life but were rarely documented in blow-by-blow detail. We are left to wonder how representative an author such as Pliny the Younger was, whether people really believed what they said in epitaphs and to what extent tradition and convention primarily governed behaviour. But these very questions are still worth raising and exploring, and they feed into wider issues about Roman identity, society and potential changes across time. It is important to see dying and death in ancient Rome as a process that stretched across individual lives, across generations and across the Roman era. A study such as this illuminates the 'Roman' way of death while highlighting the fact that the expectations surrounding the dying, the dead and the bereaved were not necessarily unchanging across time, space and social status.

1

Facing Mortality

Death is the one great certainty of life, but how and to what extent do people confront the fact of their own mortality? In modern Western society death can seem distant and removed. Death is medicalized and confined to old age; it is not part of people's daily experience. It has been argued that death is a taboo subject, something that is not openly discussed or anticipated. How a Roman thought of, experienced and prepared for death would have been very different. High levels of mortality suggest that, at the very least, death could be up close and personal; death did not strike down just the elderly, nor was it sanitized and removed from sight. Rome and its empire were dangerous places to live: cities were dirty, polluted and violent. Death took the young and old alike and must have wrecked lives on a daily basis, and not just those of its victims; by removing children, death took away the future hopes of parents, and by removing adults, death took the financial stability of any dependants. For every family, death could undermine its emotional and economic stability and threaten its very survival.

Many who lived in the Roman era must have been all too aware of their own mortality. At times Roman life can even appear a little morbid. *Memento mori* (reminders of death), an obsession with last wills, numerous monuments to the dead, gladiators fighting to the bitter end and philosophers who argued that any day might be one's last all suggest that death and the dead were close neighbours to the living, neighbours that were to be confronted rather than shunned. Yet it still remains difficult to judge how the people of Rome and its empire engaged with the concept of their own mortality, since so much of the surviving evidence presents the skewed perspective of the wealthy male élite. For the disenfranchised, slaves, the urban poor, women and children the perspective on and prospect of inevitable death is almost impossible to trace.

There were mechanisms available to assist people (especially, although not exclusively, the wealthy male élite) to negotiate, accept and engage with the death of the self and of others. Preparing for death could involve practical, emotional, spiritual and philosophical elements. Which of these were selected and in what combination would have differed for every individual. This chapter focuses primarily on the practical, and some philosophical, preparations associated with the death of the self. This is not to deny the primarily emotional and spiritual dimensions to the death experience, and these will be explored in later chapters (Chapters Four and Five). At this stage it is worth noting that Roman notions about the hereafter were often sketchy, which meant that for many people religion might not have been fundamental in how perspectives were shaped and how death was faced. Confronting death was less about spiritual preparations for the afterlife and more about accepting one's fate and making practical plans for worldly posterity. In short, there were certain things that a good Roman was supposed to do about his death, not just for himself but also for his family and heirs: he needed to write a will, plan his memorial and think about the reputation that he would leave behind.

A PHILOSOPHY OF DEATH

For the serious-minded, death defined life. The most important surviving insights about facing death originate from the pens of ancient philosophers rather than from authors on religion or from canonical religious texts. As Plato had put it, 'the whole life of a philosopher is a preparation for death'. There were different viewpoints on how death should be faced and how the fact of mortality should influence life. Most philosophers, of whatever doctrine, believed that the inevitability of death implied a responsibility to live life seriously, sensibly and virtuously, accepting that death would come to all alike.[1]

All that you see will soon perish and those who see its passing will soon perish too; and then what difference will there be between one who lives to the greatest age and the baby that dies in its cradle?[2]

Ancient philosophy sought to demystify death and challenge the traditional superstitions that surrounded it (*see* p. 112–15). A fundamental issue was whether man had a soul, or some sort of spirit or life force, that might survive death. Among philosophers at least, there were diverging opinions about whether the soul existed and about its nature and its fate at death. According to Cicero, the great orator, writer and politician of the mid first century BC, some philosophers believed that the soul was located in the heart and others that it was in the brain, while still others identified the soul with breath. Cicero continued by noting that the Stoics held the soul to be fire, while some individuals even equated the soul with musical harmony, numbers and movement. In popular beliefs the soul was thought to leave the body at death, and it could be imagined as a moth or butterfly exiting from the mouth and flying away to the kingdom of the dead. For the philosophical schools, whether the soul survived death, and what happened to it if it did, differed greatly. Followers of Epicurus and Aristotle believed that death was annihilation; followers of Plato believed that the soul was immortal; Orphic-Pythagoreans believed in cyclical reincarnation; and the Stoics believed that souls might be liberated but had little subsequent independent being. To a great extent the survival and fate of the soul were secondary issues in ancient philosophy. This is not to say that the relative views on the soul did not shape the philosophies involved and influence how people prepared for the hereafter (or not), but the primary concern was most often how to live life in the light of the knowledge that death was unavoidable.[3]

Two of the most popular schools of thought were those of the Epicureans and the Stoics. To note that these were popular is not to claim that all in the Roman world subscribed to these philosophies; the available options in both philosophy and religion were near endless (see Chapter Four). Philosophical discourse may have been common among the educated élite, but many of these individuals read widely and did not define themselves as adherents to one particular school of thought. Philosophy may have played little or no role in the lives of the wider population (see p. 22).

Lucretius is perhaps the most famed Epicurean writer of the Roman period. Little is known of his life. Lucretius lived sometime in the first century BC and was a follower of the philosophical school founded in Athens by Epicurus (341–271 BC). Lucretius wrote a substantial poem entitled On the Nature of the Universe (De Rerum Natura) that explored how man can achieve tranquillity or peace of mind. According to Lucretius, one of the greatest obstacles to the state of tranquillity is man's fear of death. This fear is addressed in the third book of the poem, where death is identified as the root cause of much unhappiness; people are so overwhelmed by the prospect of death that it brings out the worst human characteristics, such as greed, jealousy and desire, as they struggle to give their life meaning. One of the central arguments advanced by Lucretius against the fear of death builds on Epicurus' own statement that 'death is nothing to us'. The argument is made that after death man does not exist and can feel no pain or endure no suffering, thus it is irrational to fear death; if man had no sensation or existence before birth, it follows that it will be the same after death. Lucretius also argues that the underworld with all its horrors is simply fiction (see p. 112) and an illogical one at that, for how can it be experienced when one has ceased to exist? For Lucretius death is an absolute end, and beyond it there can be neither happiness nor unhappiness.

> We may be certain that there is nothing in death to be feared by us. He who no longer exists cannot be made miserable, and a man is the same as if he had never been born once immortal death has taken away his mortal life.[4]

The Stoics took a slightly more optimistic line, suggesting that the soul might survive after death but have little or no sensation and thus pursue a better 'life' without the body. The traditional view of the underworld was also dismissed as just nonsense. The Stoic school was founded in Athens by Zeno of Citium (334–362 BC), and with its austere ethical doctrines it became popular in Rome during the late Republic and flourished during the early Imperial period. Seneca the Younger (4 BC–AD 65), the emperor Nero's tutor and adviser, wrote extensively on philosophical subjects from a Stoic perspective. In his writings Seneca was less concerned with speculating about what happened after death and more concerned with how one should accept, face and prepare for death. Seneca argued that the inevitability of death meant that it was to be little feared, but it needed to be accepted and prepared for since it could strike anyone at anytime: 'You do not know when death awaits you: so be ready for it everywhere'; 'Death visits each and all; the killer soon follows the killed.' Seneca viewed death as a process; from the day we are born we are dying, and although the means by which life ends may be different, the end is one and the same. Everyone is thus equal in death, so for how long one lives is unimportant compared to the quality of the life: 'We should strive not to live long, but to live rightly.' Seneca firmly believed that moral philosophy could teach men how to die, acknowledging that his own resolve in facing death came from such philosophy: 'We must prepare for death before we prepare for life.' Seneca's beliefs were tested at his own end. Forced to suicide by the emperor Nero, Seneca was calm, resolute and brave in the face of death (*see* p. 59).[5]

The views of the Epicureans and Stoics were influential, much studied and often quoted, but this does not indicate that belief in these views was prevalent. Some of the great thinkers and influential characters of the ancient world may have studied a lot of philosophy but could still hedge their bets as to whether and in what form the soul survived, subscribing fully to neither annihilation nor continuity. What happened after death was the great unknown, but what happened in life was comparatively certain and within one's control. If philosophy taught anything, it was that life should not be blighted by the prospect of death. Death in itself was not a bad thing and should not be feared. Death could provide an end of suffering, and even if this meant that the soul did not survive, having no existence was better than having a miserable existence.

Therefore in what way or for what reason do you say that you consider death an evil, when it will either make us happy if our souls survive, or free us from misery if we are without sensation?[6]

FACING THE INEVITABLE

Moral codes based on philosophy were essential to the likes of Seneca the Younger, but we are left to wonder how and in what ways these philosophical perspectives influenced other members of society. It is hard to judge how many people actively believed in the survival of the soul or in the afterlife (*see* p. 112–115) or gave serious consideration to traditional beliefs or philosophical musings. Some authors were sceptical about the import and impact of philosophy; the satirist Juvenal (c. AD 65–130) suggested that real people got their fortitude through the school of hard knocks; the bawdy novelist Petronius (mid first century AD) had his *nouveau riche* freed slave Trimalchio claim that he had never listened to a philosopher, as if this was a positive attribute. Yet Petronius also had Trimalchio 'philosophize' about death and the frailty of life. While playing with a model skeleton, Trimalchio noted that life is all too short. Petronius was perhaps mocking both over-zealous philosophers and those who pretended to understand them or quoted from them out of context. However, Trimalchio's musings do reflect a common literary, rather then purely philosophical, thread of the need to accept death. Everyone, philosopher or not, had to remember that they were born to die and thus make the most of their allotted span. This is best immortalized in poetic mottoes such as 'seize the day' and 'death is coming'.[7]

Since life is short, cut back far-reaching hopes! Even while we speak, envious time has fled. Seize the day, putting little belief in tomorrow.[8]

Ruin to him who cares about tomorrow. Death is pulling my ear, 'Live' he says, 'For I am coming.'[9]

The brevity of life and the inevitability of death were frequently coupled with the fact that death was a great leveller. Young or old, rich or poor – all would die. This could be a form of consolation, since even the great and powerful could not escape death. Listing how kings, tyrants, the good and the evil all died, and also noting the vulnerability of man's creations, such as cities and empires, served to underline that man is mortal: 'Pale death knocks on the door of the poor man's cottage and the king's castle with equal force', observed Horace (65–8 BC). In Rome even the all-powerful emperors, who claimed descent from the gods and divinity for themselves, could not escape the inevitable. As Martial (c. AD 40–103) put it, 'the Mausoleums [of the emperors] close by command us to live, for they teach us that the very gods can die'.[10]

Forewarned was forearmed for some people who sought to know when and how they would depart life. Astrologers who predicted life's course and its end by reference to the stars might have been widely consulted. The successes of the emperor Tiberius, for example, were said to have been predicted by an astrologer while he was a baby, and as emperor Tiberius kept an astrologer as part of his household, although he later banished all astrologers from Rome. Indeed astrology had a chequered history with Roman authority; sometimes it and its practitioners were courted and at other times they were banned, depending on whether their interpretations of the stars and heavens were providing endorsement for or undermining a regime. Tiberius' own anxiety may have sprung from the astrologers' claims to be able to predict the time of the emperor's death and thus make his hold on power seem vulnerable. For some, astrology may have been little more than mumbo jumbo. Petronius poked fun at astrology and its followers by having the ridiculous Trimalchio announce that due to astrology he knew precisely how many years, days and hours he had left to live.[11]

Those who did not subscribe to astrology might still have believed in a preordained destiny – that life's course and length were controlled by forces that might be propitiated but ultimately not denied. The Fates (*Parcae* or *Moirae*) were three sister goddesses first found in Greek mythology. Nona (Clotho) spun the thread of life, Decima (Lachesis) measured the thread with her rod and Morta (Atropos) cut the thread, although sometimes the roles of the goddesses were merged. The Fates could not be cheated, and man could not live beyond his appointed span: 'none can break the sisters' iron decrees' noted Ovid. In literature the spinning and snapping of the thread of life symbolized that time was running out and that man alone was not the controller of his destiny: 'the Parcae spin the thread of doom which no god can untwist' (Tibullus); 'his day is ended, the relentless thread runs out' (Statius). Closely aligned with the Fates was Fortuna, the goddess of fortune and luck, who controlled the course of life, lifting men high and then bringing them low, and ultimately being party to the time and cause of death. As Horace put it, 'Fortuna shifts her fickle favours, now kind to me, now kind to others.' Fortuna could be perceived as a blind goddess, or at best unreliable, striking down the deserving and undeserving alike. In epitaphs Fortuna and Fate were both readily blamed for death: 'unfair Fortuna envied him' said one grieving mother who had lost her son. Yet Fortuna and Fate were also associated with a sense of resignation and acceptance: 'this is what Fate wanted' said the commemorators of 14-year-old Stephanus, while the epitaph of Claudia Secunda had her say, 'I do not want you to grieve for my end, friend, this quickly completed life was what Fate gave me.' For some, Fortuna and the Fates were regarded as powerful life-controlling goddesses to be honoured; offerings, altars and prayers were frequently made to Fortuna in particular. Petronius' Trimalchio, as well as believing in astrology, had his hallway decorated with images of Fortuna, with an overflowing cornucopia and the three Fates spinning golden threads. For others, including many authors, the Fates and Fortuna served as powerful allegories for the duration of human life and the unavoidable nature of death. The philosopher Seneca the Younger, for example, frequently referred to Fortuna in his writings; he pictured Fortuna not as an uncaring goddess, but as a symbol of the uncertainties of life and that man must make the best of whatever happens, including death:[12]

> Everything is thrown about and reversed at the bidding of Fortune and amidst this chaos of human affairs nothing is certain except that death awaits everyone.[13]

Astrology, the Fates and Fortuna were an aspect of how people faced death. The extent to which people actively believed in these forces is hard to judge; for some they were little more than allegories and symbols, but for others they were real life-giving and controlling forces. At the very least, these figures and concepts were part of the vocabulary of Roman death, allowing people to speak of the reality of mortality, to confront, to complain, to understand, even to predict how and why death affected them and those who they loved.

MEMENTO MORI

For some, inspired in part by Epicurean philosophy, if death was certain and life was short, life needed to be filled with fun – as much as, if not more than, with virtue. Any day could be one's last, so it should be enjoyed by indulging in the pleasures of life, such as the baths, sex, food and especially wine. This could be given an extra edge if death really was imminent. In their final days (31 BC) Antony and Cleopatra partied in style, even forming a society among their friends entitled 'The Order of Inseparable Death'. The hedonistic final celebrations of the doomed couple went hand in hand with Cleopatra's search for a painless means of death. The 'seize the day' theme was also taken to extremes and parodied at the extravagant banquet of the freed slave Trimalchio, the fictional creation of the novelist Petronius. Trimalchio's feast is both fabulous and grotesque – the food is exotic and decorative, and there are dancers and entertainers, baths and much wine. Yet the spectre of death is also present: Trimalchio knows via astrology how long he has to live and he has a clock and a trumpeter to remind him of the passing hours of his life. Among his guests are an undertaker, a monumental mason and another guest who has come direct from a funeral. Trimalchio even entertains his guests by reading aloud his will and planning his tomb.[14]

Trimalchio's feast was a parody, but dinner parties and banquets with their over-indulgent elements could be a favoured venue for *memento mori*. The irony that their pleasures were transient was not lost on diners, with the drunken guest raising a glass to the dead and the common fate of man:

> When men are reclining at banquet, holding up cups, with their brows shaded with wreaths, they speak from the heart and say, 'Brief is joy for poor weak men. Soon it will be ended, and thereafter not recalled.'[15]

The association between death and feasting seems to have been particularly potent in the late Republic and early Imperial period, and Trimalchio's feast needs to be seen in this context. Tableware adorned with dancing skeletons survives from this time, and one house in Pompeii had a black and white mosaic depicting a skeleton acting as a waiter (Figure 1). These images served to remind the diners that death was never far away. Trimalchio's grotesque, death-obsessed dinner even ended with a mock funeral. Trimalchio brought out his shroud, the ointments for anointing his dead body and the wine that would be poured over his bones, and reclining on his couch, as if on a bier, he had trumpet players sound out a lament. Such a scene may not be pure fantasy; apparently a certain Pacuvius, one-time governor of Syria (under Tiberius), used to hold a funerary banquet every day, at the end of which he was carried out to cries of 'He has lived'. Seneca the Younger, our source for this anecdote, was of course unimpressed by such behaviour, but he used it to illustrate the point that everyone should live virtuously since any day could be one's last. The emperor Domitian played with this same fear at a grand dinner party he held for leading citizens. Everything had a funeral feel; the room décor, the waiters and the food recalled death and the grave, frightening the guests into thinking that they were about to die. Domitian's reminders of death felt all too real, even though the guests were spared![16]

This macabre death imagery may remind us of mediaeval equivalents – images of skulls, skeletons and decaying bodies found particularly, but not exclusively, in funerary art. Yet the Roman images, literary and visual, do not invite the viewer to give serious contemplation to the future state of their body and soul. This is not to suggest that there was never a serious or sombre, even sobering, side to the imagery, but the contexts in which most of it was found suggest a certain playfulness, and that the central message was, to quote Horace, 'Seize the day'. At the very least the imagery suggests a certain acceptance of death; death was talked about and confronted even if in the somewhat intoxicating and jocular environment of the feast.

THE LAST WILL AND TESTAMENT

Philosophical preparations for death and the sometimes playful confrontation with the inevitability of death existed alongside practical planning. Cato the Elder (234–149 BC) once commented that there were only three things that he regretted in his life and one of them was that he had been without a will for a whole day. This emphasizes the importance to the propertied man of having a will and of ensuring that one's estate was in good order, loved ones provided for and memory protected. Most people probably had little or no property, thus a will would have been of no importance. If there was no will, the laws dictated that blood relatives, especially any children, would inherit whatever the deceased did own – provided, that is, he or she was free and a Roman citizen. The making of a will may have been a practice that characterized an educated, propertied, and largely male minority.[17]

A Roman will was a formal document. It had to be written in Latin, follow certain conventions of content and language, be witnessed by seven witnesses and then sealed. The majority of wills were written some years before death rather than on the deathbed itself. As a result, people revised them frequently or added codicils as circumstances changed. Revisions close to the time of death were common and could occasion speculation. Two years before his death, following his divorce, the death of his daughter and the birth of his grandson, Cicero made a new will in which his ex-wife, Terentia, was apparently most interested. The author Petronius Arbiter called for his will before he committed suicide (AD 66) and made amendments to it. Pliny the Younger noted in his letters two testators who left old wills and had thus failed to record and update their final wishes.[18]

The main beneficiaries of a will were most often the immediate family of the deceased, especially the children. A testator would need to disinherit children if they were not named as heirs or the will could be declared invalid. The will also allowed the testator to provide for a spouse and to reward friends and ex-slaves with gifts and legacies. In the 'will of Dasumius', recorded in a funerary inscription of AD 108, the testator named his daughter as principal heir, along with a friend and two women (of unspecified connection) who were to receive lesser portions of the estate. The testator also left gifts of money to a list of friends and left named items, such as gold plate and statues, to members of his household. A veteran of the fleet, Gaius Longinus Castor, who left a papyrus copy of his will in Egypt in the late second century AD, named two of his slaves, who were to be freed, as principal heirs.[19]

The will was a means to express people's wishes. The testator was supposed to make considered decisions about the fate of his estate, and it was thus often thought that the will was indicative of the deceased person's real nature and their true opinions about others. Pliny the Younger noted that there was an old saying that 'a will was a mirror of character'. Some joked that the will was the only time that a Roman told the truth, since it could be a vehicle to express praise and blame and to insult and abuse. A will allowed the dead to speak from beyond the grave, and what was said affected the living: 'The dead man lies senseless in the tomb, but his words have power', succinctly observed Augustine (fourth century AD). To leave someone a meagre legacy or to omit their name altogether from the will could be a deliberate insult. Valerius Maximus, who wrote a handbook on memorable deeds and sayings during the early first century AD, recalled several stories of testators who defied people's expectations by not naming them as heir. Valerius Maximus did not view these as thwarted inheritance hunters (see p. 30–31), but mainly as the victims of a malicious or ungrateful testator. These testators may have simply neglected to update their wills, but such cases could create strong reactions; the corpse of one testator was dragged though the streets by a rope when the crowd heard that he had not made the expected candidate heir: 'He got the heir he wanted and the funeral he deserved' (Valerius Maximus). The ultimate testamentary judgement and punishment of disinheritance was rare, but the will might identify slaves who were never to be freed or ex-slaves who were not to be interred in the tomb. In the 'will of Dasumius' (*see* p. 28) the testator named two slaves who were not to be manumitted since their behaviour had been unacceptable. We are left to wonder exactly what they had done to incur their master's displeasure.[20]

Even emperors could show an interest in the wills of their subjects. Augustus saw it as a compliment to be named as heir or left a bequest in a will, and he made sure that his response was appropriately moderate, only accepting bequests from people that he actually knew and taking care of the interests of the testator's children. The historian Tacitus noted how the omission of Tiberius from the will of Iunia, sister of Brutus and widow of Cassius, the murderers of Julius Caesar, was seen as a deliberate snub to the emperor. To criticize the emperor openly was a dangerous game. The author Petronius, forced to suicide by Nero, denounced the emperor in his will for his debauchery; this cost an innocent woman her life, since the emperor held her, rather than Petronius, responsible for revealing his indiscretions. In general for the élite of Rome, naming the emperor in the will reflected their social sphere – the emperor was in theory their peer and 'friend'. Under more tyrannical emperors, there were pragmatic and tactful reasons for naming the emperor heir. Tacitus noted that his father-in-law, Agricola (died AD 93), named his daughter joint heir with the emperor Domitian, who 'was so blinded and corrupted by incessant flattery that he did not see that it is a bad emperor who is made heir by a good father'.[21]

A good will reflected well on both the testator and the living survivors. In his letters Pliny the Younger commented upon people's wills, viewing them as a final positive or negative act of the deceased. So the elderly and infirm Domitius Tullius may not have led an exemplary life, but his will was good, giving priority to close family. An inscription set up to a certain

Murdia, which probably recalled the words of her eulogy (*see* p. 79), noted
the content of her will; this will had won the praise of her fellow citizens
due to the gratitude she showed her husband and the fair treatment she
gave to her children. Valerius Maximus told of a mother who did not do
right by her children, naming only one of her two daughters as heir. This
decision was no doubt motivated by family ill-feeling, and the slighted
daughter could have brought a legal case and challenged the will. Instead
the daughter accepted her mother's decision, and 'She showed herself
less worthy of the injury done her, the more calmly she endured it.' The
will of Mark Antony, scandalously opened by Octavian before Antony's
death, reflected badly on the testator and his intentions. Octavian's action
of reading the will was an extreme one, but it served a powerful political
purpose, since the will announced Antony's wish to be buried in Egypt
with Cleopatra. The will revealed where Antony's loyalties really lay and
that he had compromised his Roman identity.[22]

The contents of a will were nominally private, but the will might be
spoken of freely and could be changed regularly. Who was to inherit, and
how much, might be a topic of interest and gossip. Wills could be opened
and read by the testator to prove what their intentions were or to gain the
praise and affection of the beneficiaries. Petronius had Trimalchio read
out his will at the dinner party so that his household could hear how he
intended to treat them and thus give him their thanks and gratitude while
he was still alive. The biographer Suetonius noted that Julius Caesar had
often read out part of his will to his troops, the part in which he named
his son-in-law and later enemy Pompey as principal heir. Wills could be
and sometimes were changed, and this could give the testator a certain
power, as Martial noted: 'You say I am your heir, Catullus, I won't believe
this until I read it.'[23]

The hopes and expectations (often disappointed) of the inheritance
hunter or legacy hunter (*captator*) became a literary theme. These
individuals were said to prey on dying men and women who were
stereotypically childless, old and rich, trying to win their favour in the
hope of being left something in the will. Some authors noted that being

childless brought certain advantages in the shape of more 'friends' and more gifts. The early comic playwright Plautus had an elderly character joke that 'My children are all the people who send me presents . . . even though it's my property they are fishing for!' The inheritance hunter was a stock character and stereotype who illustrated the negative impact of wealth on Roman society. Whether inheritance hunting was ever commonplace or successful is difficult to gauge. In literature the *captator* was often disappointed, with the testator having the last laugh.[24]

> You change your will three times a month, Charinus, and each time I send you cakes flavoured with honey of Hybla. I give up. Take pity, Charinus, and stop re-sealing your will. Or else do what your lying cough continually promises! My cash-box and my purse are empty. Even if I was richer than Croesus, I would soon be poorer than the beggar in the Odyssey, if all I gave you was beans this often.[25]

WILLS, MONUMENTS AND MEMORY

As well as taking care of one's property and earthly goods, and ensuring the prosperity of one's family, practical planning for death could entail disposal of the body and remembrance. For the less well-off, saving for the cost of the funeral may have been an essential preparation. Funerals could be expensive, and burial clubs existed; these clubs allowed the individual to make staggered payments that were saved to pay for the funeral and burial in a collective tomb (*see* p. 68). For the wealthy, funeral and burial expenses were met from the estate and took precedence over legacies and bequests. The will could be used to make specific demands concerning the funeral. Seneca the Younger, for example, requested a simple funeral in his will, as did Atticus, the close friend of Cicero. In general most testators seem to have expected that their funeral would be conducted appropriately and rarely specified details concerning it. More testators were interested in how their remains would be marked and commemorated. Many surviving epitaphs include references to the will of the deceased, noting that the heir had discharged his or her duty by setting up a tombstone or tomb according to the provisions of the will. Some wills even made elaborate stipulations about the tomb, its location, its cost and who was to have access to it. A few surviving epitaphs record that a specified sum had to be spent on the tomb construction; for example, Manius Valerius, a military tribune and priest, stated that 50,000 sesterces were to be spent on the tomb for himself and his brother. By contrast, Lucius Tarquitus Sulpicianus, a scribe or secretary, requested that just 20 sesterces be spent on his memorial. The testator in the 'will of Dasumius' specified the sum to be spent on his monument, the time in which it was to completed and its future use by freed slaves. The heirs of Cestius, whose large pyramid tomb still survives in Rome, noted that they had completed its construction within 330 days of his death, as had been stipulated in the will. Another testator, whose will was inscribed in Langres (France), left highly detailed instructions for his memorial's design, decoration and furnishings.[26]

The will could entail additional strategies to perpetuate the memory of the deceased. A testator could make donations or set up foundations that benefited the community. The most extravagant testamentary donations were cash gifts to the populace and the gift of land, buildings and amenities. Julius Caesar left three gold pieces a man to the population of Rome as well as turning his private grounds on the banks of the Tiber into a public garden. Agrippa (died 12 BC), the emperor Augustus' right-hand man and heir, left gardens, a public bath building and money for cash gifts. Other wealthy testators from across the empire gave legacies to fund public works and to build, restore or embellish structures in their home towns, such as temples, theatres, libraries and baths. For example, a centurion from Mustis (Mest, North Africa) left money for a temple; Caius Sulpicius Flavus, a military commander, made a testamentary bequest to Vasio (Vaison-la-Romaine, France) for the building of a marble portico in front of the public baths; Pliny the Younger gave money for the building and upkeep of public baths in his home town of Comum (Como, Italy); Caius Iulius Secundus' legacy was for an aqueduct in Burdigala (Bordeaux, France); and the wishes of one testator from Trebiae (Trevi, Italy), despite

the emperor Tiberius thinking the bequest would be better spent on a
road, were fulfilled in the building of a theatre.[27]

Some testators established foundations – bequests were invested and the
income then used to fund regular benefactions. These foundations might
finance games, shows, the upkeep of public buildings or the distribution of
money, oil or food. A testator from Bononia (Bologna, Italy), for example,
made a bequest to the town, the profits from which were to be used to
pay for the citizens to have free entry at the public baths. The beneficiaries
of such foundations could be restricted to members of guilds (*collegia*)
or to the local magistrates or groups of priests. Some foundations were
explicitly linked to the cult of the dead through paying for libations, din-
ners and flowers at the tomb. These were often connected to the festivals
for the dead or the birthday of the deceased (*see* p. 100–101). Iunia Libertas
from Ostia (Italy) left some land, buildings and shops to her freed slaves
on condition that some of the profits were used to decorate her tomb
and pay for sacrifices there. A military tribune left money to the town of
Spoletium (Spoleto, Italy), the interest from which was to pay for a dinner
for the town's inhabitants to be held on his birthday. Quintus Cominius
Abascantus from Misenum (Miseno, Italy) left a sum of money to the
Augustales (prestigious priests of the Imperial cult), the interest from
which was to be used annually to adorn certain statues and to fund commemorative rites at his tomb, while any remaining money was to be used
for the upkeep and repair of the tomb. There was an element of reciprocity
in these testamentary requests. The testator was benefiting others, but
by attaching strings to the bequests also promoting their own memory.
Publicizing the act of generosity, mainly through inscriptions, might be
a way of further perpetuating personal memory and trying to enforce
the long-term honouring of the conditions. One testator of the second
century AD from Gythium (Gytheio, Greece) asked that her benefaction be
recorded by three inscriptions set up in three different places: 'so that my
philanthropic generosity should be well known and acknowledged both
by citizens and by visitors to the city . . . My idea is that I shall be immortal
by virtue of this good and kindly gift.'[28]

PRESERVING REPUTATION AND IDENTITY

Much of what could be done via the will in terms of promoting memory could be done during life. The élite were very conscious of their lasting reputation (*fama*), knowing that through their words and deeds they should leave an enduring legacy for posterity. This tradition was rooted in the Republican ideal of family honour. The leading families of wealthy office-holders, the *nobiles*, competed to display success and virtue and to emulate their forefathers. By the mid-Republic the memories of this élite group were promoted by a range of monuments, such as inscriptions, public buildings, victory monuments, honorific statues, public processions (triumphs and at games) and family tombs. These ensured that individuals and families were known in their lifetime and were remembered after death, while helping to underpin Rome's stability and continuity. As Sallust (86–35 BC) claimed, 'The memory of the deeds of others produces in the hearts of noble men a desire to fan a flame that is not extinguished until their own virtue has equalled that fame and glory.' Families might edit their own history to glorify their own line of descent, ignoring some members and promoting others. In 140 BC, for example, after his son committed suicide following an extortion trial, Titus Manlius Torquatus (consul in 165 BC) did not attend his son's funeral or allow the display of the family funerary masks (*see* p. 89). The family carried on as if this particular member had never existed. As the Republic moved towards its end, the competitive norms of display between families began to break down, and overt competition between individuals, especially military leaders, became more intense and ultimately destructive. Under the emperors, political competition among the wealthy élite was simply no longer possible in the same form. The best statues, monuments, buildings and shows, at least in the city of Rome, had to be linked to, if not explicitly funded by, the emperor. Yet the Republican ideals, including the importance of memory, persisted; a man should aspire to be worthy of remembrance through his words, deeds and service to the state (even if the latter was in reality the emperor). Only the truly great and good deserved to be remembered:[29]

The deep flood of time will submerge us; a few great men will raise their heads above it, and although destined finally to depart into the same realms of silence, will resist and for a long time battle against oblivion.[30]

This battle against oblivion began well before death. Buildings, statues, amenities and foundations were paid for and often named after the living (although during the Imperial period an individual might honour the emperor's name as well). Philanthropy and generosity could earn one a reputation to be enjoyed while alive as well as earning one remembrance after death. It was even more prestigious to have honours voted and heaped upon one by public and popular demand, both in life and at death. Julius Caesar planned to provide Rome with a new forum, temple and public library, and he presented many cities of the empire with 'magnificent public works'. These acts bought Julius Caesar popularity and promoted his name. In addition, innumerable honours were awarded to him – temples, altars, statues and privileged seats at the theatre and senate house. Caesar's immodesty in accepting so many honours was thought to have alienated people and contributed to his downfall. Yet after death Caesar was further honoured; his forum, for example, was completed, benefiting the reputation of his heir, the new emperor Augustus, as much as his own reputation. Caesar's name lived on after death, not just because of his political and military career, but also because of his surviving public works.[31]

Literature – that is, great literary works – was often perceived as even more enduring than physical monuments. Words had the potential to last forever, while stone monuments, statues and the like would decay and fall. Writers preserved memory and boasted that their works would last for all time. Horace said most famously of his poetry, 'I have made a monument more lasting than bronze.' This is a sentiment echoed by many other authors:[32]

My poems shall be so many monuments to your beauty. For neither the pyramids built so high at great cost, nor the house of Jove at Elis that copies heaven, nor the wealth of Mausolus' tomb can escape the end imposed by death. Their glory is reduced by fire or rain or they are crushed by their weight or the passage of time.

But the name that my talent has earned will survive for eternity; for such talent is without death.[33]

If you were not a great writer, you might still hope to see your name and deeds grace the pages of others. If one earned a reputation as a great soldier, hero or statesman, one could hope to be remembered and perhaps even influence that memory before death. Authors, whether historians, poets or letter writers, shaped memory, helping to decide what would be remembered and in what way. As the poet Lucan (AD 39–65) ruefully observed, writers had a certain power in making and breaking reputations: 'How great and sacred is the task of poets, saving everything from death and giving mortals eternal life.' Cicero noted this process, rather unsubtly, when writing to a historian friend of his. Cicero, himself a distinguished writer, wanted others to record his own political successes but to do so in a way that Cicero would approve of and be able to enjoy while he still could: 'I cannot wait to see the world learning about me in my lifetime and to enjoy my small glory myself before I die.'[34]

For the majority of people, the battle against oblivion was a tough fight; they would not be remembered for their words or deeds nor have their names recorded in the literary works of others. But they, or at least the moderately wealthy among them, could leave some record of their life. Wills, as noted above, could perpetuate memory by requesting the construction of a tomb or grave marker. The alternative was pre-death planning and building or commissioning one's own funerary monument. Epitaphs often contained expressions such as *vivus fecit*, meaning he or she built it while still alive. This method allowed a person to consider how he or she wished to be remembered and commemorated rather than leaving these decisions to the heirs. Trimalchio's description of his tomb is the only detailed literary example of such pre-death planning. Petronius has the wealthy, rather drunk ex-slave speak of his tomb with a monumental mason pal of his at the end of the dinner party. Trimalchio discusses the size of the plot, the sculptural décor and the epitaph in great detail, arguing that we should all pay as much attention to our tombs as our houses, since we'll be occupying the former much longer than the latter! Petronius' description was an extreme parody designed to suggest that the more showy and extravagant the tomb, the more inadequate the man, but it was perhaps only the wealthy élite, who could choose from a myriad of ways of commemorating their memory, who were disdainful of the attempts of others.[35]

REMEMBERING THIS LIFE

The pre-death construction of tombs indicates that people thought about their death and gave serious consideration to the time when they would no longer be present. However, in many respects tomb design, décor and epitaphs remained firmly focused on the living rather than on the dead. The tomb recorded what the person had been and generally engaged little with what the dead person would become or with spiritual or philosophical concerns about the soul and the hereafter (*see* p. 114). There was little that was macabre about planning for death in the Roman world. Petronius' Trimalchio may have been obsessed with death, but that obsession sprang from his fear that death would mark the end of all he had achieved; his plans for his tomb and funeral hinged on the idea of perpetuating and enjoying the here and now. Trimalchio focused on material, not spiritual, preparations as if this would allow him somehow to cheat death.[36]

We see a similar emphasis on the here and now in some epitaphs, especially those that were composed as if to speak to the passer-by. These epitaphs sought to engage the living, to encourage them to say the name of the deceased and ideally to read the epitaph out loud, thus giving the dead a voice once more and perpetuating memory:

You traveller, who make your way along the path, stop I ask, I beg you not to ignore my epitaph.

As you hurry on your way, stop briefly traveller.

Know, traveller, that your voice is mine.[37]

Most epitaphs only provided basic factual information about the commemorated person and his or her life, rarely expressing hopes for the
continuity of the soul or expected reunions with loved ones (*see* p. 114
and 186–7). Occasionally epitaphs entailed direct advice to the living, once
more echoing the message to 'seize the day' and enjoy it: 'While I lived I
drank freely. You who live drink'; 'Worn out by old age you will be like
this in the tomb.'[38]

In funerary iconography, images of the dying, dead bodies and the
afterlife were also unusual. Mythological allegories could depict the
deceased as a dying hero or born again as a god or goddess (*see* p. 110–111);
images such as upturned torches might symbolize the extinguishing of life;
and astrological symbols sometimes hinted at a celestial life hereafter,
but the use of such images was not that widespread, and the decaying
state of human remains, allegories for the separation of body and soul
and visual *memento mori* were in general not the subjects of funerary
art. A handful of funerary monuments were decorated with skeletons
(for example, an early second century AD funerary altar from Naples
depicted a skeleton reclining and holding up a drinking cup), but such
rare examples owed their inspiration to the 'eat, drink and be merry'
theme popular at this time, rather than a real or spiritual contemplation
of the fate of the body and soul. Images of the deceased alive, well and
non-skeletal, reclining as if at a feast, were fairly common (Figure 2).
These may have represented a desire for such pleasures in the afterlife,
but they may also have sought to capture the status (real or desired)
of the commemorated person while alive or played on the idea of the
survivors visiting the tomb and partaking of a feast with the deceased
(*see* p. 85–87). Indeed tombs, with their images, words and design, the
latter even incorporating dining and seating areas (*see* p. 101–102 and
173–174), promoted an interaction between the dead and the living. In
part this may suggest belief in the afterlife and the continuing presence of
the dead, but it also indicates that the creators of these tombs did not wish
the dead to be physically isolated in a completely separate world or place,
and that there was a duty to remember the dead as they had lived. In short

the ideal was that the dead would be a continuing presence among the living.[39]

CONCLUSION

Tombs were most often about remembering the dead as they had been when alive rather than as dead and decaying entities or representing them as members of a new and separate afterlife. Monuments were about memories of the past. People could plan, order or build monuments while still alive or leave provision for them in their will. Monuments came in all shapes and forms. Tombstones and tombs were complemented by statues, buildings, foundations and literary works. In planning such memorials, people were thinking, to some extent, about death and were confronting their own mortality. Philosophical debate and even astrology or belief in the Fates may have equipped some people to face their deaths and those of their loved ones. For others the prospect of death centred on more practical issues. Individuals could make decisions about the fate of their property, where their remains should lie and how their own life should be summed up and pictured. In doing so, however, people were often thinking about this world more than the next; they were thinking of future generations to come and how they could interact with or have a presence among them.

Leaving a lasting legacy and a good posthumous memory, or failing this, a simple name in an epitaph or a portrait on a tomb, staked a claim on the future. It was as if people aimed or hoped for some sort of immortality of memory in this world, perhaps to compensate for tenuous afterlife beliefs and the feared finality of death. These were, then, less preparations for the death of the self and more preparations for the perpetuation of memory.

2

Death Scenes

In the Roman world death constantly reshaped the families and the contact networks of the living. Ausonius, a statesman and writer of the fourth century AD, composed a series of poetic epitaphs to his dead relatives; these included his grandparents, parents, uncle, aunt, brother, two sisters, wife, son and grandson. All these, old and young alike, had predeceased Ausonius, but he did not reveal what had killed them. For most people of the Roman era, we simply do not know what led to their deaths. Surviving epitaphs may provide an age at death, but most do not supply information on the cause of death. Similarly, literary texts rarely focus on the everyday deaths of ordinary folk, although the same texts are often filled with dramatic or tragic death scenes. The deaths of the famous could be viewed as inspirational, and books existed that were compilations of good and worthy death stories. How someone died could be extremely revealing; it could reflect, and in literary accounts be made to reflect, the nature of the person's character and the quality of their life. Indeed, a quick survey of Latin literature would suggest that few Romans died peacefully in their beds. Instead they fell victim to violence, political intrigue and enforced suicide. The reality for the majority of the population may have been less dramatic but no less harsh. Poor sanitation, famine, malnutrition, disease, epidemics, natural disasters and warfare took their toll. We have little direct or detailed information on mundane and ordinary deaths, but age statements in epitaphs indicate that thousands of people were carried off before or during their prime.[1]

LIFE EXPECTANCY

How precarious was life in Rome and elsewhere in its empire? Did people walk the streets in fear of an imminent demise? In modern society we can estimate life expectancy and evaluate the impact of morbidity and mortality on the living. How long people can expect to live for, what will most probably kill them and the risk factors related to gender, age, socio-economic status and geographic region can all be gauged. For ancient Rome we simply do not have similar relevant statistics. This lack of data has not stopped people from trying to understand and reconstruct Roman life expectancy, and for good reasons. If we can access the Roman age structure, we can gain fundamental insights into the expectations and experiences of Roman society; age structure impacts on factors such as family continuity and economic stability that shape the roles of individuals and thus society overall.

The basis for much speculation about ancient life expectancy lies in the plentiful numbers, especially ages at death, that can be found or extrapolated from ancient sources. For example, ages at death were commonly noted on epitaphs, some population census data is recorded and human skeletal evidence can sometimes be aged. The difficulty is that this data is rarely reliable and does not automatically span the breadth of the population. The ages at death recorded on tombstones illustrate many of the potential pitfalls. It might be thought that the thousands upon thousands of ages stated on epitaphs could be used to generate some workable statistics. We could, for example, add up all the ages and divide by the total to obtain a mean average age at death. However, age statements have inherent characteristics. Many of the recorded ages were far from precise, since inscribed ages often ended in the Latin numerals V or X, suggesting that ages were rounded up or down or may simply have been guessed at. Nor do the recorded ages cover all of the population; babies and infants were rarely recorded and more males than females were generally commemorated. In fact, ages were most often given for boys and adolescents, for soldiers and sometimes the elderly. In short, epigraphic age statements characterized certain groups and are thus limited in what they now reveal about Roman demography.[2]

More profitable than calculations from ancient numbers have been comparisons between Rome and other more recent societies. The study of Roman age structure has been heavily influenced by 'model life tables', which simulate attrition rates for different populations and highlight the impact of geographic, economic and chronological factors. The closest fit for the Roman world is thought to be the life table of a developing country in the mid to late twentieth century. This comparison suggests that at birth the chances of an individual surviving into adulthood were low and that, overall, the average life expectancy of the population was around 25 to 30 years. If childhood was survived, however, a life expectancy of 40 or 50 years was possible. It seems likely that in Rome and its empire many children died, but those who survived childhood stood a reasonable chance of seeing middle and even old age. These simulations and figures may always remain speculative. There must have been substantial variations across the geographic regions of the empire, between urban and rural populations and even across the seasons of the year (*see* p. 44–45), but at the very least model life tables help us to recreate and evaluate the potential impact of death upon daily life.[3]

The lack of hard data on life expectancy serves to underline the distance between modern society and the ancient world. Exact figures may always escape us. We cannot know how many children, adults, middle-aged or elderly were present in the city of Rome at any given time. What we can say is that in Rome, and probably much of its empire, life was often short. Death was a present danger, but probably not to the extent (most of the time at least) that it paralysed society. Death, of others and ultimately of the self, was something that people had to live with, cope with and to some extent accept. Death, by its frequent presence, could be a matter-of-fact part of life.

CAUSES OF DEATH

The vast majority of surviving Latin epitaphs do not record the cause of death, but a handful of exceptions mention a range of fates. We can note, for example, the woman and child crushed to death in a festival crowd; the decorator who fell to his death while working on a ceiling mosaic; the soldier from the fort at Isca (Caerleon, Wales) who died while on a military expedition to Germany; the 10-year-old girl from Salona (Solin, Croatia) murdered for her jewellery; and a wife from Lugdunum (Lyons, France) killed by her husband. In these cases the information was provided because it differed from the norm; these deaths were unusual, and the details invoked a sense of shock and sympathy among readers – who is not still saddened upon hearing that 8-year-old Fortunatus drowned in the public baths? Most deaths, and the epitaphs that recorded these deaths, were less striking. We can anticipate that disease, underpinned by poor sanitation, urban overcrowding and malnutrition, accounted for much loss of life. Epitaphs rarely noted deaths caused by disease or infection, and although ages at death, when supplied, may be suggestive of, for example, the vulnerability of the young, they do not reveal what were the biggest killers and the impact of underlying factors such as poverty and abuse.[4]

Statistical studies of epitaphs do suggest that there were some seasonal patterns in mortality. Christian epitaphs, unlike pagan epitaphs, often included date information, and they indicate that the late summer and early autumn were periods of increased mortality in the city of Rome. The dangers of the summer had long been noted by Roman authors; the poet Horace observed how the summer heat affected the vulnerable and how 'fond mothers grow pale with fear for their children'. The summer months were best not spent in Rome. The wealthy were fortunate and could retire to their rural or suburban villas. Pliny the Younger, for example, owned several properties that afforded escape from the pressures of urban life, including the oppressive summer months. Pliny also noted that when travelling to one of his properties, some among his party were made ill by 'the intense heat'. For the elderly, the midwinter and spring were also danger times, perhaps due to the prevalence of respiratory diseases. Away from the urban sprawl of Rome, winter may have been the season of highest morbidity, although it remains difficult to generalize across the Roman Empire as to when people were most vulnerable; there was great variability in geographic terrain and temperatures, which must have created a range of disease environments. In the late first century AD, Pliny the Younger contrasted healthy and unhealthy regions in Italy, noting that at his Umbrian estate people lived to a great age and that 'my slaves are healthier here than anywhere else; up till now not a single one I brought with me has died'.[5]

What the most common killers and the diseases that claimed the most victims were is hard to judge. In literary texts symptoms are rarely described in sufficient detail to establish a clear diagnosis. Diseases of the respiratory system such as bronchitis and tuberculosis and infections of the digestive system such as gastroenteritis may have been common. Infectious diseases such as typhus, cholera and smallpox were probably big killers. It has also been argued that malaria was endemic in parts of the Roman Empire, including Rome itself. Skeletal evidence can sometimes indicate underlying medical conditions, if not the precise cause of death. Human remains from Pompeii and Herculaneum, representing a population killed by a single event, the devastating eruption of Vesuvius in AD 79, suggest that many of the inhabitants were healthy and well nourished. However, the skeletal remains also provide evidence for conditions such as anaemia, arthritis, bone tumours, syphilis, osteoporosis and rickets, as well as evidence of healed or partially healed broken bones. These conditions in themselves may not have been immediately life-threatening for the afflicted individuals, but they did have the potential to influence the quality of life and leave the sufferers vulnerable to complications and further infections. Particularly striking, and highlighting another risk to life, are the remains of a 16-year-old girl from Herculaneum who was seven months pregnant with her first child. The pelvis of this girl was so immature that it would have been impossible for her to deliver a full-term baby, and in the opinion of one scholar, 'It was much better for her to have died quickly in the eruption than slowly in labour.'[6]

Epidemics were not uncommon, and the sheer numbers of those who died in outbreaks of diseases and plagues make for shocking reading. Suetonius claimed that 30,000 people died of plague in Rome during the reign of the emperor Nero; Cassius Dio stated that 2,000 died in the city every day during the great empire-wide plague of AD 189. We may question the accuracy of these numbers, but at the very least they serve to emphasize the devastating impact of these events and make us wonder how many others died regularly in smaller, less infamous contagions.[7]

In literature the deaths of ordinary people were generally only noted and commented upon collectively when they died in such large numbers. Natural and man-made disasters might also draw comment. Tacitus observed that as many as 50,000 people were killed when a wooden amphitheatre collapsed at Fidenae in Italy in AD 27; thousands were killed in the eruption of Vesuvius (AD 79); and in the earthquake of AD 115 in Antioch (Syria), 'a multitude were killed by the falling debris'. The most frequent listing of large-scale death is found, however, in descriptions of battles. Once more we can question the reliability of the quoted figures; excessive estimates for the enemy dead and underestimates for Roman casualties could strengthen Rome's claim to supreme power. At the battle of Zama (202 BC) 20,000 Carthaginians and in the region of 1,500 Romans died; at Cynoscephalae (197 BC) 8,000 of the Macedonian enemy were killed; the defeat of Boudicca (AD 61) saw 80,000 Britons slain and only 400 Romans; in one attack against a Roman garrison during the Jewish War, 10,000 Jews were killed and only a few Romans; at the battle of Mons Graupius (AD 83) 10,000 Britons and 360 Roman troops died. Rome could be ruthless in victory and after breaking sieges might massacre all the enemy survivors. Polybius, a Greek writer of the second century BC, wrote how the slaughter after a siege inspired terror and how no one, not even dogs and animals, was spared.[8]

Rome did suffer defeats. The sack of Rome by the Gauls in the fourth century BC cast a long shadow across Roman history, thereafter imbuing the collective Roman psyche with a fear of invasion. The defeat by Hannibal at the battle of Cannae (216 BC) was also devastating; so many men were lost (as many as 50,000) and so many families were affected that the city was almost overwhelmed by grief. The loss of three legions and several auxiliary units (perhaps as many as 20,000 men) in AD 9 in the Teutoburg Forest, under the command of the general Varus, devastated the emperor Augustus; the anniversary of the defeat was made a 'black day' in the Roman calendar and the emperor was frequently heard to mutter, 'Varus, give me back my legions.' However, by the later first century BC, and certainly by the mid first century AD, we can begin to question the impact of most battle casualties on the population of the city of Rome. The army came to be increasingly recruited from the provinces of the empire rather than directly from the manpower of the city. Rome might celebrate great victories and sacrifice many men, but the battles were far removed from Italy and the soldiers rarely originated from the city of Rome itself. The exception to this could be during civil war, when conflict might rage through Italy and threaten the walls of Rome. There was nothing more disturbing than the idea of a Roman spilling a fellow Roman's blood, and literary accounts often emphasize the destructive nature of civil conflict.[9]

Political intrigue also cost many lives. Literature often focused on these events, which were famous, or infamous, aspects of Rome's rise to power and the maintenance of that power. Roman politics, especially of the late Republic, could be highly competitive, and to back the wrong man could be lethal. The suppression and destruction of political reformers such as the Gracchi and the in-fighting among the leaders of the late Republic, culminating in the assassination of Julius Caesar (44 BC), suggest the dangerous nature of the world of the political élite. Proscriptions – published lists of the condemned – were to become a particularly terrifying consequence of political unrest. In 83 BC the dictator Sulla published a list of more than 500 names in the space of three days; these people had a price on their head and the cost of sheltering them was death. The emperors could also purge opposition, expelling and executing dissidents and encouraging opponents and 'traitors' to take their own life before facing the humiliation of a trial. The tally of the aristocratic dead could stand as one of the final judging statistics of a Roman emperor. The biographer Suetonius tells that the emperor Claudius executed 35 senators and 300 Roman knights. The emperor Tiberius was particularly notorious for his 'treason trials', and after betrayal by his Praetorian captain Sejanus, he ordered the massacre of those complicit (AD 33).[10]

> The vast number of victims of the massacre lay on the ground; either sex, all ages, the famous, the obscure; their bodies scattered or heaped together. Relatives or friends were not allowed to stand by or to weep over them, or even look for too long. Guards surrounded them, watching their sorrow, and escorted the rotting bodies that were dragged to the Tiber. There they floated away or grounded, with no one to cremate or touch them. Terror had dissolved the ties of humanity and the growing cruelty drove compassion away.[11]

For the élite, execution was often by enforced suicide; the emperor got his way, and the condemned were given the chance to save face and retain some dignity (see p. 58–59). The alternative was a relatively swift dispatch by means of the sword. However, for the lesser orders execution was often slow, painful, humiliating and highly public. Criminals could be crucified, burned alive, thrown to wild beasts or used in other fatal arena entertainments. We hear of mythical re-enactments where the condemned were forced to role-play the deaths or torments of legendary characters and heroes. Some criminals could be condemned to fight in the amphitheatre, but gladiators could also be recruited from slaves and even free men. The gladiatorial profession was a disreputable one, but some gladiators could become extremely popular, win prize money and ultimately gain their freedom. Defeat in the arena did not automatically mean death, and surviving tombstones to gladiators suggest that some at least received a decent burial (Figure 3). This was not the case for most of the condemned criminals, whose bodies may have been dragged from the arena and dumped in the river Tiber at Rome or left to rot on the cross if they had been crucified. The spectacle of the executed could provide a powerful deterrent: after the suppression of the slave revolt led by Spartacus (71 BC), 6,000 of his followers were crucified along the Appian Way from Capua to Rome.[12]

Death for many, whether by execution, battle wounds, accident or disease, would have been prolonged and painful. Doctors were common, but medical knowledge was rudimentary. Complications might follow procedures. Verginius Rufus, the mentor and friend of Pliny the Younger, failed to recover from a broken thighbone that had been badly set (AD 97). An epitaph to a young man in Rome stated that 'the doctors operated on him and killed him'. Pliny the Elder (AD 23–79) also expressed concern at doctors and their search for cures:

> Doctors risk our lives while they are acquiring their skills; their experiments cause deaths; and yet for doctors, and only for doctors, there is no punishment for killing a man. In fact they pass on the blame, criticizing the deceased for his want of moderation and self-control.[13]

Doctors might have often been limited in the practical help and pain relief that they could give. People with disease, even if it was not immediately life-threatening, might consider suicide to escape the pain. Pliny the Younger wrote of a friend who, if his illness was diagnosed as terminal, would prefer to take his own life, and of another friend who, in the face of continuing pain and discomfort, starved himself to death. Pliny the Elder noted that 'life's supreme happiness was a sudden death'; he continued to note famous cases of people dying unexpectedly as they went about their daily business. Many of these were struck down presumably by heart attacks or strokes. Pliny the Elder's own death was unexpected and dramatic; he was overcome by noxious fumes as he tried to assist people escaping from the eruption of Vesuvius. His nephew, Pliny the Younger, recorded that his collapse was sudden and that when the body was found Pliny the Elder looked as if he were asleep rather than dead. A quick and relatively painless exit was an ideal, but in a world without adequate pain relief, it may have eluded many.[14]

THE DEATHBED

Despite much evidence to suggest its horrors, the deathbed and death scenes could be readily idealized. To die well, to achieve a 'good death', there were certain requirements: one should be at home, or at least with one's loved ones, and one should be brave and resolute and utter some wise or witty parting words. A close relative, preferably a mother or spouse, would then catch the final breath with a kiss, before closing the eyes and calling aloud the name of the deceased (the *conclamatio*). Any pain, suffering or anger that the dying might have experienced was little mentioned. It was not that real pain was denied or ignored, but it showed strength of character to confront suffering with bravery. Emotional extremes could characterize the bereaved (especially women), whereas the dying (especially men) were supposed to be calm and resigned. Valerius Maximus, writing in the early first century AD, summed it up and also hinted at the interest the deaths of others occasioned as a final judgement on life and character: a man was regarded as fortunate if he gave up life calmly (*placide*), and 'The greatest importance is attached to how a life begins and how it ends.'[15]

In AD 14 the 65-year-old emperor Augustus lay dying. At the time of his death he was staying at the family home in Nola (Italy), and he would breathe his last in the same room in which his father had also died. On his final day Augustus attended to his appearance before speaking to his friends and asking them whether he had played his role in life well: 'If so clap your hands and dismiss me from the stage.' He died kissing Livia, his wife of 43 years, saying, 'Do not forget our marriage.' So Augustus passed away of old age, at home with his friends and family, in his own bed. He was calm and collected and had sufficient time to put his affairs in order and speak appropriate words to those around. This was a good death. In fact it was the sort of death that Augustus had longed for, quick and painless, which considering his meteoric and ruthless rise to power, he was probably grateful for. Augustus' mind did wander just before he breathed his last, in imagining that 40 young men were carrying him off, but as fitted such a great man, this was a premonition rather than a delusion – 40 soldiers of the Praetorian Guard carried him out for his lying-in-state.[16]

We find similar elements in other deathbed scenes, and not just those of élite men. By the first century AD the domestic deathbed was also idealized for women and children, although their decorous behaviour was described by men to reflect positively upon their male relatives. Pliny the Younger wrote of the demise of a 13-year-old daughter of his friend Fundanus. Pliny commented on the child's cheerfulness and the brave and comforting words she spoke to her loved ones. The orator Quintilian (c. AD 35–90), in his account of the death of his elder son, noted the boy's courage, his struggle against his illness and his thoughtfulness for those around. In his poetic account of the final moments of Priscilla, Statius noted that the woman was surrounded by friends and family, and how she embraced her husband and spoke comforting and uplifting words to him. The bravery inherent in these accounts hints perhaps at the underlying suffering of the dying and certainly at increasing weakness. Statius skilfully evoked Priscilla's gradual loss of sensation, her failing eyes and her dulled hearing. However, extreme pain and any loss of dignity or self-control were absent in these idealized accounts. As non-family, it is unlikely that Pliny and Statius would have been present at these particular deathbeds, so they were creating a picture, using reports from those who were present, which flattered the memory of the deceased. Nevertheless in all three accounts the deathbeds were represented as busy places, with various people – family, friends and slaves – milling around. For a death to be subsequently admired, and also to avoid accusations of foul play, it needed to be well witnessed. For the powerful, the deathbed crowd may have become overwhelming. Suetonius observed that Augustus dismissed some of his entourage before dying peacefully in Livia's arms. In his dying moments (AD 19) Germanicus, (the nephew of the emperor Tiberius), who had allegedly been poisoned, conversed with his friends and his wife, although the historian Tacitus also noted that Germanicus spoke to his wife privately, as if amongst the throng husband and wife had to struggle to find a final intimate moment. We can also note that doctors were frequently in attendance. They were at the sickbeds, and probably the deathbeds, of Priscilla and the children of Fundanus and Quintilian. Statius observed that, despite their skill, the doctors could do nothing to save Priscilla. The daughter of Fundanus obeyed her doctor's instructions, and Quintilian's son earned the admiration of his doctors for his bravery. These accounts suggest that, to some degree, the deathbed was medicalized; doctors were an expected presence and played a role in supporting the dying. They may have been offering pain relief (however basic), giving advice or simply judging when the moment of death was imminent.[17]

In surviving epitaphs there are few references to the deathbed or the final hours of the dying. Epitaphs tended to describe the living person rather than the dead or dying one. As noted previously, epigraphic references to causes of death were rare and pathos was more often created from the perspective of the survivors. Epitaphs may have noted that someone died young and the anguish this created (*see* p. 61), saying nothing of how, where or with whom the person died or how he or she had faced death. For the youthful, death was sometimes described as sudden or unexpected: 'Death silently and suddenly crept up on you.' A more mature person might be imagined as accepting death calmly, or at least with resignation, having led a full life: 'I beg you not to cry but rather to speak kindly to my spirit.' The epigraphic silence on the details of the deathbed may reflect the fact that most epitaphs were commissioned and composed by family members, some of whom might have been present at the deathbed itself and felt it unnecessary to comment further. Equally the domestic deathbed was not, in general, the subject of funerary art, although a few exceptional reliefs suggest that the 'good death' was not just an élite literary construct. These rare images of the deathbed often depict the final moments of children, and it was perhaps a tribute to a child to idealize the scene while also emphasizing the pathos of the loss and the grief caused by premature death. In one example from Rome, now held at the British Museum (Figure 4), a dead girl, pictured as if sleeping, lies on a high backed couch, beneath which are a dog and footstool, with the girl's slippers resting on the latter. Mourners flank the couch, and two seated figures, probably the girl's parents, rest their heads in their hands. Close to the couch, three female figures with their arms outstretched may be calling out the name of the deceased. We cannot be sure of the exact moment that the relief is intended to represent: is this the moment of death, the immediate aftermath of the death, or the display of the body that preceded the funeral? Whatever its precise timing, the overall impression is of a domestic scene centred on familial grief and loss, which underlines that the ideal was to die at home, with calmness and dignity, surrounded by loved ones, who could then mourn for the dead appropriately.[18]

It is rather ironic, but perhaps unsurprising, that some of our most fundamental insights into deathbed traditions arise from situations where ideal expectations were transgressed or it was feared that they would be transgressed. To be away from home, to be absent from loved ones at the moment of death, could be a real fear. The exiled Ovid (exiled in AD 8), living on the Black Sea, knew that his death there would be very different to the death he would have experienced in Rome. What Ovid had taken for granted – what others would have at death – was now beyond his reach: the familiar home, his own bed and the presence of his wife. When the time came, who would weep for Ovid and who would close his eyes? Separation could also affect the bereaved, who might try to compensate for their absence by bringing the remains home or by commemorating the dead with a cenotaph. The remains of Drusus the Elder (died 9 BC) were transported back to Rome, yet it apparently remained a great source of sadness to the empress Livia that she was not present at the deathbed of her son and thus able to catch his final breath. The separation added to the poignancy of Livia's grief, but in other respects Drusus had a good end, and his brother was with him at the last (see Chapter Three). Tacitus argued that his father-in-law, Agricola, met a good death (AD 93), despite rumours of poisoning, since he died at home with his wife at his side and he spoke and acted with courage. Yet the absence of Tacitus and of Agricola's daughter left a certain sadness:[19]

His daughter and I have suffered more than the bitterness of a father's loss: it is an additional grief that we could not sit by his sick-bed, comfort his failing spirit, and take our fill of last looks and embraces. We would then have received some final message, some words to keep in our hearts. It was our own peculiar sorrow and pain that through the circumstances of our long absence we lost him four years too soon. I do not doubt, best of fathers, that all tributes were given in your honour by the devoted wife at your bedside. Yet some tears that should have been shed over you were not shed; and as your eyes sought the light for the last time there was something for which they looked in vain.[20]

A good life should have a good end with a good send-off. In a 'good death', whatever its root cause, pain and suffering were little acknowledged; instead the dying were imbued with bravery, resignation and calmness of mind. The witnesses to this end – family, close friends and doctors – could take inspiration from the dying while performing their own roles of hearing last words, catching the final breath and closing the eyes. The ideal was that the dying and dead were treated with respect. For the living who contemplated death, matching and achieving this ideal could be a cause for anxiety. Equally, the bereaved could be haunted by thoughts that they had failed their loved ones. Death, if it was unexpected, untimely or on a distant shore, could deprive both the dying and the bereaved of their expected roles.

DYING WELL

It was inevitable that not everyone died peacefully in their beds surrounded by their loved ones, but even if some of the expected norms and ideals were not met, the dying could still die well. For the aristocratic élite, at least, a death of distinction could be achieved, whatever the circumstance, provided that one acted with calmness, courage and dignity.

It was among the army that the ideal of a courageous death was forged, especially for military commanders, some of whom literally sacrificed themselves for the good of Rome. In 295 BC at the battle of Sentium, the general Decius Mus declared that he would offer himself to the enemy to dissuade his men from fleeing. After a ritual of prayers, Decius rode into the enemy line and threw himself upon their spears. The Roman army was then victorious. This act, known as a *devotio*, was a deliberate voluntary sacrifice, but although it was much admired, it was extremely unusual. Commanders did sometimes die in battle and were often portrayed as doing so bravely. Even the defeated Varus, who witnessed the massacre of so many of his troops in AD 9, retained some dignity by committing suicide rather than facing capture. But in many ways, for a military leader to die in battle was a problematic ideal. The death of a general was often a sign of a Roman defeat: for the commander to die bravely, often by committing suicide before capture, was the only way for him to salvage some honour in an otherwise far from honourable situation.[21]

In Roman warfare the ideal was to fight, win and survive. The emphasis fell on victory, not on the victims who fell to create that victory. Soldiers killed in battle were far removed from the niceties of death at home. On the battlefield there was no place for relatives and final farewells. There was some honour in dying for Rome; 'In victory death is glorious', argued Cicero, and soldiers who died in battle might be described as achieving a special place in the afterlife. 'Souls so released are set among the stars', claimed the future emperor Titus as he rallied his troops to battle. But this rhetoric was far removed from the reality. Military personnel suffered violent and bloody deaths, with their broken bodies often rapidly buried *en masse* and the graves left unmarked. The bodies of common soldiers who fell in battle were not returned to their loved ones. Their memories were not recalled by monuments, and there were few posthumous rewards for bravery. There was little that was good about death in battle, but the generalized quality of military virtue and bravery did contribute to idealized death scenes. To die well, one should exhibit the courage of a soldier. Indeed one reason why gladiators were admired was that despite their debasement, they were trained to look death unflinchingly in the eye.[22]

Courage in the face of death was much lauded. If death was sudden, unexpected or violent, one could still achieve dignity by exhibiting bravery. As his assassins approached, Cicero did not flee, but bared his neck (43 BC). Julius Caesar, who had wanted death to be swift and unexpected rather than slow and lingering, accepted his violent fate calmly, with no expression of pain (44 BC). Subrius Flavus, an officer of the guard implicated in a conspiracy against the emperor, rebuked Nero and objected that the grave dug for him was too small before offering his neck and ordering the executioner to strike firmly. When Caecina Paetus was condemned to death for involvement in a conspiracy against the emperor Claudius (AD 43), his wife, Arria, gave her husband courage in the face of death by plunging a dagger into her own breast and then handing the dagger to her husband, saying 'Paetus, it doesn't hurt.' Seneca the Younger summed up the ideal way to face death from a philosophical perspective: 'It is not a matter of dying earlier or later, but of dying well or ill.' Seneca also noted that a more mundane demise still gave opportunity for bravery: 'There is a place for virtue even in a sickbed. It is not only the sword and battle that show the soul lively and unconquered by fear; a man can display bravery even in his bedclothes.' Seneca lived up to this ideal of dying well in his own death by suicide, despite it being protracted and painful (*see* p. 59). Under the emperors many executions among the élite were by enforced suicide; these self-inflicted deaths still needed to be met with bravery and resolve.[23]

The exact definition of a 'good death' might differ according to both how the person had lived and how they died. The emperor Augustus hoped for a quick and painless end (*see* p. 50), focusing on the physical aspects of dying. A physically 'good death' was rapid and without suffering, and it might even happen amidst the pleasures of life, such as eating or drinking (compare the Epicurean perspective in Chapter One). For some, especially philosophers, a 'good death' related more to one's state of mind than one's physical suffering, and dying in a state of moral purity was the ideal. For others a good death equated to a noble or brave death, sacrificing oneself for the state or for others and confronting death with courage. These ideals about the 'good death' were not incompatible. In general, all the ideals promoted the idea that death should match life and should measure up to the individual's bravery, happiness or morality in whatever combination. For many people who were not philosophically minded nobles risking their lives for the state and emperor, the 'good death' aspired to was probably one that was as comfortable, painless and dignified as was humanly possible.[24]

SUICIDE

Suicide was a source of ambivalent attitudes in the Roman world; it could be constructed as either a good or a bad death. On the one hand, suicide could be viewed suspiciously, as an act motivated by a guilty conscience or weak resolve. On the other hand, suicide was viewed as a brave and respected choice made in the face of real adversity. As with so much in the Roman world, who one was and where one stood in the social pecking order could dictate whether death by suicide was celebrated or maligned.[25]

Suicides were traditionally among the discontented dead; unable to enter the underworld, their spirits could threaten the living. Virgil suggests that those who killed themselves because they hated life occupied a separate horrid and swampy place in the underworld. Certain social stigmas could also be attached to suicide. Legal texts indicate that those who had hanged themselves or committed suicide from a sense of guilt were not to be mourned for. This suggests that motives for suicide might be scrutinized; was the act prompted by known or unknown criminality? We can see similar concerns in the rules of a burial club (*collegium*), which would not pay out funeral benefits in the event of a member committing suicide. This might have been because suicide was viewed inauspiciously, but it is perhaps more probably related to fears that the society's funds would be abused. Why those who hanged themselves were stigmatized is less clear. An Italian benefactor who donated land for a public cemetery stated that those who hanged themselves were not to be buried there. In Puteoli (Pozzuoli, Italy) the directions for a firm of public undertakers (see Chapter Three), noted that hanged bodies needed to be cut down promptly. The method of suicide may have been a matter of honour. A real man fell upon his sword, cut his wrists or took poison; hanging was the mark of the poor, dishonourable and truly desperate.[26]

Motive and method could make suicide a bad death, but rarely was it condemned as an evil that transgressed the laws of nature. The Jews, a minority group in the Roman Empire, and some Epicurean philosophers did question one's right to end one's life, but for many, at least among the educated élite, it was simply a question of freedom of choice. If life became unbearable due to ill health, the political climate or loss of honour, one could choose 'this path to freedom'. This is not to say that suicide was taken lightly; it was the characteristic of a wise man not to give up life too quickly or too freely, but to apply reason and wisdom to the situation in which he found himself. Among the élite, then, suicide was rarely seen as the negative act of the desperate, but a rational choice, and in politically unstable times it could be the ultimate means of self-definition.[27]

Suicide could be a matter of aristocratic honour, power and even privilege. To take one's own life rather than risk capture, humiliation, death and possible corpse abuse at the hands of one's enemies or opponents was the honourable option. A noble suicide could make a fitting end to a noble life, or even add a crowning dimension. The most lauded Roman example was Cato the Younger, who fell upon his sword rather than surrendering to Julius Caesar at Utica in 46 BC. Cato even defied his friends' attempts to save him by tearing his wounds back open, such was his determination to die. We can note also the account of the death of Brutus, the assassin of Julius Caesar, who killed himself after defeat by Mark Antony in 42 BC. In his final moments Brutus was surrounded by good friends, and he spoke rationally and acted bravely, so his death encompassed elements of the typical 'good death' scene. Indeed some of these political suicides entailed a deliberate element of spectacle, almost stage management, at least in the surviving literary descriptions. These brave deaths could only become an example to posterity if they were suitably witnessed and recorded.[28]

An enforced suicide ordered by the emperor could be more problematic, since it could be a symbol of the emperor's power rather than the free choice of the individual; yet suicide still allowed the victims to salvage elements of their dignity. Seneca the Younger, the great Stoic philosopher who had invested much time in thinking about death (see Chapter One), a one-time tutor and adviser to the emperor Nero, was ordered to commit suicide in AD 65. Seneca was with his wife and friends, and he spoke wisely and faced his prolonged death (through cutting his wrists) with bravery and dignity. It was a death to match his life. The same applied to Petronius Arbiter, a man of high living and the probable author of the bawdy novel *The Satyricon*. When, in AD 66, he was ordered to take his life by the emperor Nero, in whose court he had served, Petronius spent his last hours in idle chit-chat, eating, sleeping and listening to silly poems; in his will he denounced the corruption of the emperor. The account of Petronius' death is constructed not just to reflect his life, but also to reverse the normal élite, philosophically driven ideal suicide.[29]

For the majority of the inhabitants of Rome and its empire, as always the reality may have been far removed from the noble ideal. Many who committed suicide would have been more concerned with escaping real pain and horror than with creating an honourable and dignified spectacle. Seneca the Younger told of two gladiators who committed suicide on their way to the arena, one by placing his head into the moving wheel of a cart, another by choking himself to death with the stick and sponge used in Roman toilets. Pliny the Younger wrote of a couple who jumped to their deaths from a cliff because of an awful disease that afflicted the husband. Seneca and Pliny spoke of these deaths admiringly. Both acknowledged the desperation of those involved, but in creating ideals that conformed to the élite stereotype for suicide, both were inclined to overlook the lives, suffering and degradation of those beyond their own social and economic circle. At the hands of Seneca and Pliny, these suicides became uplifting or inspiring anecdotes for the educated literary élite. In an epitaph from Mogontiacum (Mainz, Germany) dating to the first century AD, we see perhaps some of the harsher social realities. A freed slave herdsman was murdered by his own slave, who then drowned himself in a river rather than face the punishment for his deeds. Here suicide was not glamorous or idealized, but a desperate act in a dangerous and violent world.[30]

BAD DEATHS

The most horrific deaths were inflicted on society's outcasts, criminals in particular. The punishment was not just the physical pain, but also the removal of all the usual norms for death, burial and remembrance. There would be no loved one to catch the final breath, to wash the body and to dispose of it properly. It was only a minority who confronted such a terrible end, but the prospect of a 'bad death', or at least that the death might be marred by the lack of some of the idealized elements, may have been a real fear. As noted above, loved ones might be absent or the death might occur on a foreign shore. These were not necessarily out-and-out bad deaths, since the dead might still be buried decently and mourned for appropriately, and sometimes the remains were even returned home. It was the contravention of the burial norms that could be the cause of most anxiety. Shipwreck and death at sea could be particularly problematic in this respect and thus dreaded. Not only was the deceased deprived of the essential niceties in such an unpredicted death, but he or she was also left unburied. Cicero claimed that those lost at sea were regarded as properly disposed of because the bones did not lie above the earth, but not everyone might have been convinced by this, and some still worried that the body would be washed ashore. Virgil has Aeneas meet a comrade in the underworld who is trapped in an unpleasant zone because, having died at sea, his body lay unburied on a beach. Propertius has the drowning Paetus pray that the tide will cast up his corpse as a comfort to his mother. Petronius' heroes in *The Satyricon* are involved in a shipwreck and tie themselves together, hoping that if their bodies are found some stranger may bury them. Horace imagines a drowned man, his body swept to shore, pleading with a passer-by to throw a few handfuls of earth over his corpse.[31]

Death at sea might be classed as a *mors acerba* (bitter death) or a *mors immatura* (premature death). Such deaths encompassed unexpected or accidental deaths and the deaths of the young. These dead, especially children and young adults, were perceived as having been taken before their time, while still in the prime of their lives. The youthful could be made to speak pitifully through their epitaphs: 'I died a premature death', explained a 22-year-old man. The commemorators of one child exclaimed, 'May a premature death never cause sorrow to you.' The death of one's child or children, whether they were infants or adults, could cause particular anguish (see Chapter Five). Parents believed that it was against the laws of nature for their children to predecease them. In his epic poem, Lucan had a father kill himself rather than perform the last rites for his dying son: 'You are still breathing, you may still survive me.' Some epitaphs noted that in burying and commemorating a child, the parent did for the child what the child ought to have done for the parent. The idea of a premature death was not, however, just confined to the young. Pliny, in writing of his sadness at the death of the aged Verginius Rufus, noted, 'To me it is as if he was taken before his time.' To describe a death as bitter or untimely, labels that could be made to fit just about any death, emphasized the grief, disappointments and anguish of the living, but these deaths were not necessarily constructed as bad deaths for the dying. Quintilian and Fundanus grieved for their children and saw their expectations thwarted (*see* p. 51). Pliny wrote that Fundanus had been planning his young daughter's marriage; now, instead of ordering jewels and fine clothes for the wedding, he was ordering incense and spices for the funeral. Nevertheless the actual deaths of the children were constructed in idealized terms: despite their youth, they died well (*see* p. 51). Equally, even though Verginius Rufus died from complications following a fall that caused a 'slow and painful' death, Pliny stressed that the way he faced his death was to be admired.[32]

By contrast, some deaths were shocking and awful for both the dying and bereaved (if there were any). A bad death contravened all, or at least most, of the idealized expectations, and in literature such bad deaths generally happened to bad characters. Whereas a good death reflected a good life, a bad death reflected a bad life. To die well even in potentially awful circumstances symbolized the brave and resolute (*see* p. 55–56); whereas to be afraid, to chatter nervously or to weep uncontrollably in the face of death was characteristic of the weak and the dishonourable. Messalina, the wife of the emperor Claudius, who had cheated on and plotted against her husband, made a bad end (AD 48). It could so easily have been different, since at the last Messalina was with her mother and had an opportunity to turn the sword on herself; instead the distraught empress was weeping and wailing, and she faced insults from her executioners before they ran her through with the sword. The emperor Nero, who fled Rome on being declared a public enemy (AD 68), was ill-prepared for his death; Nero prevaricated, muttered to himself and finally had to be helped to drive the dagger home. At least both Messalina and Nero were with family or followers and their bodies were allowed decent, if not celebrated, burial. In many cases members of the élite not only failed to show courage, but they were treated as little better than common criminals. When Sejanus, the captain of the guard and right-hand man to the emperor Tiberius, was denounced in AD 31, he was dragged to his death and his body was exposed. The emperor Galba was beheaded and the head was abused (AD 69). The emperor Vitellius, who pleaded for his survival, was tied up, dragged through the streets half-naked, abused and tortured before his execution, after which his body was dumped in the river Tiber (AD 69). There was heavy symbolism in how these death stories were told. These were the most powerful men in the state, and both their abuse of power and their fall from power were graphically mirrored and illustrated by the means of their death and subsequent corpse abuse.[33]

These deaths, as with the opposing idealized death scenes, were of course literary constructs. This is not to say that they were complete fabrications, but we can question who exactly would have seen these deaths, good and bad, and how they would have reported what they had seen. Tacitus hinted at some disparity in his account of Galba's final moments, noting that opinions differed as to the manner in which Galba faced his death. So much of Galba's posthumous reputation hinged on this crucial moment and on who witnessed it and how it was subsequently reported by admirers and detractors. Seneca the Younger also claimed that men were conscious of how their deaths would be judged and evaluated, especially if they opted for suicide: 'Someone will say that my behaviour was not brave enough; another that I was too headstrong; a third that another type of death would have shown more spirit.' Indeed a simple polarity between good and bad deaths does not always hold true; there could be shades of grey in between. A few characters managed to retrieve something good and honourable amidst the horror and humiliation, and some inadequate characters were allowed to redeem themselves in death. The emperor Otho, far from Rome's best ruler, killed himself with bravery (AD 69). Having accepted defeat, Otho put his affairs in order, wrote farewell letters to his nearest and dearest and stabbed himself without fuss. Otho was greatly mourned and became more admired for his death than his life. Other great characters endured unfortunate ends. Pompey the Great was murdered in 48 BC, and his head was sent to Julius Caesar for display. This was a bad end that resonated with Pompey's latter-day misfortunes, but the deception in his death and the abuse of his body did not reflect well on the victors. Pompey may have made mistakes, but did this end match his life? Cicero similarly met an unpleasant death (43 BC). He was proscribed by Mark Antony, hunted down and beheaded, and his head and hand were then displayed in the Roman Forum. Accounts say that Cicero bared his neck to the executioner with bravery, and subsequently Mark Antony was vilified by some for his treatment of the great orator. What befell Cicero and Pompey was shocking. These men did not deserve such bad deaths and corpse abuse, so what happened to them was problematized in ancient accounts. Just as good and bad deaths could reflect good and bad characters, these troubling ends could become emblematic of troubled eras in Roman history. Death stories became a commentary not just on the morality of individual characters, but also on the morality of the times.[34]

CONCLUSION

There were many ways to kill a Roman. Exactly what killed most people
and how long they were likely to live for escapes us. We do not have hard
and fast facts and figures, only the hints and observations, often skewed
for particular ends, found in surviving ancient sources such as epitaphs
and literature. So often we are presented with ideals about how one should
die rather than the realities of how one did. Most of these ideals were
focused on men, especially the élite, and the need to face death, whatever
the circumstance, with the courage of a soldier, with calmness and resolve.
However, these ideals were readily domesticated, with the deathbed centred on home and family, and with women and children complementing
their men-folk by dying well. In general the surviving death scenes tend to
present polarized perspectives; death is either sanitized or shocking.

In literature, in particular, death scenes were constructed to suit the
needs of the author, the political climate or both. Some people just had
to die well, others badly. How these people actually died has become so
distorted that the reality now often lies beyond our grasp. Sometimes,
however, we do gain insights into how deaths were deliberately reinter-
preted or rewritten. Cato the Younger's suicide may have become much
lauded, but his opponent Julius Caesar apparently wrote a work against
Cato that may have put a very different spin on his death. It does not
survive. We can also see contrasting perspectives in the death of Domitius,
a follower of Pompey, who died at the battle of Pharsalus (48 BC). In
Julius Caesar's account, Domitius was cut down while running away like
a coward; according to the poet Lucan, he gladly died among his peers.
These two authors were writing different genres, in different periods and
from different perspectives, and how they represented the same death took
on contrasting roles. What we are left with is ideals and counter-ideals
that are suggestive of the importance of death and dying in the Roman
world, especially the perception that dying was bound to the identity of
the individual. In short, it did not matter what killed you, but how you
faced death and then died.[35]

3

Funerals and Feasts

In 9 BC Drusus the Elder, the stepson of the first emperor, Augustus, suffered a severe fall from his horse. Drusus' brother, the future emperor Tiberius, rushed to the Rhineland to be at his side, but the injuries were to prove fatal. The body was returned to Rome, accompanied by Tiberius, who walked all the way. At Ticinum, in northern Italy, the emperor joined the entourage for the remaining journey to the capital city. The body, surrounded by the *imagines*, or images of Drusus' ancestors, was taken to the Roman Forum, where a eulogy was delivered by Tiberius. A second speech was made in the Campus Martius, where the body was then cremated, and the remains were placed in the Imperial mausoleum (Figure 13). Drusus' death was a bitter loss, the unexpected demise of a young man in whom not just his parents, but also the whole empire, had pinned future hopes. Drusus had died away from home without his mother's or wife's final embrace or kiss, yet his sudden end was in many respects a good death; Drusus had died in the service of the state, confronting enemies, and his brother at least had been present during his final moments. The way Drusus was treated after death, with the winding cortège and the grand funeral, was a tribute and an honour, a respectful end for a greatly respected man.[1]

Surviving detailed descriptions of Roman funerals are exceptional. People rarely commented upon what to them was common knowledge and practice, thus understanding the events immediately after death, those leading up to the funeral and the funeral itself can be a problematic process. The written sources that do mention death and funeral rituals may also distort reality, representing the rarefied world of the élite, giving explanations for anachronistic customs or providing imaginary poetic death scenes and funerals that inverted or challenged norms. These snippets of literary evidence are complemented by a few visual sources and a vast quantity of archaeological evidence. The latter provides a wealth of material from the funeral process, such as cremated and inhumed remains and grave goods or offerings. In piecing together this literary, visual and archaeological evidence there is a danger, however, of creating a composite Roman funeral that may never have been a reality for most of the inhabitants of the city of Rome, let alone the empire. It needs to be remembered that the literary evidence is biased toward the élite and can be chronologically widespread, while archaeological evidence for burial, although originating from across the empire and providing useful indications of cultural conformity and diversity, is not always easily related to the rituals and human actions that created it.

Nor should we lose sight of the temporal, regional, ethnic and economic differences inherent throughout the empire. In other words, how does the description of the funeral of Drusus the Elder, a noble dying at the end of the first century BC, relate to a simple, now unmarked, cremation burial found in Britain, dating to the late first century AD? Did the funeral of this lone Briton involve a procession and a eulogy? Who attended and organized his or her final rites? It is now impossible to answer these questions, but posing them highlights that we have no or few details for the vast majority of the millions of funerals that took place in the Roman period. In much of what follows in this chapter, the literary, visual and to some extent archaeological evidence is mainly drawn from Rome and Italy, but it still remains challenging to gauge the full impact of factors such as chronology, status and gender on the details of funeral rituals.

Despite the caveats in the evidence base, we can still note that for most of the inhabitants of the Roman Empire, of whatever period and background, the funeral was an important and essential ritual. Funerals in all cultures enable people to say farewell to the dead and to renegotiate their place in society. Death dislocates both the deceased and the bereaved from their usual roles in the social structure, placing them in a liminal state; the deceased are gone but their physical remains are still present; the bereaved are isolated and struggle to participate fully in their usual roles in the community. The funeral finally separates the dead from, and restores the bereaved to, the world of the living. Funerals in Rome and its empire, as in other periods and cultures, served to unite society, demonstrating its common beliefs and core values, while underlining differences and roles based on age, gender, wealth and status.

EXPENSES AND UNDERTAKERS

Roman funerals could be expensive. Individuals might leave instructions in their wills or with loved ones specifying their wishes, including how much was to be spent. Marcus Aemilius Lepidus, a leading politician of the second century BC, argued that the funerals of great men were not made noble through extravagance but through the display of ancestral images (*see* p. 89), and he instructed his sons that his funeral was not to be too expensive, setting a financial limit of a million asses. It has been calculated that a million asses would have supported 800 peasants at subsistence level for a year! This tale suggests that funerals, in their cost and trappings, were expected to reflect the standing that the deceased had held within Roman society. Needless frivolity might be frowned upon by some, but funerals were related to the status and identity of the deceased and what they or their family could afford. This is further underlined by legal texts: funerals were to be paid for from the estate of the deceased, and what was a reasonable expense depended upon wealth and status.[2]

It is difficult to know what entailed the largest expense at the funeral. Marcus Aemilius Lepidus stated that he did not wish to have extravagant purple cloth on his bier, but what the million asses was to be spent on was not noted. Clothes, perfumes, incense, mourners, musicians and food probably topped the list of expenses. This is not to argue that a funeral had to be extravagant, and funerals held for the majority of the population were probably modest and comparatively inexpensive. A fancy bier, fine shroud, costly perfumes, noisy musicians, hired mourners and undertakers were not essential. In Rome, family and friends traditionally performed the key roles of washing the body, mourning the body, carrying the body and burying or cremating the body. It is probable that many families, especially among the less well-off, did as much as they could themselves, hiring only the basic equipment and manpower.

However, the existence of funeral clubs (*collegia*) into which members paid regular contributions suggests that even for the poorer elements of society a funeral and burial did entail certain essential, or at least desired, costs. In funeral clubs people grouped together, paying a small monthly subscription, so that the club funds could then pay out a sum of money at the demise of a member. These clubs allowed individuals to anticipate and save for the cost of a funeral, and they probably also helped in the organization of funerals, with the club providing some of the necessary equipment and manpower. The regulations for one club, based at Lanuvium in Italy during the second century AD, noted that members had to pay an initial entry fee (100 sesterces) followed by a monthly subscription (5 asses), and then at their death the club would pay out a lump sum (300 sesterces). The club also undertook to pay for bodies to be returned home if a member should die some distance from the town and to hold a funeral for an image of the deceased if the body was unavailable. The latter was to cover the possibility that a master might not hand over the body of a slave. This emphasizes the social milieu of such clubs and also that some slaves had disposable income to pay for membership. Clubs could also be sponsored by wealthy patrons who contributed to club funds or provided a tomb for burial of club members. The club gained financially, while the patron gained a reputation for philanthropy and potentially a retinue of grateful followers. The purpose of such clubs might be, prima facie, to provide support for burial, but there was also a social side, with regular meetings, comradeship and internal club hierarchies. A member of the Lanuvium club was expected to donate an amphora of good wine on joining and another if he or she should gain freedom. Raising a glass to both the dead and the living was a central activity.[3]

The truly impoverished would have been unable to save regularly, and using a *collegium* or undertakers was impossible. There was little by way of state help. Towards the end of the first century AD, the emperor Nerva introduced a funeral grant of 250 sesterces for the Roman plebs. The motivation behind this gesture is unclear, and we do not know for how long it lasted or who exactly benefited. Before and after this, many corpses, especially of slaves, non-citizens and the destitute, might have received very basic disposal, if any at all (*see* p. 157–9). Not until the time of Constantine (emperor AD 306–337), who organized groups of undertakers in Constantinople to provide funerals for the poor, was the issue of funding urban funerals again fully confronted.[4]

For those who could afford to employ them, undertakers may have taken substantial costs. Libitina was the goddess of funerals; she was not worshipped, but she was associated with a grove outside the Esquiline Gate of Rome where items and services for burials could be purchased or hired. Among the funeral specialists were *pollinctores* who prepared the body, *vespillones*, who carried coffins and corpses, *fossores* who dug graves and *ustores* who cremated bodies. There were also flautists (*tibicines*), horn-players (*tubicines*), mimes, dancers, dirge-singers (*praeficae*) and mourners for hire. A *dissignator* might also organize and direct the proceedings, especially the funeral procession.[5]

The extent to which these death specialists were employed and the exact nature of the undertaking business are not well documented. Some of the best insights come from two inscriptions found at Puteoli (Pozzuoli, Italy) and Cumae (Cuma, Italy), which set out regulations for funerals that were normally contracted out to firms of professionals. The undertaking contractor was supposed to maintain a certain number of staff and to conduct funerals in order of request, although priority was to be given to organizing the funerals of the town councillors (*decuriones*). It is notable that the same firms were also involved in the punishment of slaves and the execution of criminals. Undertakers and executioners were much maligned and shunned elements of the community, and many of those employed in these roles would have been slaves. The regulation from Puteoli noted that the undertaker's workers had to bathe separately from others, that they were only to enter the town on business and then they were to be marked out by wearing a colourful cap. Death could bring a sense of pollution, both physical and spiritual, which affected undertakers (and executioners) as handlers of corpses. In literature, undertakers might be on the end of biting comments. Not only were they ill-omened, but they also made a profit out of the grief and misfortune of others. Horace noted people's fear of, and the ominous presence of, the black-dressed undertaker; Martial made jibes at the associations between doctors and undertakers, both pedlars of death; and Valerius Maximus was surprised that some undertakers charged only a nominal fee after the death of some Republican heroes: 'Those who lived for nothing but profit despised profit.'[6]

It is apparent then that people could choose to employ undertakers to assist with the handling and preparation of the corpse and with its final disposal. The specialist skills of these undertakers suggest a range of options, from complete coverage of all that needed to be done to a more limited use of just some services. The familial role in the disposal of the dead was idealized and for some always remained of primary importance, but from the late Republic, specialists tapped into this potential market and into the desire for both display and convenience. The specialized roles allocated to undertakers suggest a highly professionalized service, even if it was much maligned. Certain skills might have been increasingly monopolized by these experts, and thus it might not have always been possible or ideal for the family to do everything themselves. For example, building and tending a funeral pyre that would burn efficiently required a certain level of expertise and access to the necessary resources. The regulations from Puteoli and Cumae suggest that by the early Imperial period the relationship between undertakers and clients needed to be legally formalized; by this time the death specialists were well established and thus frequently employed by those who could afford all or some of their services.[7]

PREPARING THE BODY

At the moment of death, certain key actions were taken. The last kiss, the closing of the eyes of the deceased and the calling out of their name confirmed death (*see* p. 50). The body may have been moved at, or just before, the moment of death and placed on the ground, perhaps to symbolize that man returned to the earth at death. Artemidorus, in a work on interpreting dreams (second century AD), noted that 'The dead like babies are wrapped in cloth strips and are placed on the ground; and the end is to the beginning as the beginning is to the end.' The body was then washed in warm water, anointed and garlanded with flowers. A coin could be placed in the mouth as a symbolic fare for the underworld ferryman (Charon). The jaws were then bound, and the body was wrapped in a shroud or other suitable clothing. The role of preparing the body was traditionally attached to the women of the house, but male *pollinctores* could be employed. These *pollinctores* probably took their name from the powder (*pollen*) applied to the face of the deceased to conceal the discolouration of death. A death mask of the deceased may have been made at this time for use in the production of future portraits. The wealthy would already have had their likeness taken, and their *imagines* (*see* p. 89) may have already been produced, so such masks may have been the preserve of those middling classes desperate for a final memento of the deceased. However, the possibility that these masks may also have played a role in the funeral ritual, the mask being placed over the face of the corpse during its period of display, cannot be ruled out. Indeed the handful of surviving examples of 'death masks' have been found interred with the remains of the deceased, thus precluding their use, or at least long-term use, in portrait production.[8]

The acknowledgement of a death meant that the family became a *familia funesta*, obliged to undertake the funeral and also prohibited from usual activities. The presence of the corpse brought a sense of pollution, both physical and spiritual, to the house, home and family, and the subsequent rituals sought to redress this pollution. The direct handling of the corpse by women and paid undertakers meant that the pollution affected the men of the house least of all. A death in the family could be particularly problematic, however, for men with a public religious role. When the dictator Sulla was presiding at the festival of Hercules in 82 BC, he was unable to visit his dying wife and was forced to divorce her and have her removed from his house. Sulla was respecting religious scruples and apparently subsequently grieved for his wife deeply, respecting her with a lavish funeral. The emperor Tiberius, a stickler for traditional behaviour, also took his religious role and that of others seriously. When Tiberius delivered the eulogy for his son Drusus in AD 23, a veil was placed between him and the body 'so that the eyes of a high priest might not look upon a corpse.' Tiberius also criticized his nephew, Germanicus, a priest, for handling the bones of the dead when he buried the victims of the Varian disaster.[9]

Once prepared, the body was displayed in the atrium of the house. The body was placed on a funeral couch (*lectus funebris*) with feet towards the door and was surrounded by flowers and burning incense as the household mourned and visitors paid their respects. The corpse might be dressed in finery, with symbols of office on show. Juvenal joked that in his day (late first century to early second century AD) people only wore their togas when they were dead! The appearance of the dead contrasted with that of the bereaved, who wore dark clothing and might dirty their hair with ashes, pull at or even cut their hair, beat their breasts and scratch their cheeks. Such dramatic gestures were particularly characteristic, although not exclusively, of women. In many respects the mourners marked their state by doing the opposite of what was usually expected, such as not washing or not eating, and by wearing dark clothing, which was usually associated with the poor. Hired mourners could also be employed to complement and support the family mourners, taking on some of the demeaning work, singing dirges and laments in praise of the deceased and shouting and wailing to express the grief of the bereaved.[10]

Lucian, writing in the early second century AD, provides a useful summary of the preparation of the body and the behaviour of the bereaved. To this Greek satirist it was all a bit farcical and melodramatic. Lucian claimed that 'the same stupid customs prevail everywhere', but it is difficult to judge whether everyone everywhere in the empire did follow similar practices.

> Then they wash them, as if the lake in Hades wasn't big enough for people there to wash in! Then having anointed the body, which is already speeding to decay, with fine perfumes, and crowning it with beautiful flowers, they lay the dead in state, dressed in splendid clothes, which are probably thought to stop them getting cold on the journey and from being seen naked by Cerberus. Next come cries of distress, wailing women, weeping everywhere, the beating of breasts, tearing of hair and blood marked cheeks.[11]

A rare sculpted relief originating from a tomb in Rome depicts a body lying in state (Figure 5). A deceased woman is laid out on a bed with a double mattress. The bed is surrounded by torches, and at the foot is a flute player. Behind the bed a male figure holds out a garland toward the deceased, and two female figures, with their hair untied, beat their breasts. At the bottom of the scene, in front of the bier and shown in smaller scale, are further mourning figures also beating their breasts. It is difficult to judge whether the figures in the relief represent the family of the deceased or hired mourners. The flute player suggests the presence of at least some funeral specialists and the singing of laments and dirges, while the presence of members of the household is suggested by three figures at the bottom right of the relief who wear the pointed caps of freedmen, indicating that these former slaves had been freed in the last will and testament of their owner.[12]

While the corpse was displayed, plans for the funeral would have been advanced. For the well-to-do, heralds may have been employed to announce the death on the streets and to encourage people to attend the final rites. An announcement of a death has been found painted onto a house wall in Pompeii. How much time elapsed between the death and the funeral would have varied. For most families, who lived simply, display of the body would have been impractical and unhygienic, and the funeral probably rapidly followed death. For the élite, the body may have been displayed for up to a week. The Romans were familiar with embalming (and mummification) through contact with Egypt and the Greek east, but these practices were not extensively adopted. When Nero's wife (Poppaea) was embalmed, 'stuffed with spices', in AD 66, the historian Tacitus described this as unusual and foreign. Perfumes and the burning of incense may have sufficed to disguise odours. The Elder Pliny noted that certain spices were associated with death and vast quantities of these were used every year at funerals.[13]

THE FUNERAL PROCESSION

Following any lying-in-state or display, the body was conveyed from the home to the grave or site of cremation. For the élite the body may have initially been transported to the Forum for the delivery of a eulogy, but most bodies were probably taken directly for disposal. Cemeteries were located outside of the walls of Roman towns (see p. 154–5), so this journey may have been a lengthy one. The procession (pompa) consisted of the bier, musicians, mourners, family and friends. In terms of expense and duration, it may have constituted the major part of the ritual. The dead and the bereaved could not be missed. The streets would have cleared at the sound of the musician's trumpets, horns and flutes and the shouts, wails and singing of the hired mourners. All would make way for the decorated bier, the dark-clothed mourners and an entourage of people bearing torches and incense burners. The processions of the élite, at least during the Republic and early Imperial period, were rendered even more of a spectacle by the parade of the imagines. These were masks representing the facial features of the ancestors of the deceased, which could be worn by actors. The deceased himself might even be brought back to life by an actor or relative wearing his mask. The funeral could thus become a mix of sombre procession and carnival parade.[14]

A fundamental source for, and a unique representation of, a funeral cortège is a sculpted relief from Amiternum (near L'Aquila, Italy) that dates to the mid first century BC (Figure 6). The deceased lies on a bier with a double mattress that is shouldered by eight pallbearers. Around the bier is a canopy decorated with the moon and stars. Resting on the canopy is a helmet, perhaps indicating that the deceased had served in the army. Behind the bier follow nine mourners who are grouped together, almost stacked upon each other. The lowermost mourner carries a container, probably for incense. Immediately in front of the bier are two women, possibly representing hired mourners; one is pulling at her hair, while the other has her arms upraised in grief. Two tiers of musicians head the procession, including three horn players and four flute players.[15]

The body of the deceased would be carried on a bier, which in the case of cremation would be burned on the pyre. Excavated debris from pyres suggests that biers were made from wood, but they could be decorated with bone, ivory and bronze. The bier might also be draped with cloth. Marcus Aemilius Lepidus, as noted above, did not want expensive materials for his bier. On the relief from Amiternum (Figure 6), the canopy decorated with moons and stars may be intended to imply opulence and the presence of rich fabrics. The bier would be carried by eight bearers, ideally drawn from members of the deceased's family. It was an honour for sons, heirs and even freed slaves to carry the dead. It was noted that Quintus Metellus Macedonicus (consul in 143 BC) not only lived to a great old age and died among his family, but also was carried out by his sons and sons-in-law, who included a praetor, three ex-consuls and one ex-censor. This was a distinguished man, carried out by even more distinguished relatives.[16]

The bier was accompanied by mourners. Some of these would have been women hired to make symbolic gestures of grief, such as pulling their hair and beating their breasts. Among the well-to-do and élite it may have been deemed more appropriate to pay people to weep and wail than make a personal public show of emotion (*see* p. 128). Some of the mourners may have sung or chanted laments praising the dead and emphasizing their passing. Family and friends – those genuinely bereaved – probably followed behind the bier. Having a lengthy procession and a well-attended

funeral was viewed as a symbol of worldly success and an expression of
public respect:

> He was buried very well. He had a bier with beautiful linen. The mourning was very
> good since he had left several of his slaves their freedom, but his widow was a little
> mean with her tears.[17]

As Petronius does here, some authors claimed that wealthy men, desperate
to leave a final good impression, freed their slaves in their will to boost
the number of free men who would follow their bier to their grave. The
emperor Augustus tried to stop such extravagant displays by restricting
the number of slaves that could be freed by will.[18]

Torches may have accompanied the procession, lighting the way and
helping to clear the streets. The presence of the torches may indicate that
all funerals were originally held at night, but equally their use may have
had symbolic or protective origins, lighting the way of the deceased to the
next world or warding off evil spirits. Night-time funerals were associated
with children, whose rapid removal and disposal could symbolize their
marginal status (*see* p. 137). This is not to say that all children were
cremated or buried at night, and a hasty disposal under the cover of dark,
even of a youngster, might arouse suspicion. This was the case with the
funeral of Britannicus (AD 55), who was said to have been poisoned by his
stepbrother, the emperor Nero.[19]

For many the funeral procession would have been simple and rapid.
Musicians, hired mourners and elaborate biers would have been an
unnecessary expense for the poor. It is possible that the burial clubs
owned some basic equipment to be used by members, such as a bier, cloth
and incense burners, and no doubt the fellow members of the *collegium*
swelled the ranks of the funeral procession. The regulations for the
collegium at Lanuvium (*see* p. 68) suggest that members would be paid,
or at least nominally rewarded, for attending fellow members' funerals.
For those who had made little or no provision, the procession would have
been functional and rapid. A combined stretcher and coffin, known as a
sandapila, might be used to transport the body. The narrow shape of this

and the lowly nature of its servile bearers could be a way of insulting the well-to-do. After his assassination, the emperor Domitian was carried out in a *sandapila*, and the poet Martial insulted a certain Zoilus by comparing his pretentious litter with a *sandapila*. Once more we access the experiences of the non-élite, and a large part of the population, through indirect rather than direct evidence. For most authors the ways of poverty were often shameful, although simplicity and modesty could sometimes act as a foil, albeit an artistic or ironic one, to needless extravagance.[20]

> Do not let my funeral procession make its way with many masks, nor let there be a trumpet making a vain lament for my end. Do not allow a bed with an ivory pillow be prepared for me, nor let my dead body lie on a bier embroidered with gold. Let there be no procession of incense-bearers, but only the humble rites that mark a poor man's funeral.[21]

FUNERAL SPEECHES

What happened when the grave or pyre was reached remains largely unknown. Certain rituals may have been performed, including animal sacrifice and the distribution of food (*see* p. 85>), although the exact timings often remain unclear. In the case of cremation, the bier was placed on the pyre, the body was anointed and the eyes were opened. The deceased was kissed by a loved one, who would then ignite the pyre. The name of the deceased was then called out, and in military funerals and those of some emperors, the pyre was circled three times. Whether there was a specific religious aspect to all this and whether set prayers or exact formulae accompanied the actions remains a mystery. Pliny the Elder referred to the custom of opening the eyes of the dead and provided a ritual explanation, stating that it was important that the eyes be displayed to the heavens.[22]

The aspect of the pre-disposal ceremony or customs about which we know the most was not religious. A speech or eulogy could form part of the proceedings, and this was very much focused on praising the deceased and offering comfort to the bereaved rather than providing spiritual guidance. For the élite this speech (*laudatio funebris*) was a mark of distinction, which could be sanctioned by the state. The speech was delivered in the Forum prior to arrival at the cemetery. For others a speech may have been made at the graveside or pyre. We can note that for Drusus the Elder, there were speeches both at the Forum and at the pyre. The delivery of two speeches reflected the importance of Drusus, and the account indicates that the grave site or pyre was an accepted venue for speech-making.[23]

A eulogy may not have been appropriate for all, as it was in principle a mark of distinction, but we can imagine that simple comments, generic praise and lament may have been uttered at the graveside of many people. Lucian's satirical lament by a father for his son, although delivered in this case at the laying out of the body, is suggestive of the tone. The father bewailed his own loss and noted all the experiences that his son would be deprived of, such as marriage, children, work and partying. For the political élite the speeches were part of the funeral spectacle (*see* p. 89–93) and the eulogy provided an opportunity to recall the successes of the deceased and to place these in the context of the family's position within the political framework. This was particularly the case during the Republic, when the speech was delivered by a close male relative and had the potential to inspire those around. Under the emperors the tradition of speeches for prominent people continued, but they were often now delivered by a fellow leading citizen rather than by a family member, thus blunting their political edge. In his first-century AD work on oratory, Quintilian noted that 'Funeral speeches are often imposed as a duty on those holding public office, or entrusted to a magistrate by decree of the Senate.' At the end of the first century AD Pliny the Younger noted that the funeral of Verginius Rufus (AD 97), a man who had saved the empire by putting down a Germanic revolt, was foremost a credit to the emperor, and the speech was delivered by the serving consul. In Imperial Rome familial praise of the dead may have been better placed in private contexts. In public any praise had to be tempered by the knowledge that the emperor was not to be surpassed.[24]

It is perhaps ironic that some of the best preserved examples of eulogies honoured women rather than men. Two of these speeches date to the late first century BC, a time of political change when it may have been easier to note traditional female virtues rather than male virtues. In the eulogy of Murdia we hear of the fair and equal treatment demonstrated by this woman, through her will, toward her children, and we also hear of her commitment to the idealized virtues of wool-working, obedience, chastity and modesty. The speaker noted that such speeches for women often said similar things: 'The praises awarded to all good women are usually simple and identical . . . it would be tiresome to find new praises for a woman, since the course of her life has little variation.' The second surviving speech to an unknown woman, although she is often called Turia, detailed more of her life events. Once more the traditional virtues of chastity, obedience and wool-working were praised, but 'Turia' was also presented as a woman with true strength of character who had defended her father's will, pleaded for the life of her husband and protected her home against plunderers. This life and the speech were a reflection of troubled times at the end of the Republic, but they suggest that eulogies, despite formulaic elements, could be centred on the individual and their contribution, even if these aspects were primarily viewed from the perspective of familial virtue and honour. In praising these women the male speakers also praised themselves and their families.[25]

The eulogies to Murdia and 'Turia' both survive because they were inscribed onto funeral memorials, forming part of the epitaph. It underlines the commemorative aspect of speech-making that this final, needs be selective, account of a life could form an essential part of a posthumous legacy; in the words of the husband of 'Turia', 'the thought of your fame gives me strength'. Perhaps for men, the really prominent among them that is, eulogies were more often published in book form than put up as inscriptions. Pliny the Younger planned to publish a eulogy written in praise of a friend's son. This eulogy may not have been delivered at the actual funeral, but it suggests that literary praise of the dead both preserved memory and flattered and comforted the survivors (*see also* Chapter 5).[26]

DISPOSAL OF THE BODY

Disposal was the climax of the funeral. During the Roman period bodies were either burned (cremated) or buried (inhumed). Practices such as embalming and exposure of the corpse were known of and persisted in certain parts of the empire, but they were not widely practised. How a society disposed of its dead was seen as a cultural indicator. Cicero noted the particular traditions of the Egyptians and Persians, and the satirist Lucian dismissively joked that 'The Greek burns, the Persian buries, the Egyptian salts.' Lucian's list may simplify a range of customs, but it serves to highlight that some practices were viewed as culturally specific and that part of being Roman, or at least Graeco-Roman (remember Lucian came from the Greek east), was accepting and conforming to the dominant method of disposal, even if this method did in reality vary across time and space.[27]

Some authors dismissed or belittled human anxieties about the fate of their corpse. When you were dead, the argument went, you would not know or care about what happened to you, and ideas about protecting the soul were just superstitious nonsense. The philosopher Lucretius, who believed that death was not an evil (*see* p. 20), asserted that it made no difference whether a body was inhumed, cremated, embalmed or exposed; people were fools for believing that their body would still feel or experience these fates. Most people, however, did care what happened to the bodies of themselves and their loved ones, and great importance was placed upon decent disposal. To be inadequately buried, for a body to lie exposed or even worse to be mutilated was seen as a great indignity. Criminal punishment often entailed the denial of disposal. This was a way of destroying the identity of the deceased and meant that their soul would not achieve rest. An aspect of selecting suicide for some was that it gave them power to ensure that their body was disposed of properly, if somewhat hastily, rather than falling into enemy hands. Tacitus explained the popularity of suicide during the emperor Tiberius' reign of terror:[28]

This mode of death was popular due to fear of the executioner and because a man sentenced to death legally forfeited his estate and was forbidden burial, whereas he who passed sentence on himself was rewarded for his speed by burial and recognition of his will.[29]

The most basic requirement for disposal was that the body should be covered with earth, and even a few handfuls of dust in a symbolic gesture could suffice. Horace imagined a drowned sailor, his body washed up on the shore, demanding that a passer-by put right the wrong done to his body: 'It will not take long. Throw over three handfuls of earth, then hurry away.' Burial in the earth may have retained its symbolic significance even when cremation was the dominant rite. Cicero referred to *os resectum*, the act of severing and burying a bone taken from the body prior to cremation. Varro noted a similar rite, although he related the disposal of the bone to the purification of the bereaved family. There is little further evidence for the act of *os resectum*, and we are left to wonder how and when the bone (probably a finger bone) was removed and then how, when and where it was disposed of. The essential factor was that the casting of earth over cremated or inhumed remains made the places where they were buried religious and therefore protected.[30]

Why there were shifts in use between cremation and inhumation in the Roman era is largely unclear. The laws of the Twelve Tables (c. 450 BC) acknowledged that both rites were possible. The earliest burials that have been excavated in Rome, dating to around 1000 BC, were cremations. However, Cicero and Pliny the Elder both believed that inhumation was the most ancient rite, widely practised from the time of King Numa (seventh century BC). The inhumation of bodies was certainly in vogue during the early and mid Republic, but by the first century BC cremation had become the dominant rite in Rome, although inhumation was retained by some of the older families. Ancient commentators suggest that cremation was adopted because people feared that inhumed bodies might be exhumed and abused. By the first century AD any variation from cremation could be seen as unusual. When the emperor Nero's wife, Poppaea, was embalmed and interred in the Imperial mausoleum in AD 66, this was seen as 'foreign' and not the usual 'Roman custom', while the author Petronius described inhumation as a 'Greek' practice. Indeed while cremation flourished in the first century BC and first century AD in Rome and most parts of the empire, there were exceptions. There was no law against inhumation, and it was the preferred rite among Jews and Christians. The rite also persisted in parts of Italy and elsewhere in the empire, especially in the east. From the early second century AD inhumation once again increased in popularity, affecting Rome and gradually those provinces where it had not been practised before. During the third century inhumation came to be virtually universally used across the empire. Once more the exact reasons for the shift remain unclear, but a change in fashion rather than a change in beliefs seems most likely.[31]

In cremation the body, still on the bier, was placed on a pyre (*rogus*) built of wooden logs, each layer placed at right angles to the previous one. Kindling wood, papyrus and incense might be added to help the flames take hold. Pyres could be large and elaborate, and Pliny the Elder suggested that they could be painted and decorated. The pyres built for emperors and other leading figures may have been particularly impressive; the emperor Pertinax's pyre, for example, was a three-storey tower. The site of the cremation, as well as the site of the burial of the ashes, was subsequently preserved and monumentalized for some emperors. For most people pyres were probably located within the cemetery, where there would have been an area set aside for cremation (*ustrina*). Some large tombs and enclosures could have had their own area for this purpose. In some cases the pyre may have been located at the exact place of burial (*bustum*), with the remains even falling into a grave beneath. Some ancient commentators noted the difference between an *ustrina* and a *bustum*, but direct archaeological evidence for cremation and burial at the same spot is limited.[32]

Items and offerings could be burnt with the deceased. Perfumes and incense might be added to the pyre; these assisted burning and disguised odours but could be an expensive offering. Pliny the Elder noted that cinnamon and cassia were particularly associated with the dead and were burned in large quantities at funerals. Cypress trees may have been planted to disguise odours in areas used for cremation, or cypress branches may have been arranged around the pyre. Cypress branches were also placed outside the homes of the bereaved (*see* p. 122). Pots, glassware, jewellery, food and small animals might be placed with the body on the pyre or thrown onto it as it burned. The origin of this practice was presumably the belief that these burnt offerings would accompany the deceased into the next world, feeding and clothing them and symbolizing their earthly wealth. Whether most people actually took the offerings so literally is hard to judge. The offerings may have been regarded more as an act of respect or it may have been cathartic for the bereaved to throw items onto the pyre, and some items, especially pottery, could be deliberately broken beforehand, symbolizing the finality of the separation of the dead from the living. The extravagant inclusion of property on the pyre (or in the grave) was, however, unusual. Expensive items such as jewellery were expected to be handed down to the next generation, not destroyed at death. It may have been appropriate to dispose of a young or childless girl or woman with some jewellery, but in general excessive disposal of property was viewed as needless extravagance or characteristic of certain groups, such as the Gauls. In his account of his Gallic Wars (mid first century BC), Julius Caesar noted how traditions could differ:

> Funerals, considering Gallic civilization, are splendid and expensive. Everything that the dead man is believed to have held dear, including even living animals, is cast into the pyre; and not long before now, only a generation ago, slaves and dependants known to have been loved by their masters were burnt with them at the conclusion of the funeral rites.[33]

One testator from Langres in France, a man presumably of Gaulish descent, seems to have maintained aspects of this tradition into the late first century AD, requesting that his hunting equipment, bathing items, chairs and clothes be cremated with him. More often such wanton destruction of property was seen as uncalled for or mocked, and a contributor to legal compendium *The Digest* noted that 'It is not right to bury jewellery, or similar things with the dead, as some simple people do.'

The fact that a showy pyre, richly perfumed and decorated, still appealed to some is suggested by the poet Statius' description of the pyre for Atedius Melior's favoured slave, which was heaped with purple cloth and stuffed with herbs and incense and onto which gifts were thrown. To act so was to risk censure. Pliny the Younger was appalled by the sacrifice of Regulus' son's pets around the boy's pyre, viewing it as little more than a showy and melodramatic gesture.[34]

The pyre would have stayed alight and required attention for some hours to ensure that the body was adequately burned. For a corpse to be left half-burned was offensive to the living and an insult to the dead. In two of his speeches Cicero made political capital, at the expense of his enemies, from funerals that had contravened tradition, even claiming, no doubt rhetorically rather than factually, that bodies had been incompletely cremated. Of the body of Clodius, Cicero stated that it was 'half-burned' and then torn to pieces by dogs. The ignominy attached to half-burning is also suggested by the reaction to the death of the unpopular emperor Tiberius, when a mob threatened to seize his body and half burn it.[35]

Once the fire had burned down, the pyre was drenched with wine. The remains of bones and ashes were collected and placed in a container, which was delivered to the closest female relative prior to burial. The container for the ashes could be a pottery urn, glass vase, lead canister, marble ash chest (Figure 12) or ossuary altar. The latter was free-standing, but the other receptacles would be buried directly in the ground, or they might be placed in a niche in the walls of a house tomb, enclosure or columbarium (Figure 10).[36]

In inhumation the body was buried directly in the ground, wrapped in a simple shroud or encased in a coffin made of wood, lead or stone. Some bodies were not covered with earth, remaining above ground on shelves in constructions such as house tombs or being placed on earth-cut shelves in underground *hypogea* and catacombs. Large stone and marble sarcophagi could be located above ground or within tombs, and this might especially be the case with ornately decorated examples (Figures 4 and 8), since the fine sculpture could then be viewed (if often only by a limited audience).

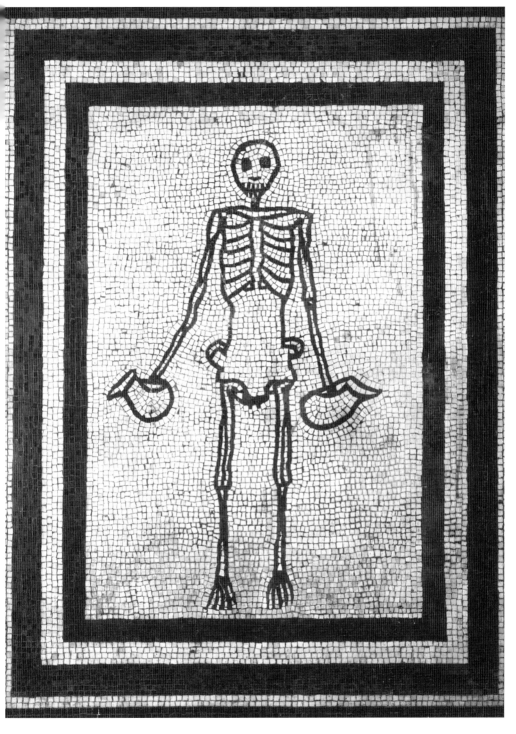

1. Black and white mosaic depicting a skeleton carrying wine jugs. House of the Faun, Pompeii. First century AD. Held at Museo Archeologico Nazionale, Naples. Photograph: Alinari.

2. Stele of Curatia Dinysia (*RIB* 562). The deceased is depicted reclining on a couch, holding up a drinking cup. Chester. Second century AD. Held at Grosvenor Museum, Chester. Photograph: Grosvenor Museum.

3. Stele of the Thracian gladiator Aptus (*CIL* 12, 3329). Nîmes. First century AD.
Held at Musée Archéologique, Nîmes.

4. Marble sarcophagus depicting a child's deathbed. Rome. Second century AD. Held at the British Museum, London. Photograph: British Museum.

5. Relief from the tomb of the Haterii depicting a body surrounded by torches, mourners and musicians. Rome. First century AD. Held in the Vatican Museums. Photograph: Alinari.

6. Relief of a funeral procession. Amiternum, Italy. Mid first century BC. Held at Museo dell'Aquila. Photograph: Alinari.

7. A pipe for libations leading to a cremation grave protected by tiles. The Via Triumphalis necropolis, Rome.

8. Sarcophagus depicting the abduction of Persephone by Hades, with Demeter giving chase. Rome. Late second century AD. Held at Galleria Uffizi, Florence. Photograph: Alinari.

Grave goods similar to those that might be burned on the pyre, such as jewellery, coins, pots and lamps, might be placed with the inhumed body, but as with cremated remains, these offerings were rarely extensive.

FEASTS

Events immediately after the disposal are unclear, and their exact nature and timing may have varied according to whether the body was inhumed or cremated. The utterance of some standard or formulaic words (*novissima verba*) may have ended the ceremonies at the point when the pyre was lit or grave filled in. Evidence for these words is limited, but they may have included a final farewell (*vale*) to the deceased and an instruction to the mourners to leave. Cicero noted that a sacrifice of a sow to the goddess Ceres (*porca praesentanea*) took place at the grave, and it was this act that made the grave legally a grave. Did this sacrifice happen after or before a body was inhumed; and in the case of cremation did this take place before or during the cremation or afterwards, once the remains had been collected and 'buried'? We simply do not know, but it is perhaps more likely that the sacrifice occurred at the beginning of the cremation ritual, with the sacrificial meat being divided between the dead, the bereaved and Ceres, with the deceased's portion then being burned with the body and the family consuming theirs at the pyre-side. Late commentators also refer to a meal known as the *silicernium* that 'purged the family of their grief', but they do not state exactly where and when it was held. The immediate family of the deceased may have fasted in the days between the death and the funeral, and a symbolic meal at the time of disposal may have marked the end of this period of their mourning. It is possible that only close family and friends lingered as the grave was filled in or the pyre died down and the final rituals were performed. It is worth noting in particular that cremation may have been a lengthy process, and it is hard to imagine that many mourners would have remained at the pyre unless they were offered food and refreshment at this stage. Thus it seems most likely that any food consumed at the pyre or graveside on the day of the funeral was largely symbolic. The major feasting occurred some days afterwards and may not have been solely centred on the grave or pyre site.[37]

Immediately after the funeral, those who had participated were supposed to be purified with fire and water (the *suffitio*), and the house of the deceased was to be cleaned by sweeping. As with the *silicernium*, evidence for these cleansing rituals comes only from late commentators, and it remains hard to judge whether these rituals were widely practised. For the family, days of rest and mourning (*feriae denicales*) followed the funeral. On the ninth day after burial, further cleansing rituals, a sacrifice and a feast (*cena novendialis*) near the tomb brought this period of mourning to a close. The dead and the living were symbolically united at this ninth-day feast and at subsequent festivals. Tombs could include dining areas, wells for drawing water and even barbeques for cooking food. Families and other bereaved could visit tombs, make offerings to the dead and also dine and picnic with the dead at certain festivals or on personal anniversaries (*see* p. 99–102). However, the food offered on these occasions to the dead, both in its type and presentation, served to underline and mark the separation of the dead from the living. Food burned on the pyre symbolized the deceased's last meal and final consumption of sacrificial meat; thereafter the food offered to the dead only needed to be simple. Certain foodstuffs, especially salt, lentils, eggs and beans, were associated with offerings made to the dead and thus these could take on negative or ominous connotations. The lentils and salt, 'symbols of mourning', served up to Crassus' troops before fighting the Parthians (53 BC) proved to be a bad omen. The simplicity of the food offered to the dead meant that a comparison with it could also be a way of insulting people's style of entertaining. A senator was criticized for slurring a priest's banquet by describing it as like a 'funeral feast'; Juvenal joked that at a rich man's dinner party the poor guest's meagre portions were like a 'funeral offering'. Food and drink given to the dead could also be viewed as polluted, and the living were not supposed to eat it, although the offerings might still be a source of temptation for the hungry homeless. The poets Catullus and Tibullus both refer to women searching for and taking food from cemeteries.[38]

The ninth-day feast may have been the first formal occasion on which the grave was visited, the dead honoured and the living entertained. One of Trimalchio's dinner guests arrived late and drunk after attending a ninth-day funeral feast; he listed the extravagant food, including pork, sausages, bread, honey, nuts, apples, cheese, snails, eggs and even bear meat, that the guests had consumed, mentioning only briefly, and then with some regret, that half the wine had to be poured over the remains of the deceased. Whether this feast, in part or entirety, took place at the tomb is unclear. We can imagine that if the deceased had been cremated and not yet interred, the event could have been held at home, the deceased being treated as a symbolic guest of honour. However, tombs often had space for diners (*see* p. 173–4), and such a fancy dinner party held in or near the tomb underlines that the tomb and cemetery could be the focus for merriment as much as for solemnity.[39]

Feasts, including the ninth-day feast, held after the funeral and aimed very much at entertaining the living could be extravagant events, providing an opportunity for the bereaved to display status and impress both peers and social inferiors. This was taken to the extreme in commemorative banquets organized by Rome's élite. These banquets may have been held some time after the death. They were far removed from the cemetery and were intended to further the political careers of surviving family members. These were huge acts of largess; basically, an individual paid for the citizens of Rome to party, citing the memory of a deceased family member as an excuse. As early as 328 BC, at least according to the historian Livy, a magistrate sought electoral favour by distributing meat to those who attended his mother's funeral. In 58 BC Quintus Arrius held a lavish banquet to commemorate his father, motivated no doubt by the prospect of standing for election to the consulship the following year. Conversely, the meagre banquet organized by Quintus Tubero to honour Scipio Aemilianus in 129 BC was said to have cost him his election to the praetorship. Gladiatorial contests arose in a similar fashion. These were first presented at the funeral of Decimus Junius Brutus Pera in 264 BC, and they became impressive and extravagant shows. In theory they were commemorative events to honour the dead, but in reality they were a way for the survivors of the dead to court popular support. Julius Caesar, for example, held gladiatorial shows and naval battles in honour of his daughter in 46 BC, eight years after her death. Élite funerals and commemorative events, at least during the Republic, were events that could unite the community while simultaneously enforcing the social hierarchy.[40]

For the less well-off, any feasting to mark the death was probably associated with the ninth-day event and would have been relatively modest. The early laws of the Twelve Tables (c. 450 BC) suggested that things could get a little boisterous and sought to prohibit continuous drinking rounds. Many centuries later, Augustine (fourth century AD) noted that some Christians continued the tradition of drinking and feasting at the tomb on annual festivals, even honouring the dead with offerings. For Augustine the riotous behaviour that could ensue was not a suitable way to respect and remember the dead.[41]

Funerals and the following events were clearly social occasions: opportunities for people to meet up, to be entertained and even to flirt. The poet Ovid noted that grieving widows with their dishevelled hair could be rather attractive! People who attended funerals and the ninth-day feast hoped to be well fed and entertained in payment for their presence and commemoration of the deceased. There was an expectation that the dead would have a good send off. Horace teased that 'The neighbourhood praises a funeral put on with style.' This expectation could gain a macabre twist with people not just planning their final parting and party but trying to enjoy it all, and the attention, while still alive. Such mock funerals could also serve the more serious purpose of acting as a *memento mori*, a reminder that all men will die (*see* p. 25–36); indeed perhaps this message was always inherent in the rituals of feasting and offerings that promoted contact between the living and the dead.[42]

FUNERALS AS SPECTACLES

When done on a grand scale, a funeral involved an element of spectacle and entertainment. This is not to dispute that a funeral could be a sombre event. We can note, for example, the mass sadness recorded at the funerals of Drusus the Elder (9 BC) and later at that of his son Germanicus (AD 19). But large numbers of participants at such funerals became an audience wishing not just to show their last respects, but also to be impressed, entertained and even inspired. An élite funeral of the late Republic and early Imperial period involved the same basic elements as a funeral for any other member of society. In essence the body had to be prepared, displayed, carried to the grave and then disposed of. It was through additional features, and also sheer scale and grandeur, that élite funerals became memorable shows that often entailed political messages. Two elements in particular made these funerals stand out: the funeral speech delivered in the Forum and the parade of ancestral masks (*imagines*). A fundamental source is the description of a Republican funeral written by the Greek historian Polybius in the second century BC. Polybius noted that the whole population of Rome attended such events and would listen to a close relative, often the son of the deceased, deliver a eulogy from the rostra in the Roman Forum. In recalling the achievements and virtues of the deceased, the speech had the power to incite such sympathy that 'The loss seems not to be confined to the mourners but to be a public one which affects the whole people.' Polybius also noted that an image of the dead man, a mask, was made and carefully stored in the family home. At any subsequent family funerals, the mask and those of other deceased family members were worn by actors dressed up as the deceased men. These actors processed with the bier and sat to listen to the eulogy in the Forum as if in death all the generations, past glories and achievements of the family were reunited:[43]

> It is not easy for an ambitious and virtuous young man to see a finer spectacle than this. For who would not be impressed at the sight of the masks of all these men who have won fame in their time, now gathered together as if alive and breathing? What spectacle could be more noble than this?[44]

Stirring speeches and lineage-promoting masks were no doubt complemented by ever-increasing extravagant funeral display. We see an extreme
example in the funeral of the dictator Sulla. At his death in 78 BC Sulla was
voted a 'public funeral' by the Senate, which was paid for by the treasury
and to which all citizens were invited. Sulla's body was carried to Rome
on a golden litter. Once it reached the city it was accompanied by 2,000
gold crowns, gilded standards and silver shields. So many spices were
donated that a large figure of Sulla was fashioned out of frankincense
and cinnamon. The cortège included senators, *equites*, priests, priestesses,
thousands of soldiers and the common people, all accompanied by
trumpeters. Echoes of such public funerals are found in the towns and
cities of the empire, where a public funeral could be provided by the
local council (*ordo decurionem*) and was usually given to members of
that council and their relatives. Funerary inscriptions record individuals
honoured in this way and sometimes provide additional insights into the
provision of incense and the erection of commemorative statues. In the
local area these funerals must have seemed the equivalent, if not quite the
equal, to the grand funerals held in Rome.[45]

In Rome itself, funeral display, at least of the competitive kind, may
well have reached its peak during the late Republic. Cicero noted that the
early law of the Twelve Tables (c. 450 BC) had attempted to curb funerary
expenditure and frivolity, limiting expense to 'three veils, a purple tunic,
and ten flute-players' and stating that women should not scratch their
cheeks or wail. Cicero believed the provisions a good thing since, 'It is
according to nature that differences in wealth should cease with death.'
However, the laws clearly had little weight in Cicero's day (first century BC).
In the late Republic a death in the family was an opportunity to court
public support through a range of commemorative events. The feasts,
banquets and gladiatorial games that were used to promote the careers and
prestige of surviving family members have already been noted. The funeral
itself was an opportunity to display wealth and the competitive side of
family prestige. As the Republic headed towards collapse, political tensions
could run high at such public gatherings, and riots occurred at several

funerals. The funeral of Clodius (52 BC) led to the burning down of the senate house; the crowd seized Caesar's body and cremated it in the Forum (44 BC). To be sure these events were sparked by uncertain and unstable political times, but they illustrate how funerals gave opportunities for both individuals and groups to find a public voice. The funeral of Julius Caesar, with a stirring speech by Mark Antony and the display of images of his murdered body, was pure theatre designed to illicit a dramatic response from the audience.[46]

With the transition from the Republic to the Imperial period, élite funeral display began to change. The funeral of Julius Caesar had demonstrated how potent these events could be. Tiberius, the successor of the first emperor Augustus, was very careful in his organization of his predecessor's funeral. Tiberius did not wish to witness riots or undignified behaviour, as they might undermine his own authority and right to rule. A new emperor, not the mob or political rivals, needed to be in control of how an old emperor was disposed of. It would also become increasingly clear that competing with the emperor, including in the funerary sphere, would be unwise. The most elaborate funerals were to become the prerogative of the emperor and members of his family. An *iustitium*, or cessation of all public and legal business in Rome, was declared after an emperor or an important member of the Imperial family died. This in effect extended mourning from beyond the confines of the family to all the population. The funerals of the emperors drew upon Republican models for the funerals of the élite. Speeches and the parade of *imagines* remained important. In fact the display of the latter at funerals probably gradually declined among other élite families who did not wish, or at least perceived it as unwise, to promote their familial lineage above that of the emperor. Funerals of emperors also gained a new twist in symbolic suggestions that the emperor was not actually dead but immortal.[47]

The funeral of the first emperor, Augustus (AD 14), for which he left instructions but which was, no doubt, also stage-managed by his widow Livia and her son Tiberius, set the precedent for future emperors. The funeral needed to be impressive but still rooted in Republican traditions.

Soldiers were present to ensure appropriate behaviour. The bier, carried by magistrates, was made of ivory and gold and had gold and purple hangings. Several effigies of Augustus, made of wax and gold, were displayed, and numerous masks (*imagines*) of his ancestors and of illustrious Romans formed the procession. Two orations were given in the Forum. After these the body was carried to the Campus Martius for cremation. The widowed Livia stayed by the pyre for five days, then the bones were collected by members of the equestrian order and placed in the Imperial mausoleum. The extravagant show culminated with a new twist (at least according to the much-later Cassius Dio): the release of an eagle from the pyre. In its flight the eagle was supposed to represent the ascent of Augustus to the heavens. The idea of the transition from man to god (*apotheosis*) became a common element of Imperial funeral spectacle, with eagles flying from the pyre or individuals claiming that they had witnessed the ascent of the emperor's spirit. The *apotheosis* of an emperor was not, however, automatic. The emperor's immortality lay in the hands of his successor and nominally, at least during the early Imperial period, in the vote of the Senate. The funerals of emperors reflected their ability to rule well, or at least their ability to ensure the succession. A good rule (including having provided for the succession) meant a funeral with all the trappings plus the prospect of divinity; a bad rule meant an ignominious death, corpse abuse and no funeral at all.[48]

Almost two hundred years after the funeral of Augustus, the significance of the rite was clear. Inhumation may have replaced cremation for the masses, but the Imperial funeral, with cremation at its heart, was a recognized act of legitimization. A new emperor had control over both the body of his predecessor and the old emperor's new status as a prospective divinity. In AD 193 the funeral of the emperor Pertinax was organized by the emperor Septimius Severus. Pertinax had died some months earlier, and his successor had been overthrown by Septimius Severus, who now needed to establish his rule as the rightful successor to Pertinax. With no body available, a richly dressed effigy of Pertinax was made and displayed in the Forum. People processed by the effigy, which was surrounded by images of distinguished Romans, as if paying their last respects. Septimius Severus read a eulogy, and then with the crowd wailing and lamenting, the effigy was born on a bier to a pyre, which was three storeys high and adorned with ivory and gold. The consuls set fire to the pyre, and an eagle flew out and away. Thus Pertinax was made immortal and Septimius Severus emphasized that the seat of power was rightfully his. This was not so much a funeral as a ceremonial institution that was integral to the safe transfer of power.[49]

CONCLUSION

Reconstructing all the details and rituals that constituted a Roman funeral is a problematic process. Snippets of information survive about specific rites such as the *silicernium* or *os resectum*, and even 'facts' such as that the dying should be rested on the floor or the dead placed with their feet toward the door are in reality often only supported by a handful of sources. Equally, many things may have been done because of tradition rather than active belief that the rituals were essential. It is impossible for us to judge, for example, whether a coin for Charon or food offerings were provided from genuine belief that these were essential to the dead or simply because it was a matter of convention. In short we are left to wonder how reliable the available information is and whether aspects of the rites were minority or majority practices or, in the case of some rites, were even only confined to Rome's distant past.

The dangers of weaving the evidence together to create a sort of identikit Roman funeral were noted earlier. In seeking to give an impression of how the dead body was treated and disposed of, it is almost impossible not to be drawn into assembling the evidence to provide a narrative account of the body's journey to the grave. This may not always be the ideal way of handling the evidence, but at least the process reveals that funeral rituals were affected by social factors such as wealth, status, gender and age.

The identikit Roman funeral, even if largely a creation of modern

scholars, is not one that simply fitted all. Evaluating the available evidence
for Roman funeral rituals also highlights that there was change across
time. Authors and commentators might discuss and explain the rites,
indicating that the traditions were believed to be important and that a
Roman funeral was a defining and central element of Roman identity,
but things did change. We can note, for example, the increasing use of
undertakers, the declining use of the *imagines* and shifts between cremation and inhumation. Nevertheless a sense remained, even if somewhat
illusory, of the importance of tradition and continuity.

What is clear, despite potential changes in the details, is that the
rituals marked the separation of the dead from the living and allowed
the survivors to renegotiate their position in society. Death could be
threatening and frightening; the body had changed from a living being,
something that was needed and vital, to little more than unwanted matter.
The corpse and those who came into contact with it could be perceived as
physically and spiritually polluted. Once more we can question whether
the dead were really viewed as a spiritual threat, but the general idea of
pollution came to symbolize the unease and uncertainties that death
brought. The stigmas attached to undertakers, the distinguishing dress,
behaviour and actions of the bereaved and the traditional cleansing rituals
created a distance between the living and the dead and between the non-
bereaved and the bereaved. The rituals were a journey that reintegrated
(or symbolically purified) the bereaved, returning them to their normal
life, and delivered the dead to their new place among the ancestors.
Through spatial and temporal dimensions the funeral rituals removed
the polluting corpse from the world of the living. The body was physically
transferred from home to cemetery; its journey might be via the atrium
(if 'lying-in-state'), the streets (procession) or the Forum (for an élite
eulogy), and it would finally reach the grave or pyre. This journey could
be a rapid one or take several days, but the ninth-day sacrifices and feast
ensured a temporal turning point for the bereaved; internal grief might
remain, but the source of pollution was gone. The dead were no longer,
physically, with the living.

The funeral rituals also had the potential to mirror and reinforce the major social divisions in Roman society, helping to underpin social structures and roles and also confirming their potency. The perceived differences between men and women, adult and child, rich and poor, the powerful and the powerless were all echoed in the rituals. Roles were assigned according to the age, gender and social position of both the deceased and the bereaved. Note the expectation that women would weep, wail, loose their hair and wash and dress the dead; that men would act as pallbearers and deliver eulogies; that small children might be buried at night; that slaves were suited to certain undertaking roles; that once freed, ex-slaves could mourn or act as bearers; and that the poor were little cared for in death, while the wealthy élite could make a grand and glittering final exit.

It is the funerals of the élite and the relatively well-to-do about which we know the most. The few accounts and images that we have emphasize the element of display, but also the fact that funerals, even if underlining social differences, were a shared experience. A good send-off could draw a crowd, and the grander the deceased, the more diverse a cross-section of the populace in attendance. The élite could exploit this audience. In the Republic the procession of the *imagines* and in the Imperial period the *apotheosis* of the emperor are suggestive of the entertainment value of funerals. A death was an opportunity to create an eye-catching pageant and spectacle that could reinforce the superiority, even divinity, of the ruling powers. In the Republic, funerals promoted a common heritage between the spectators and their leaders, and in the Imperial era the funerals of emperors promoted stability and continuity at a time for potential unrest. In short, in their attendance and in their expression of grief, real or not, the people of Rome could be united. In all this there may have been a level of cynicism among some; there may have been a realization that people were being manipulated, that their favour was being bought and that emperors were not really gods at all. However, funerals could always evoke mixed reactions; funerals could be serious, tear-jerking occasions, but also they could be a time for fun, food and frolics. With elements of spectacle, feasting and the mocking role of mimes, élite and Imperial funerals could entail a satirical or carnival-like atmosphere. Signs of *apotheosis* that challenged the divide between human and divine were then the ultimate aspect of what might be termed funeral theatre.

4

Heaven and Hell

*To the good memory of Mellonius, a sub-deacon, who lies
in this grave. He crossed over in peace on the sixth day
before the kalends of February [27 January].*

*Here lies Felix, a senator and tribune, who lived 61
years, and was received by God on [?] of October, in the
consulship of Bassus and Anthiocus [AD 431].*[1]

In Rome of the fourth and fifth century AD, the Christian faith provided
its adherents with meaning to life and death. Death was a migration from
this world to the next, and the deserving dead would be received by God
or welcomed by angels and would 'live' in heaven. Death was not the end.
If we wind back the clock three or four centuries to a pagan pre-Christian
Rome, there was rarely such certainty about what lay beyond the grave.
Many people may have simply believed that death was the end, that it was
annihilation, and neither soul nor body would survive. Others did have
hope, if often ill-defined, for the continuity of the soul. Some believed that
the dead were set among the stars or gods or that they occupied a murky
underworld kingdom. For some these hopes and beliefs were strongly
held, underpinned by adherence to particular cults and religious practices,
the details of which often now escape us. What is clear is that 'what did a
Roman believe happened after death?' is not a straightforward question
to answer. There was not one view that held sway.

THE PRESENCE OF THE DEAD

The oldest traditions and rituals, apparently dating to Rome's earliest days, suggest that the dead were always ascribed some sort of presence, force and influence, although it is often unclear where the dead were imagined to reside or the exact form this presence took. Simple offerings were made to the dead at certain key locations, including tombs and houses, suggesting that the dead could be viewed as separated from the living but also present among them. The dead were honoured and respected as ancestors but also placated as a potential threat. The rituals suggest a need to acknowledge rather than ignore the dead; that Rome's future, and that of individuals and families, was intimately bound to those who had gone before.

One striking but somewhat obscure rite was associated with the *mundus*. This rite was described by late sources who were interpreting the works of earlier authors, and we are left to question whether it was of relevance, or even still practised, in the Rome of the late Republic and of the emperors. Festus, who wrote on words and their meanings, explained that in the centre of the city of Rome, on the Palatine Hill (although others located it in the Forum), was some sort of chamber or pit, the *mundus*, with a key stone known as the *Lapis Manalis*. This stone was supposed to be removed three times a year (on 24 August, 5 October and 8 November) so that the dead could briefly access the world of the living; these days were thus inauspicious, and no state business was to be performed. Another late author, Macrobius (quoting the first century BC Varro), noted that 'When the *mundus* is open, it is as if a door stands open for the sorrowful gods of the underworld.' Plutarch suggested that it was Romulus, Rome's founder, who created the *mundus*, encouraging the first inhabitants to cast soil from their native lands and the first fruits of the harvest into the pit. The *mundus* was then associated with fertility as well as death, reinforcing the connections between the earth, the dead and new life, which may have been particularly potent at the foundation of a city. The creation of a *mundus* may have been an aspect of the rituals associated with the foundation of Roman towns, but in reality little is known about these gateways to hell and whether the rite of opening them was much respected.[2]

More widely attested were the annual festivals for the dead, including the festivals of roses (23 May) and violets (22 March), when graves and tombs were adorned with flowers, and also the *Parentalia* and the *Lemuria*. Once more these festivals were believed to have their origins in Rome's dim and distant past, and their exact role (especially of the *Lemuria*) in Rome of the late Republic and the Imperial period is unclear. The most detailed description of the *Parentalia* and the *Lemuria* is found in *The Fasti* of the poet Ovid, a work centred on key dates in the Roman calendar. Ovid, writing under the emperor Augustus, may have reinvented the significance of these festivals in light of the new emperor's emphasis on piety to the ancestors and the gods. Rome's rulers often looked to the past, including to traditional rituals and beliefs, to give legitimacy to their rule.[3]

The *Lemuria*, held on 9, 11 and 13 May, was a time for the spirits of the dead to walk, specifically to wander around the house. The associated rites were private and domestic in character and happened at night. Ovid tells that at midnight the house owner was supposed to get up, barefooted, wash his hands, throw black beans over his shoulder and say nine times, 'I send these and with them I redeem myself and my family.' The shade was believed to collect the beans and follow behind unseen. The ritual ended with further purification by water and a clash of bronze accompanied by a demand for the shades to depart: 'Ghosts of my fathers, leave.' In the context of the *Lemuria*, the presence of the dead was a shadowy and potentially malign one; the dead were not welcome in the places of the living. Yet in other respects the homes and houses of the living did give space to the dead. Each home had a *lararium*, the shrine of the protective household gods or spirits who may have been closely aligned with the dead ancestors. Houses might be handed down through the generations and display portraits and images of previous occupants. The past, enshrined in the ancestors, was important, and family descent could be crucial to the identities of the living. Ovid also noted the festival of *Caristia*, which was held immediately after the *Parentalia*. The *Caristia* was a time for families to assemble and take stock of past, present and future generations by giving thanks to the family gods, remembering the dead and celebrating the young. In house and home the dead were revered, respected and remembered, but as the *Lemuria* suggests, not always wanted. It was crucial to recall the dead, but there was always something faintly threatening and, moreover, unknown and uncertain about the dead and their possible continuing presence.[4]

The *Parentalia*, or *dies Parentales*, was associated with the graves and tombs of the dead. It was held between 13 and 21 February. The last day (*Feralia*) was for public ceremonies, while the other days were focused more on the family. This was a time for individuals to remember parents and other deceased relatives. The details and origins of the *Parentalia* are once more described in greatest detail by Ovid. The festival was apparently an inauspicious time, especially for marriage, since the souls of the dead were free to wander among the living. It was a time to honour the dead with prayers and offerings: garlands, corn, salt, bread soaked in wine and violets. Ovid claimed that the custom was introduced by Aeneas in memory of his father and that to neglect the custom was to risk the anger of the dead. Ovid even recalled a legend that once when the rite had not been performed, Rome had grown hot from funeral pyres and ghosts had howled through the streets. Unlike the rituals surrounding the *mundus* and also the *Lemuria*, observance of the *Parentalia* is well attested. People sometimes left instructions in their wills, publicly inscribed, that their graves should be decorated and offerings should be made at this annual festival. Iunia Libertas from Ostia, for example, left property to her freed slaves, some of the profit from which was to be used for the decoration of her tomb and for sacrifices there on the *Parentalia* and also on the days of roses and violets. Quintus Cominius Abascantus, from Misenum (Miseno, Italy), left money to the local *Augustales* (honorary priests of the Imperial cult) during the mid second century AD on condition that annually on the *Parentalia* his tomb would be decorated with violets and roses, oil would be poured over his remains and the *Augustales* would dine at his tomb and also organize wrestling matches there. Abascantus was clearly a man of some importance, or at least regarded himself as such, and to him the *Parentalia* seemed more of a public spectacle than a private rite, although the essential features of making offerings to the dead and visiting the grave were included. The dining and wrestling proposed by Abascantus suggest that visiting tombs and graves was not necessarily sombre or serious. Few tombs may have been honoured as lavishly as that of Abascantus, but the *Parentalia* was a time when families met in the cemetery, made offerings and showed their respects, but also picnicked, chatted and maybe even enjoyed themselves as they remembered the dead.[5]

The *Parentalia* allowed communication between the living and the dead, as did other festivals and personal anniversaries, such as birthdays. The tomb was the focus for these commemorative rituals, suggesting that the dead were regarded as having some sort of continuing existence at, or in close proximity to, their grave. Tombs could be regarded as the homes of the dead and made to appear as houses, with windows, doors, mosaic floors and painted wall décor. Petronius had the wealthy freedman Trimalchio joke, 'It's a big mistake just to have nice houses when you're alive and not worry about the one we have to live in for much longer.' The poet Statius described the tomb that Abascantus had built for his wife Priscilla as like a house. Epitaphs sometimes called the tomb or grave the 'eternal house' (*domus aeterna*), and other phrases such as 'eternal rest' (*quieti aeternae*) and 'here rests' (*hic requiescit*) evoked the image of the dead resting or sleeping in the tomb for all time. Other epitaphs were more explicit; that of Lucius Runnius Pollio from Narbo (Narbonne, France) stated, 'I continue drinking in this tomb more eagerly because I will sleep and remain here for ever'; an epitaph from Rome described the tomb as an 'eternal house in which future life must be passed'. For others death and the grave were a welcome escape and a new world that offered sanctuary: 'I fled the miseries of sickness and the great ills of life; I am now free of all its pains and enjoy a peaceful calm' claimed the epitaph of Publius Atilius from Comum (Como, Italy), while a 6-year-old child from Ravenna (Italy) is made to observe 'life was pain, death gave me rest'. The common formula 'may the earth lie lightly upon you' (*sit tibi terra levis*), often shortened to the letters STTL, suggested the hope for rest but also that the dead might still have sensation. The offerings that could be made

to the dead – drink, food and sacrifices – indicate that the dead could be
perceived as requiring sustenance. Tombs could be equipped with wells,
barbeques and benches to encourage the living to visit the dead and
perform tomb cult. Libation tubes allowed wine and liquid offerings to
be poured into the ash container or grave of the dead person (Figure 7).
Graves were regularly to be decorated with flowers and garlands, and
lamps may have been kept alight. At the grave the living and the dead
could be physically and emotionally united. The poet Ovid imagined Anna
visiting the grave of her sister, the Carthaginian Queen Dido, and kissing
the ashes and offering some of her cut hair. Such close physical proximity,
with the actual touching of human remains and personalized offerings,
may represent poetic fancy, but the bond that the living should feel for the
dead was often celebrated. An epitaph from Rome suggests the types of
things the living expected, wanted and promised to give: 'For many years
your husband will be able to give you the garlands and offerings which he
has vowed, and so that the lamp may ever be kept alight with nard.' The
antithesis of all this was that those who were unburied, due to accident or
punishment (*see* p. 80 and 179), could be regarded as restless and homeless
since they had no grave – no home – to house their remains and spirit and
thus no venue for tomb cult and remembrance.[6]

Whether people believed that the dead resided at the tomb or whether
references to home, rest and sleep became little more than comforting
euphemisms is almost impossible to judge. It is difficult to evaluate what
motivated people to visit graves and perform the traditional rituals. Was
the *Parentalia* observed because of deep-seated belief that the dead needed
to be placated or fed, or was it a matter of observing tradition and convention? Did people believe that the dead were present and appreciated the
offerings, or were the gifts symbolic marks of respect? Were such festivals
primarily about remembering the dead (as Abascantus from Misenum
seems to prioritize) and in the process promoting the unity and identity
of the living family or community? These may remain unanswerable
questions, but posing them underlines that tomb cult may have been
multifaceted and may have fulfilled different roles for different people.

THE UNDERWORLD

Thus far we can trace a certain intimacy and co-dependence between the living and the dead, in particular enshrined in certain traditional rituals and ceremonies. Leaving the question of belief aside for the moment, in Rome's distant past the dead were imbued with some sort of continuing presence that demanded acknowledgement and respect. These earliest rituals may not have depended on a well-developed sense of where the dead went to or resided. There were fears that the dead might enter the spaces of the living, but more generally the dead were associated with their graves and tombs. The idea that the tomb served as a home for the dead persisted for centuries, but, simultaneously, other locations, spaces and worlds were imagined for the dead. Explanations were gradually adopted, adapted and invented as to where the souls or spirits of the dead resided. One of the earliest and most persistent, which provided a ready vocabulary for the afterlife, was the myth of Hades, the underworld kingdom of the dead.

Festivals such as the *Parentalia* and *Lemuria* may have had a Roman origin and character, but when it comes to the afterlife in general, it is impossible to unravel the interrelationship between Greek and Roman traditions. Whether spiritual or philosophical models for the fate of the dead are explored, the Roman view was heavily dependent on the Greek one. The essential reference point for the underworld in the Greek tradition is Homer, an elusive (in terms of precise chronology and production) poet or poets, whose works were perhaps first composed in the eighth century BC. The earliest account of the world of the dead is found in Book 11 of *The Odyssey*. Homer's central character, Odysseus, tells of his visit to an underworld to consult the seer Teiresias about how he can reach his homeland of Ithaca. Having made a sacrifice at the entrance to the underworld, Odysseus is surrounded by the souls of the dead, including those of people he had known in life (an unburied comrade, fellow Trojan warriors and his mother), and the seer Teiresias, who foretells Odysseus' future. Odysseus also witnesses Minos (son of the god Zeus) passing judgement on the dead and some mythological characters enduring excruciating punishments for their crimes against the gods. The geography of the Homeric underworld is vague and rather static; Odysseus views the souls rather than moving across the terrain, and although there are hints that the dead are judged and the good separated from the evil, there are few indications as to how the underworld is organized and structured. In an earlier book of *The Odyssey*, reference is made to the Elysian Fields at the limits of the earth, where the exceptional and heroic dead are honoured with an easy life, but in Book 11 the dead, even the good among them, have become pale shadows of their former selves, fluttering spirits lacking vitality and living in a gloomy, somewhat disordered world. The Homeric vision of life after death offers little to the ordinary man; it is a world occupied by heroes, the famous and the infamous. It provides no insight as to whether normal mortals can be accepted and whether they will suffer rewards or punishment according to how they have lived.[7]

With time the Homeric basis to the underworld was elaborated upon, and the moral and judgemental aspect of the kingdom was brought to the fore. The underworld had its own geography (although it would be hard to draw a reliable map!), and it had familiar places, faces and names. We can piece together a picture from various sources, including numerous authors of the Roman era, who range from poets such as Ovid and Virgil (*see* p. 105–106) to satirists such as Lucian, thus encompassing romantic poetic fantasies and disbelieving, tongue-in-cheek satires, all written up to a thousand years after Homer. The essential features were as follows. The underworld was called Orcus or Hades by the Romans; the Greek terms Tartarus and Erebus could also be employed, although these names were more often associated with the regions of punishment. Hades (also known as Pluto or Dis), a brother of Zeus, was king of the underworld, and his queen was Persephone (Proserpine in Latin), the daughter of Demeter. Hermes often acted as a guide, leading souls from this world to the underworld. The kingdom was surrounded by great rivers: Styx (the river of hate), Acheron (the river of sorrow), Lethe (the river of forgetfulness), Cocytus (the river of wailing) and Phlegethon (the river of fire). The river

Styx (and sometimes the Acheron) faced new arrivals, who could only cross the water with the help of a ferryman, Charon. Once across, the souls must pass through a gate of adamant guarded by a nephew of Pluto called Aeacus (although this character was sometimes placed among the judges) and by a three-headed dog (Cerberus). The dog was friendly to those who entered, but it would not allow anyone to leave or run away. Minos and Rhadamanthus, sons of Zeus, judged the souls. Those who had lived virtuously were sent to the Elysian Fields, whereas evildoers were handed over to the Furies (Allecto, Megaera and Tisiphone) and taken to the place of the wicked (Tartarus), where they were punished in proportion to their wrongdoing. Descriptions of Tartarus often focused on infamous bad characters of Greek myth such as Ixion, who for attempting to rape the goddess Hera was strapped to a wheel rolling in every direction, and Sisyphus, who for trying to cheat Death was forced to roll a huge rock uphill, only to have it roll down again. Those who had led normal lives, following a middle path of no great wickedness or great good, were little commented upon, although they could be pictured as wandering relatively freely about the underworld kingdom. The souls were often thought to be shapeless phantoms that vanished at the touch and were sustained by the offerings made by the living.[8]

The earliest and fullest exploration and creation of the underworld in Latin literature, one that aimed to give Hades a truly Roman twist, is found in Virgil's *Aeneid*. Virgil was writing at the cusp of a new age, under the first emperor Augustus, when art and literature were written in the image of the new age or channelled to support and promote that age. In *The Aeneid* the hero Aeneas escapes from Troy to Italy, where his descendants will one day found the city of Rome. This is an epic tale that promotes the connections, values and beliefs that unite Rome's past, present and future. In Book Six, the Sibyl, or prophetess of the god Apollo, helps Aeneas visit his father in the kingdom of Hades. After sacrifices and prayers, Aeneas and the Sibyl are able to enter a cave (Avernus) that leads them to the lower world. Aeneas sees the Acheron, the ferryman Charon, the river Styx and crowds of souls waiting to cross. The Sibyl explains that only those who have been buried properly can make the journey and thus rest in peace. The Sibyl convinces Charon to transport the living Aeneas across the Styx and then drugs the guard dog Cerberus. Aeneas first encounters souls who have met an untimely death, such as infants, suicides and those wrongly condemned. The next area is occupied by those who have died for love, where Aeneas meets Dido, whom he had abandoned in Carthage. The next group of souls are those famed for their exploits on the battlefield, who are much lamented on earth. Close to here the road divides, one path leading to Elysium and the other to Tartarus. Aeneas, from a distance, is able to view Tartarus, 'seething with flames and rolling clashing rocks in its torment'. It is an impregnable fortress guarded by one of the Furies, Tisiphone, and from it emanate the sounds of clashing chains, whips and groans. The Sibyl notes that Rhadamanthus rules in Tartarus, punishing criminals and traitors – not just the infamous sinners of Greek myth, but also those who harmed family, hoarded money, committed adultery, fought unjust wars or broke pledges to their masters. The Sibyl and Aeneas continue on their journey until they reach the 'happy fields' of Elysium, which are occupied by the fortunate souls. In Elysium the air is pure. There is green grass, dancing, music, sport and feasting, all enjoyed by those who died for their country and by priests, poets and scientists – in short, by those who had benefited others or are remembered for their merit. Eventually Aeneas finds his father, Anchises, who is surveying purified souls who are about to drink from the river Lethe and return to earth. Through this device, the introduction of reincarnation into the traditional realm of Hades, Virgil, in the voice of Anchises, is able to prophesize the future, pointing out souls who will become great Romans, including the emperor Augustus. Aeneas then leaves the underworld through the gate of ivory, the exit of 'false dreams'.[9]

Virgil's underworld has a defined geography with different zones to which souls are allocated according to the nature of their mortal life (and in some cases their cause of death). The account is moral and judgemental, and it promotes the values – devotion to family, mankind, the state and the gods – that Virgil's peers, at least the educated male élite, were supposed to subscribe to in the age of Augustus. Virgil's view of the underworld, and its place in his epic poem, was undoubtedly inspired and influenced by Homer. Just as the hero of the great Greek epic traverses the world of the living and the dead, so must the hero of the great Latin epic. Yet Virgil's description was also influenced by other sources and writings on the afterlife (*see* p. 107–108). In Virgil's work there was a greater sense of right and wrong, of rewards and punishments, and there were suggestions that souls could change their state rather than being confined in a dim underworld for all time.

CELESTIAL KINGDOMS

The afterlife was not always perceived as being centred on an underworld kingdom. Souls might go up rather than down; they could be pictured as soaring rather than sinking. In the fourth century BC the Greek philosopher Plato ended his dialogue between Socrates and Glaucon, *The Republic*, with the 'Myth of Er'. In this story the soldier Er came back from the dead and told what he had seen in the other world. According to Er, souls were judged in relation to their mortal existence; the just were sent upwards into the sky and the unjust downwards into the earth. The latter suffered in the underworld in proportion to the sins of life, while the former had a happy and beautiful existence in an upper world. Once the souls had been rewarded or punished for the behaviour of their life, they were brought before the Fates and they chose a new life, before drinking from the river Lethe and being sent to their rebirth. The sense of the purification of the souls and their reincarnation in this Platonic vision may well have influenced Virgil's later description of the underworld (*see* p. 105–106). We see a similar fascination with the purification and reincarnation of the soul, in a celestial setting, in *The Divine Vengeance*, written by the Greek author Plutarch in the early second century AD. Plutarch told of another near-death experience, that of Aridaeus from Soli, who had a vision of the afterlife and as a consequence became a reformed character. Aridaeus claimed that his soul had gone up among the stars, where he saw other souls moving about aimlessly and crying in terror. Other higher souls were joyful, and among these Aridaeus recognized a kinsman who renamed him Thespesius and then served as his guide. Aridaeus saw souls being punished between lives, suffering pain and torment according to their sins. Among those so treated, Aridaeus saw his own father, who had murdered some visitors for their money, a crime that had gone undetected on earth but for which ultimately he did not escape punishment. Indeed Aridaeus noted that the souls of those who had pretended to be good and virtuous in order to disguise their wickedness were punished most severely. After punishment some souls were forced into the new bodies of all manner of living things. Aridaeus even saw the soul of the emperor Nero about to be reincarnated as a frog![10]

Morality was the defining feature of such visions of the afterlife. The dead were divided, with their souls systematically categorized and then dispatched to the appropriate region. In such accounts the emphasis often fell on punishment. The 'Myth of Er' detailed the sufferings of the sinners but only mentioned the fate of the good souls, and their flight upwards, in passing. Similarly, Plutarch noted in *The Divine Vengeance* that there were 'higher souls' but focused on the souls that were far from pure. There was less moral and dramatic mileage in good people and pure souls! Heaven was boring, 'hell' was much more interesting and fun to describe. Elysium, or the Elysian Fields, was portrayed as the nice bit of Hades or sometimes even as a separate kingdom altogether, the 'Isle of the Blessed', which, if not actually in the sky, was certainly removed from the traditional gloom and doom of the underworld. It could be a bucolic land of feasting and plenty. Lucian poked fun at the ideal – this was a place where people wore clothes spun from spider-webs, enjoyed beautiful feasts and drank from fountains of enjoyment and laughter. It was all too good to be true.[11]

Not all who held that the soul went upwards reinvented Hades in the sky, with zones for the good and bad and the spectre of reincarnation. Visions of the heavens and the place of the soul could be deliberately non-specific. People might believe, or wanted to believe, that the soul was liberated at death and even that it was immortal, but its disembodied state was hard to picture. Theories and ideas were often connected to philosophical musings about the soul, its place in the universe and the order of the planets, stars and heavenly spheres. We see the importance of these theories of the universe in Cicero's 'Dream of Scipio'. In this, Cicero provided a Latin parallel to the 'Myth of Er'. Scipio Aemilianus (185–129 BC) experienced a vision of his adoptive grandfather, Scipio Africanus (236–183 BC), who showed him the place of the earth in the universe. The overall message was that in the great scheme of things, man and the earth are insignificant, but the possibility that human virtue will be rewarded and that the soul is immortal and 'godlike' was also emphasized.

> Be certain of this so that you will be even more eager to defend the Republic: all those who have saved, helped or extended their country have a special place fixed for them in the heavens, where they will enjoy a life of eternal happiness.[12]

In this context 'heaven' was enshrined as a place for the righteous and illustrious, and the sense of immortality and unending glory were to be a source of inspiration to the great and the patriotic.

Cicero's 'heaven' was vaguely conceived; we gain no insights into what 'the special place' entailed. For a select few, visions of life after death had a more defined divine and celestial connotation. The emperors, or at least those emperors who were perceived as having ruled well, were made gods at their death. An eagle could be released from the pyre, carrying their soul skywards, or their spirit was imagined to have risen heavenwards in the sun's chariot. A comet seen at the death of Julius Caesar was thought to be his soul. The poet Ovid imagined the goddess Venus carrying Caesar's soul high into the heavens:[13]

> Venus take the soul from the murdered body and make it a star, so that always the divine Julius will, from his high temple, shine down upon the Capitol and Forum.[14]

There was undoubtedly much of the political rather than the spiritual in the divine imagery of Rome's rulers, but it may have had some influence upon popular beliefs about the nature of life after death. Funerary portraiture could show the dead of more modest backgrounds in the guise of a god or goddess. The tomb of Claudia Semne, set up by her husband sometime in the mid second century AD, was to be decorated with statues of her dressed as the goddesses Venus, Fortuna and Spes. Perhaps her husband, a former slave of the Imperial family, was inspired by images of the emperors and members of their family in the style of gods and goddesses or with divine attributes. Sculpted reliefs on sarcophagi could also suggest parallels between the life and the afterlife of humans and the divine. Dating mainly to the second and third century AD, detailed scenes adorned the front of sarcophagi, depicting well-known episodes from myths. One favoured theme was the story of Endymion, a mortal who was beloved of the moon goddess (Selene) and was forced to sleep eternally. Images of the sleeping figure of Endymion encompassed ideals of love and devotion and the hope for eternal rest and sleep for the deceased. The myth of Adonis was also popular; this was the tale of a mortal lad loved by the goddess Aphrodite but fated to die while hunting a wild boar. On sarcophagi the story was reduced to a series of emblematic scenes: the departure for the hunt, the wounding of Adonis by the boar and his death in the goddess's arms. These scenes represented virtue, courage, love and devotion – all qualities that the deceased may have had or aspired to. Another favoured theme was the abduction of Persephone (Proserpine) by Hades and the chase given by her mother, Demeter (Ceres). These sarcophagi often depicted Hades at the centre of the design, holding the struggling Persephone in his chariot, while Hermes led the way to the underworld. Demeter followed, holding torches to light her path, in a dragon-drawn chariot (Figure 8). Images of Persephone encapsulate the grief of the survivors, a fear of death and the human struggle against it, but they also show hope and a sense of new birth, since according to the myth Persephone was allowed to return to earth every spring.[15]

Sarcophagi with mythological allegories emphasized overall that even the gods could not change the course of fate: all mortals will die. Simultaneously, however, by devotion to the gods, Adonis, Endymion and Persephone earned immortality. These reliefs can be read on different levels. On the one hand the images suggest that death was viewed as inescapable and final and that there was a real gulf between the living and the dead; on the other hand the images encompassed hope for continuity, immortality and even resurrection. To be sure these images may have become convenient shorthand, little more than a vague hope for peace in death, rather than a reflection of real belief in immortality or divinity. But such mythological allegories and the *apotheosis* of the emperor do suggest some fluidity in Roman beliefs about the nature of death and the god-human relationship.[16]

For some people, celestial kingdoms and idealized views of a happy life after death were related to the 'mystery cults', which were widely practised in the Roman Empire, especially from the first century AD onwards. These cults, in origin centred on divine figures such as the Greek Demeter and Dionysus, the Persian Mithras and the Egyptian Isis, gave the individual followers hope for this life and the next. Members of these cults joined a group of people who shared and promoted a view of the life or world to come. There would be an initiation ceremony at which the mysteries were revealed to the initiate, who would be purified, regenerated and somehow touched by divine immortality. Direct evidence for what adherents of these cults believed and expected is understandably extremely limited. In Apuleius' *Metamorphoses* the hero becomes an initiate in the cult of Isis but makes it clear that it would be sacrilege to speak of what was revealed to him; he does, however, indicate that he was brought to 'the boundary of death' and met the gods 'face to face'. That initiates hoped for special treatment or special passage through the underworld is suggested by a handful of inscribed gold tablets placed in the graves of followers of the Orphic branch of the cult of Dionysus, some of which date to the Roman period. These tablets were written to remind the soul or spirit of the deceased initiates what to say and do when they arrived in the afterlife.[17]

People could choose, then, to believe that the soul did not descend to a grim underworld but went to the happy fields of Elysium or a celestial afterlife. The heavenly fate of the soul might be imprecisely conceived, but for some the soul was reincarnated until it was pure; and for others the soul gradually dissipated, ultimately merging with the divine principles of the universe; while for others still the soul was set among the stars or received by the gods.

BELIEF AND DISBELIEF

To what extent people actually believed in an afterlife – in Hades or a celestial kingdom – is a tough if not impossible question to answer. It is clear that the creators of the surviving literary visions of heaven and hell were mainly poets and philosophers who did not always believe in what they wrote. These were stories or myths that provided useful allegories for mortal life and insights into universal truths about the human condition. The 'afterlife' often formed part of moral and philosophical dialogues, allowing the authors to explore the consequences of human choices, actions and behaviour. We can note once more that Virgil had Aeneas leave the underworld by the gate of 'false dreams', throwing into question all that he had seen in the underworld. Cicero described accounts of Hades as 'the monstrosities of poets and painters'. Many of the intellectual élite were quick to dismiss the traditional view of the underworld and all its familiar characters. These were just stories told to children, images originally designed to frighten people, which had little value by the time of Rome of the late Republic.[18]

Some individuals believed categorically that there was nothing after death. This view was particularly expounded by followers of Epicurean philosophy, such as Lucretius, who dismissed Hades as little more than nonsense and denied the survival of the soul (see Chapter One). Others argued that man's impossible quest to know what happened after death and arguments that death was not the end were part of human vanity: 'These are childish delusions and the invention of mortality greedy for unceasing life', argued Pliny the Elder. However, as Seneca the Younger so wisely noted, 'The fear of going to the underworld is equalled by the fear of going nowhere.' It was easy to dismiss Hades, but less easy

to surrender completely the hope that there might be something after
death, however ill-defined it might be. Thus philosophers, the foremost
of thinkers, often argued for the continuity of the soul, even if they
disagreed about what happened to it, while the Mystery Cults, which
promoted some sort of life after death, seem to have grown in popularity
in the first and second centuries AD. In the Roman world people could
choose to believe in nothing – in annihilation after death – or hope for
something, a hope which could embrace a wide spectrum of possibilities.
Acknowledged uncertainty, or even indecisiveness, characterized some
authors who appear to have hedged their bets about what they did believe,
and it could be argued that an open, or at least questioning, mind was an
asset. We can note, for example, how Cicero explored and acknowledged
different possibilities in his writings. In the *Tusculan Disputations* Cicero,
as noted above, roundly dismissed Hades, and in *The Republic* (Scipio's
Dream) he promoted a celestial resting place for good souls. However, in
a speech against Mark Antony, Cicero pictured the latter's soldiers being
punished in the underworld for fighting against Rome. Cicero belittled
or exploited the different possibilities and imagery to suit his rhetorical
or philosophical agendas.[19]

Moving away from the intellectual élite, it is more problematic to trace
how the prospect, or absence, of life after death impacted on people's
lives and thought processes. The élite could be patronizing, claiming
that the common people believed in the myths and silly tales. The Greek
historian Polybius, commenting on Roman institutions, noted the role of
superstition in holding the state together, arguing that one way of keeping
the common people, the masses, under control and in their place was
the prospect of punishments in Hades. Polybius was admittedly writing
in the second century BC, and the subsequent decline and fall of the
Republic may have helped to undermine the potency of the myths. If the
intellectual élite were publicly questioning the veracity and usefulness of
the myths, did this filter down and influence other social groups? It has to
be acknowledged, at the very least, that the traditional view of Hades may
have had a separate existence to its intellectual literary one; not everyone

was reading Virgil or agreeing with Cicero. The places and characters of
Hades, be they Charon, Cerberus, Lethe, or Elysium, may have been part
of the common currency of many people, part of how people spoke of
and viewed life and death, acting as a shorthand for varied hopes and
expectations that we can no longer re-create with accuracy. Currency
of expression, however, was not necessarily the same as belief. Epitaphs
are perhaps the most revealing source for what people beyond the élite
subscribed to. Admittedly most epitaphs revealed nothing or very little
about what the deceased and their commemorators expected or hoped for
the dead. Those epitaphs that did address the fate of the dead expressed a
range of views and perspectives. There were few detailed references to the
underworld, but some epitaphs made mention of hopes for the afterlife:
hopes that the dead person was in Elysium, in the sky or among the gods.
For example, a slave called Antigenides, from Pisaurum (Pesaro, Italy),
was made to observe, 'I now live in Tartarus, by the waters of infernal
Acheron and under dark stars. I have escaped the uncertainties of life.'
Iulius Gallanius from Haïdra (Tunisia) 'is not held in cruel Tartarus but
occupies the Elysian Fields.' A 6-year-old child from Rome was 'received
among the gods'. Lucius Aviancus Didymus, from Rome, deserved much:
'As he lived honestly and worshipped the sacred gods he ought to see the
Elysian Fields after death'; and Tiberius Claudius Tiberianus claimed that
he now 'lingers in the vale of Elysium'. Some epitaphs also promoted a
sense of continuity by supporting the image of the tomb as the home of
the dead, a final dwelling place (*see* p. 101). Others explored the prospect
of reunion with loved ones, even if this entailed more of a physical than a
spiritual reunion. 'My bones mixed with my daughter's lie together. This
will be a comfort to me', said one man in Rome; while one late epitaph
(fourth century AD) noted that a woman was to be remembered in various
cults, but she was also made to hope for a reunion with her husband of 40
years: 'I am and was and shortly after death shall be yours.'[20]

Other epitaphs, however, dismissed the prospect of any sort of life after
death. Hades, claimed one epitaph, simply did not exist: 'There is no boat
in Hades, no ferryman Charon, no Aeacus holder of the keys, nor any dog

called Cerberus. All of us who have died and gone below are bones and ashes: there is nothing else.' Another announced succinctly, 'I am mortal, I am not immortal' (Mutina – Modena, Italy), while the epitaph of Flavius Agricola observed, 'When death comes, everything will be consumed by earth and fire.' The commemorators of Prima Pompeia expressed their cynicism: 'Fortune promises much to many and delivers to no one. Live in days and hours for nothing lasts.' Some epitaphs concisely summed up a sense of annihilation, a sense that we come from nothing and return to nothing: 'I was not, I was, I am not, I don't care.'[21]

One of the most interesting aspects of epitaphs in terms of the afterlife, but in many respects the most puzzling, is the common use of the expression *dis manibus*. The words *dis manibus*, meaning to the spirits (*manes*) of the dead, became the standard opening phrase, followed by the name of the deceased, on epitaphs across much of the empire during the first century AD. Its usage became so common that it was often abbreviated to the letters DM. Yet it is hard to reconstruct why people chose this phrase so often or what they understood it to mean. How did people think of or imagine these spirits? Was the phrase used unthinkingly, purely as a matter of course and convention? Was the expression popular because it was suitably vague, acknowledging the possibility of continuity but without too much fuss or defining detail?

We could, and have (*see* p. 102), asked similar questions about rituals and tomb cult. Did people believe that the dead benefited from the flowers and offerings? Or were they purely symbolic? What we can say is that ideally there was to be a continuing relationship between the living and the dead. Epitaphs and tombs promoted interaction. Epitaphs spoke to the living, acting as reminders of the common fate of man (see Chapter One), and tombs could encourage the living to stop, sit and read the epitaph or to visit with flowers and food. The living were expected to honour the dead, tend their graves and remember. Some sort of belief in the continuity of the dead may have motivated the living, but this was probably entwined with other factors such as superstition, duty, tradition and the desire to remember and respect the dead.

GHOST AND SPIRITS

Traditional ceremonies, literary images of Hades and even philosophers and epitaphs that dismissed it all each suggest in their own way the importance attached to the dead. Whether people believed in continuity or not, whether they put flowers on a grave or not, the dead were present in memories, buildings, literature, tombs and rituals. The past was everywhere and the dead were part of it. A series of traditional and formal rituals and ceremonies set up boundaries between the living and the dead and sought to control contact between them. The idea that the dead might cross these boundaries was a source of popular stories and literary inspiration. Ghost stories were frequently told, although, as always, we are left to wonder at the extent to which they were believed in. Ghost stories were entertaining and dramatic, but they also played on superstition and uncertainties about the fate of the dead. As with other aspects of afterlife traditions, the existence of ghosts was squarely dismissed by some and believed in by others, while some choose to keep an open mind. Pliny the Younger, in recounting two tales about spirits, said that on balance he did believe in them, demonstrating that the existence of the spirit world was an area for debate.[22]

Those who were believed to return from the dead were often people who were perceived as being trapped between this world and the next; they had not been buried properly or had experienced violent or premature death. More often ghosts were seeking something from the living, especially that their bodies should be properly disposed of or their murderers brought to justice. Livy imagined Verginia, killed by her father to save her honour, roaming through the houses of those involved in her death until they were brought to justice. In Apuleius' *Metamorphoses* a father appeared to his daughter telling of his murder and who was responsible. Pliny the Younger wrote of a house haunted by the ghost of a man who was murdered on the premises and hurriedly buried. It is notable that most ghost stories were not set in or near tombs or cemeteries. Ghosts were believed mainly to seek out the living in the spaces of the living, invading their homes and sleep; dream apparitions of the dead were a particularly common literary device. The dead might upbraid the living. Propertius dreamed of his dead lover, Cynthia, who returned to complain about his lack of fidelity and the paltry nature of her final rites. But sometimes the dead might bring comfort; in one epitaph from Spain a wife wished that her husband might return: 'If tears are of any use show yourself in visions.'[23]

The literary accounts may be little more than good stories, urban myths and convenient dramatic devices to allow the dead to communicate with the living. However, other evidence suggests that there could be real fears and superstitions surrounding ghosts and spirits. The fact that some people believed the dead were imbued with special powers that could be harnessed by the living is confirmed by the recovery of spells and curse-tablets (*defixiones*) that could make requests to the dead for assistance. The dead and the gods of the underworld could be asked for help in matters of gambling, the recovery of property, revenge and love. The burials of those who died premature or violent deaths, whose souls were thought to be discontented and trapped between the world of the living and the dead, may have been particularly targeted as a means for conveying messages to the gods. One lead tablet found in a cemetery not far from Rome cursed a woman: 'Just as the dead man who is buried here can neither speak nor talk, so may Rhodine die ...' Small pots have been found inserted into graves from Roman Egypt; these pots contained wax tablets invoking the gods' help in matters of love. One pot also contained a female figurine pierced with 13 needles.[24]

Miracle workers who could both raise and lay spirits practised in Rome and its empire. In the Pliny story of the haunted house, a visiting philosopher became an exorcist, clearing the house of the malevolent ghost. Real or alleged miracle workers included Apollonius of Tyana (first century AD), who, amongst other miracles, summoned up the ghost of Achilles and removed a spirit that had possessed a boy. People might be sceptical about such powers, but the evidence suggests that individuals could build an aura around themselves and be trusted by the susceptible. Those practitioners who claimed to be able to raise the dead, most frequently to predict the future, were a striking aspect of Roman life and literature. Accusations that people dabbled in such black arts could be an effective rhetorical device. Cicero accused individuals of practising necromancy, including, in 56 BC, a certain Vatinius: 'You are accustomed to call up the spirits of the dead.' The emperors, particularly the less successful among them, could be associated with these foreign and strange practices as a symbol of their weakness and desperation. The emperor Nero had killed his mother and felt that he was harassed by her ghost; he used a Persian magician to summon her spirit so he could beg for forgiveness. The Emperor Otho, who killed his predecessor Galba, was haunted by his victim and sought to propitiate the ghost, perhaps by using necromancy. The emperor Caracalla (reigned AD 211–217), who murdered his brother Geta, was so tormented that he called up the ghosts of his brother and father, but received little comfort from them. What are we to make of these stories? On the one hand they are extreme and fanciful tales told as clear indications of wicked, corrupt and even seriously disturbed minds; on the other hand the stories suggest a thought world that imagined fluid boundaries between the living and the dead.[25]

The world of witchcraft and wizardry, whether believed in or not, created some of the most graphic and entertaining images in Latin literature; to raise up the dead and hear them speak and walk again was the stuff of high drama. This was taken to its height in Lucan's poetic description of the Thessalian witch Erictho, who reanimated the corpse of one of Pompey's dead soldiers to foretell the future. Erictho was pictured as having a close affinity with death and the dead; she lived in a tomb, was on good terms with the gods of the underworld and scavenged for body parts at deathbeds, funerals, cemeteries and public executions: 'She turned every death to her advantage.' To reanimate the corpse, she filled the body with hot blood and many magical ingredients and invoked a range of underworld powers. Reluctantly the soul returned to the corpse and prophesied the fall of Pompey. Once his job was done the soldier walked to his own funerary pyre, which was lit by Erictho. The poet Horace also created some striking scenes of witchcraft centred on Canidia and Sagana, who summoned up the spirits of the dead to answer their questions and also sacrificed a young boy whose body parts would be used in their magic and potions. Facing death, the child cursed them soundly:[26]

> I shall pursue you with terrors and no sacrifice will bring release from my terrible curses. Moreover when I have been forced to die and have breathed my last I shall come to you as a Fury by night. My ghost will, with hook-like claws, tear your faces because such power belongs to the spirits of the dead; and I shall settle myself in your tormented hearts, driving sleep away and bringing terror. The crowd from every side will throw stones at you filthy hags, and once you are dead the wolves and vultures of the Esquiline will scatter your bones; and my parents, who will have the misfortune of surviving me, will enjoy that sight.[27]

CONCLUSION

Ghost stories, more perhaps than traditional accounts of the afterlife, suggest that the dead did have a continuing, if shadowy, presence in the Roman world. This presence was something that many people may have believed in without questioning the details or wishing to understand its precise nature. This is not to say that all thoughts about life after death were characterized by ghosts, spirits and superstitions. Traditional Roman religion, rituals, philosophy and personal belief all allowed a place for the dead. There were choices to be made by the individual as to what to believe – choices that some, maybe even the majority, avoided confronting in full. People could opt to have precise beliefs and to follow certain cults, but it was also possible to take a pick-and-mix approach to beliefs about the dead and the soul, adapting what was believed, hoped or wished for according to circumstance.

It is easy from a modern twenty-first century perspective, living in the shadow of monotheism, to be cynical about Roman religion and cult. We can view the ceremonies as being underpinned by little more than vague superstitions and unquestioning tradition. Is it likely that any self-respecting Roman really believed tales about Rome growing hot from funeral pyres because the dead were angry with the living? As we have seen, the Romans of all walks of life could be just as sceptical and cynical; and the fact that belief (or indeed non-belief) was often personal and private, and even optional, may strike a chord with a modern viewer. But there is a danger that we will impose modern preconceptions about faith and the afterlife onto the Roman world and too easily dismiss the genuine fears and uncertainties that surrounded death and the dead.

To end this chapter we can return to the canonical Latin description of Hades: Virgil and Aeneas' visit to the underworld. This can be dismissed as little more than poetic fantasy or it can be held up as an evocative summary of what at least some people believed. What is apparent is that Aeneas' visit is both poignant and powerful: it served to link the living with the dead and to entwine Rome's past, present and future. Even if the kingdom of the dead was little more than literary fancy, the dead were always present in the Roman world, and they needed to be acknowledged, honoured and respected.

5

Mourning the Dead

People grieve and cope with their grief in a variety of ways. In the modern Western world, grief has become an industry; 'grief counsellors' assist the bereaved through the 'grieving process', with recognized stages such as anger and denial. However, it is also acknowledged that not everyone's experiences can be so neatly schematized or pigeonholed. Grief may be appropriately viewed more as an illness than a process – an illness for which the cure is not set or even certain. Some individuals may attain a level of acceptance and 'move on', but others maintain continuing bonds with the dead. How does the modern belief that 'everyone is different' help, if at all, in the study of grief and mourning in the Roman world? In a society with a high mortality rate, was there any place for grief? If grief was tolerated, was it viewed as a process to be controlled or as an illness to be cured?[1]

Death may be a universal factor of life, but different societies and cultures have different ways of expressing loss and grief. Everyone in their lifetime will suffer bereavement, but will everyone 'feel' the same? Therein lies the challenge: how do we access emotion in a past society, and is it even realistic to try? It may be possible to explore how people were expected to mourn and how they gave public expression to loss, but relating this evidence to the individual's emotional reality is problematic. Mourning and grief can be two separate and different experiences; public behaviour may not mirror private thoughts.

It is not that there is a shortage of evidence for grieving and mourning Romans. We have many literary, artistic and even everyday expressions of loss, such as condolence letters, consolation poems, philosophical discourses, poetic laments, epitaphs and tombstones. The challenge is the evaluation of how these distort and idealize the impact of grief, acting as a veil to conceal or even to create emotion. We may be moved by the poetry of Statius or Ovid, but what we have is an artistic construct, not an expression of the poet's own suffering. Equally we may tire of the repetitive and unoriginal nature of the language of epitaphs, but this does not mean that the sentiments expressed were not heartfelt. For grief, the most extreme of emotions, it will always be a challenge to bridge the gap between evidence and real people, but we should not be tempted to stop trying. At the very least the evidence suggests that people felt their losses and sought to give expression to them, and perhaps most telling of all, that there could be debate and discussion in Roman society about how people should mourn – that is, how they should show or not show their grief in public. It was acknowledged that not everyone behaved or reacted in the same way; in the Roman world, grief was perceived as a mixture of both raw emotion and expected behaviour.

RULES FOR MOURNING

The recently bereaved wore the marks of grief: internal suffering was signalled by exterior appearance. The house of a bereaved family, the *familia funesta*, was marked at the threshold by a branch from a cypress tree, which was consecrated to the spirits of the dead. The bereaved wore dark clothing and might have a dishevelled appearance, with hair dirtied and let loose. The bereaved might abstain from food and washing, and they might make dramatic or noisy gestures. In many respects the state of grief was marked by behaviour that reversed normal expectations: dark instead of light clothing, dirt rather than cleanliness, emotional display rather than emotional restraint. This inversion of norms and the display of symbols of grief were easily read by onlookers and passers-by, who could then act with appropriate respect. There may also have been an element of superstition involved, since the bereaved were perceived as polluted or ill-omened due to their contact with the dead, thus social interaction with them was to be limited. Note how undertakers were much maligned and how the high priests of Rome were not supposed to see or touch the dead (*see* p. 72). Until the dead were buried and the bereaved had performed the essential rituals, the bereaved were, in principle, isolated from the wider community. Nine days after the funeral, the house was cleaned and a sacrifice and feast were held near the tomb (*see* p. 86). These rituals may have lifted the sense of pollution, but the extent to which nine days marked the end of the formal mourning period varied according to gender and the degree of relationship between the mourner and the deceased.[2]

From early times there were laws that stipulated how long people should be mourned for and who should mourn. Mourning was supposed to be in proportion to the age and status of the deceased. King Numa (c. 715–673 BC), Rome's legendary second king and reformer, stated that children aged less than one year were not to be mourned for, and older children up to the age of 10 were to be mourned for no more months than the number of years lived. Numa also said that no mourning was to exceed ten months, and this was also the minimum time set for widowhood; if a woman took a new husband before this time was up, she would have to sacrifice a cow and calf. Designated periods for mourning were still advocated during the later second and early third century AD and were summarized (with some modifications of Numa's rulings) by Paulus, a writer on legal matters. Paulus noted that parents and children aged over 6 could be mourned for a year, children under 6 for only one month, a husband for ten months and close blood relatives for eight months.[3]

To what extent these laws were enforced, were practically enforceable or were ever intended to be enforced is uncertain. In general the laws probably acted as guidelines for public roles and appearances and were intended to suggest upper limits to mourning rather than to designate time spans that had to be fulfilled. Paulus noted that anyone who broke the restrictions, presumably by mourning in excess but possibly also by mourning too little, would be placed in public disgrace. How could those who wished to mourn for longer be prevented from doing so and how were those still in mourning identified? According to Paulus, those in mourning were to dress plainly, with no purple or white clothes or jewellery, and they were to avoid dinner parties. It seems then that the dress and demeanour that the bereaved adopted immediately after the death could be extended, but, with the exception of widows, this was not presumed to be essential. People could opt to display their grief for the designated periods, after which the marks of bereavement (dress and limited social interaction) were to be curtailed, unless one wished to risk public criticism. People might continue to grieve in private, but public display was, in principle, limited. The laws stress maximum rather than minimum periods for mourning, and for men in particular the briefer the period of mourning the better.[4]

The exception to all this, and the rule of the greatest significance, was the ten-month period before remarriage for widows, which was designed to avoid any disputes over paternity of children born after the death of the deceased husband. This law was enforced long after the time of King Numa. In 40 BC Octavia, the sister of the future emperor Augustus, married Mark Antony after a special senatorial decree allowing her to reduce her mourning, since her previous husband had been dead for less than ten months. In 17 BC women's mourning was suspended for the celebration of the once-a-generation Secular Games. In AD 37 the emperor Caligula, desperate for everyone to join in some theatre celebrations, 'postponed all law-suits and suspended mourning', which allowed women who had lost their husbands to marry before the set time, unless they were pregnant. *The Digest*, a compilation of Roman laws, noted that 'It is customary to obtain the emperor's permission for a woman to marry within the statutory time. A woman is not penalized for betrothal during the period of mourning for her husband.' It is apparent that rules associated with mourning primarily impacted upon women, especially widows, and only in special circumstances or through special dispensation were widows' weeds to be removed before the ten months was up. By contrast, *The Digest* stated that 'husbands do not have to mourn for their wives'. A husband might choose to show his grief by mourning in public, but no law demanded this of him.[5]

IDEALS FOR MOURNING

The laws reflected and enforced the social distinctions inherent in a patriarchal society. Expected roles were assigned according to gender and status, and they were underpinned by stereotypes as much as by the law. How one mourned, or more accurately how one was expected to mourn, was dictated by learning, culture and gender. Seneca the Younger, writing in the mid first century AD, said, 'Despite suffering the same bereavement women are wounded more deeply than men, barbarians more than the civilized and the uneducated more than the learned.' Plutarch, writing in the early second century AD and in a Greek context, said, 'Mourning is feminine, weak and dishonourable, since it characterizes women more than men, barbarians more than Greeks and inferior men more than better men.' Not everyone would have agreed with these views, but they reflected the dominant perspective of the male élite minority, who viewed grief, or more accurately the public expression of grief, as a weakness. In particular we can see a frequent contrast between the behaviour of men and women, although we need to remember that these ideals related to public behaviour and did not necessarily reflect true emotional states or private sentiments. Seneca the Younger was clear on gender distinctions, arguing that the traditional laws were to stop women mourning for more than a year, whereas no limits were set for men because it was dishonourable for a man to mourn at all! Open mourning could be described as 'womanly'; it was behaviour that particularly characterized a bereft mother. The subtext was that a woman's dramatic reaction to a loss was understandable and to some degree acceptable, and thus, in contrast, a similar reaction was not acceptable for a man.[6]

Tradition dictated that women played a prominent role in public mourning and funeral ritual. Mourning was one of the rare occasions that women had an accepted place and role in the public gaze. Women's actions and appearance gave expression to the family's and community's grief. Women wailed, cried and sang laments; they beat their breasts, scratched their cheeks and pulled at and dirtied their hair. Women would usually give the last kiss to the dying, wash the dead body and, finally, receive the ashes. These were established duties that could place women in an ambivalent position. On the one hand women could be seen as taking on the dirty and polluted tasks associated with death; on the other hand women were playing a vital role in the important transition from life to death – a role that was essential for the well-ordered running of society. Death could be both degrading and empowering for women, thus men sought to monitor and ultimately to restrain the female role in public mourning. Mourning, when done on a grand or dramatic scale, had the potential to become political and competitive; the behaviour of women reflected on their fathers, husbands and sons and thus ultimately on the state. The legal restrictions on mourning periods, as noted above, were aimed particularly at women. The early laws of the Twelve Tables (c. 450 BC) also sought to stop excessive displays and prohibited women from tearing at their cheeks and wailing too loudly. We can also note that after Rome's overwhelming defeat by Hannibal at the Battle of Cannae (216 BC), mourning was restricted since there was a real fear that the grief of women, symbolizing the suffering felt throughout the city, was becoming self-destructive and crippling. Women could be prevented from mourning those who were condemned or damned; a decree issued to condemn Cnaeus Calpurnius Piso following his suicide in AD 20 stated that he was not to be mourned by the women of his house (*see* p. 180). Mourning was one of the duties of a woman, but the nature and extent of that mourning could be controlled by men.[7]

For men, at least men in the public eye, a stiff upper lip and a back-to-business attitude was the expected reaction to a private bereavement. There were numerous literary anecdotes of men who put their public duty before personal loss. Seneca the Younger listed examples in his consolation to the bereaved Marcia: Pulvillus, a Roman priest, was performing a ritual when he heard news of the death of his son, and he carried on regardless; Lucius Bibulus, a consul (51–50 BC), lost two sons, but he resumed his official duties the day after he heard of their murders; and three days after learning of the death of his daughter, Julius Caesar was back serving as a general. Valerius Maximus, in his work on memorable deeds and sayings, devoted a section to fathers who mourned their sons admirably. These included Aemilius Paullus, who celebrated a triumph for defeating the king of Macedon in 168 BC. Aemilius Paullus had four sons, two of whom he gave to other families in adoption; a third died three days before his triumph and the fourth died three days afterwards, but instead of complaining, Aemilius Paullus noted that it was better for him to suffer misfortune than for Rome and its people to do so. It is not that these men were unfeeling or were judged to be so; instead they earned praise for their self-control and public service. The ideal was that a brave man was not susceptible to distress. Cicero noted that, 'The unconquered must despise human concerns and consider these beneath them.' For a Roman gentleman any grief needed to be private, controlled and clearly separated from public roles and responsibilities. In addition, it is worth noting that some men may have found consolation in their public duties; meaningful activity may have provided therapy and escape from private torment. One of Cicero's excuses for feeling the loss of his daughter Tullia so intensely was the decline of the Republic and his own political role – now neither home nor forum could offer Cicero comfort. Pliny the Younger, despite being greatly distressed at his wife's death and avoiding social contact, still busied himself with defending the reputations of his friends.[8]

The traditional élite ideals were stark. Both men and women were expected to conform to certain conventions and expectations, and to deviate from these could cause criticism. In simple terms, on suffering bereavement women should express emotion and men should suppress it. However, the reality could be somewhat more complex, a balancing act of conflicting emotions and duties played out on a public stage. It was not easy to live up to the ideals. Were the anecdotes about men taking their grief so bravely admired because they were in fact unusual? Perhaps most men failed to have such self-control or at least the opportunity to exhibit it in such a public manner. Equally, women might be portrayed as expressing emotion, but part of the characterization of grief as womanly (by men) was the hint or suggestion that female shows of grief were insincere. The subtext was that women might express grief openly, but men felt grief more deeply in their own, more conservative, way. The stereotyping was, then, underpinned by a realization that there could be a mismatch between ideals and reality, between public behaviour and private sentiment. In addition, the nature of the public stage for grief, and of public expectations within and beyond the élite, may not have remained static. We can note, for example, that élite women were increasingly expected to conform to male stereotypes, controlling their emotion and retaining dignity. The dominant association of women with death and mourning appears to have been eroded during the late Republic and early Imperial period. The increasing use of undertakers and hired professional mourners reduced the need for the female relatives of the deceased to make dramatic displays of grief themselves or to be so intimately involved in the preparation and tending of the corpse before disposal. This is not to say that women were no longer expected to mourn or express their grief; mourning was still perceived as womanly, but for the well-to-do a greater level of self-control and decorum was expected. Extreme female reaction to loss could now be seen as demeaning. At the death of her lover Mark Antony (31 BC), the Egyptian (and thus distant, exotic and very un-Roman) queen Cleopatra was pictured as tearing her clothes, beating and cutting her breasts and smearing herself with the blood from Antony's wounds; Plutarch observed that the self-inflicted wounds were so severe that they subsequently made Cleopatra ill. We can contrast this with the empress Livia's reaction to the death of her son, Drusus the Elder (9 BC). In literary accounts Livia, in the privacy of the palace, was allowed to feel her loss, and even to weep, but in public she was a model of decorum and self-control. Élite women could find themselves in an uncomfortable and often contradictory position; as mothers, wives and daughters they were expected to lead the mourning and to express their loss, but simultaneously grief was now more to be suppressed than flaunted.[9]

Equally, however much the stiff upper lip might be lauded, men could sometimes benefit from a softer touch. Both men and women needed to show a genuine sense of loss, while exhibiting bravery and decorum.

How a male mourner acted could be part and parcel of peer evaluation; it was an aspect of the social code. Not to adhere to the associated expectations could lay one open to criticism; getting public grieving correct was important, and those who got it wrong were mocked. But getting it right could be far from easy; too much emotion and you were an embarrassment, too little and you could be seen as devoid of feeling. Some, like the historian Tacitus' father-in-law, Agricola, were portrayed as getting the balance just right; at the death of his young son (AD 84) Agricola accepted his loss 'without the showy bravery of many a man or collapsing into tears and grief like a woman.' Many others were judged less successful in their mourning, often mourning too much. The emperor Gaius (Caligula), at the death of his sister Drusilla, was painted as a man out of control. The emperor failed to attend the funeral, shut himself away in his villa, sought solace in gambling, neglected his personal appearance and criticized those who did not show enough sorrow. The emperor Nero was condemned for his immoderate grief at the death of his four-month-old daughter. Pliny the Younger mocked his enemy Regulus for his dramatic mourning at the death of his young son, which Pliny regarded as insincere (*see* p. 1). A Roman gentleman should not grieve like a common woman. However, sometimes men could be criticized for mourning too little. After the death (AD 19) of his nephew and heir, Germanicus, the emperor Tiberius appeared cold, distant and unmoved, at least in the historian Tacitus' account. The populace reacted negatively to Tiberius' lack of emotion at the loss of their favoured prince; a touch of humanity could go a long way. Indeed in some rhetorical contexts, especially the courtroom, men might display emotion, adopting dark clothing and a dishevelled appearance to evoke sympathy, and they would aim to move the audience to tears with tales of bereavement in order to win cases.[10]

In art both men and women could be depicted as mourners. Admittedly mourning was not a particularly common theme for depiction, and it is difficult to judge the social milieu of those images that do survive. In the Haterii relief (Figure 5), men are part of the scene, although it is hard to establish whether these are undertakers or family members. A man

adorns the body with a wreath, and other male figures beat their breasts.
A small figure at the head of the couch hugs his knees in an almost foetal
position, the simple cap on his head suggesting him to be a freed slave. In
the Amiternum relief (Figure 6), dramatic displays of grief, symbolized by
raised hands, are restricted to women, and similar gestures are represented
on a child's sarcophagus that shows the moment of death or the laying-out
of the body (Figure 4). However, in the latter scene the couch is flanked
by seated figures of a man and a woman, both shown in a similar pose,
with their gaze down and heads resting upon a hand. These must surely
represent the parents of the deceased, and there is little distinction here in
how the male and female gestures of grief are depicted. Dramatic displays
with unbound hair and raised arms may have characterized hired mourners, mainly female, but the family members, men and women, could be
shown expressing their loss in a similar style. In some contexts men, as
much as women, could be portrayed as active mourners, displaying grief
and evoking sympathy.[11]

The ideals associated with male and female mourners may have
softened and moved closer together in the century following the collapse
of the Republic. In some people's eyes it was better for women to wail a
little less and for men to be a little less stoical. The contrast between élite
and non-élite ideals may have also been challenged; and the differences
between how the common people as opposed to the élite mourned may
have been reduced. Tacitus' account of the aftermath of Germanicus'
death, written in the late first century or early second century AD, may be
particularly telling since it was deliberately distorted to put Tiberius in a
bad light. It is not what Tiberius did or did not do, but how Tacitus chose
to interpret his behaviour and more importantly that of the common
crowd. Tacitus portrayed Tiberius as an unpopular emperor, someone
who upheld traditional values at the expense of the people. However,
it is possible that Tacitus was also reflecting some genuine tensions in
the presentation of mourning, or at least in how the élite were expected
to present their grief in public. After all, the restraint and decorum of
a Roman gentleman may have been of little relevance to the mass of

Rome's population. The majority of Rome's inhabitants were probably not influenced by philosophy and had no public role to uphold or in which to find solace. For these people, distinctions between private grief and public mourning may have been of little importance. The traditional élite perspective polarized society by how they grieved: the élite, especially men, had emotional control and dignity underpinned by philosophy, while the common people, especially women, lacked self-control and indulged their grief. But this stereotyping and criticizing of people, in élite sources, suggests that there could be debate and discussion about mourning and about deviation from the ideals.

The élite ideal may have been increasingly challenged in the early Imperial period, being perceived as too distant and too cold. There seems to have been a reduction of the stereotypical emotional polarity between the élite and the plebs and between men and women. Under the rule of the emperors, the public role of élite men was somewhat reduced, and there may have been less comfort and distraction to be found in public duty. This is not to say that all traditional ideals were abandoned and that it was now fine to weep in public. The heart on the sleeve did not simply replace the stiff upper lip, but there was perhaps a greater awareness of different responses to loss – that the philosophical model was not the only one – and also the importance of evaluating the audience for one's grief, which was not just restricted to the élite. Tiberius' error, in Tacitus' eyes, was that he misjudged public sentiment; he failed to look beyond the boundaries of class and convention and 'grieve' in a way that was in tune with the wider populace.

Just as bad characters in literature of the Roman period often met bad deaths, they also often made bad mourners, and just as good characters met good deaths, they also made good mourners (compare Chapter Two, 'Dying Well' and 'Bad Deaths'). A bad mourner was someone who cried too much and made a show of themselves in public, and someone who failed to put public duty before private emotions. Some people were inherently 'bad mourners' because they were not imbued with the importance of public duty; these included the common masses, women

and non-Romans. Of course, as with the good–bad death spectrum, some
people were allowed to thwart expectations. Women of distinguished
birth, for example, could exhibit manly traits, and some men of high birth
were weak and womanly. Ideals, however, were there to be challenged and
reinvented, and they were probably only admired and propagated by a
minority. With the shift from the Republic, with its élite ideals of male
virtue enshrined in public office and duties, to an Imperial era, where one
man held sway and courted popular approval as much as élite approval,
what it was to be a good mourner was open to question and negotiation.

CONSOLATION AND PHILOSOPHY

It was in philosophy, more than in religion, that comfort for one's losses
was to be found. Philosophy could teach the individual to be strong, to
face life's troubles and disasters with equanimity; and there was no greater
challenge than accepting the death of both oneself and others. From an
early date philosophical rationale was applied to the bereaved. The genre
of consolation was invented, so to speak, by Crantor, a Greek philosopher
of the fourth or early third century BC who wrote a work 'On Grief' that
was popular thereafter. This work does not survive, but its influence
was felt in many consolatory writings, treatises and letters composed
during the Roman period. There were several philosophical schools of
thought in the Graeco-Roman world, but the authors we will consider
here, Cicero, Seneca and Pliny the Younger, were heavily influenced
by Stoicism. However, in the philosophy of grief, aligning oneself to a
particular school of thought was perhaps less important than the overall
consolatory messages, especially that death was not an evil, so the dead
should not be mourned for. Consolatory essays and letters often ranged
across philosophical schools, drawing inspiration from varied individuals
and scholars for how best to deal with life's greatest tragedies.[12]

Much of this philosophy was the product of, and intended for the
consumption of, the male, educated élite. In male friendship groups it was

common practice to offer support and advice in times of trouble, such as political disappointments, exile and bereavement. This consolation often took the form of letters, with the writer acknowledging and sympathizing with the recipient's bereavement but also displaying his rhetorical abilities and philosophical learning by exhorting the bereaved to be strong. The letters were not always overtly philosophical, but they were often formulaic and underpinned by a shared value system in which philosophy provided a common language for advice and comfort. The letters tended to draw upon similar arguments: life is short, the dead are better off than the living, time lessens sorrow and grief accomplishes little.

In 46 BC Cicero wrote to his friend Titius following a bereavement. In the letter Cicero did not reveal who had died; we may assume that Titius had lost a son or sons. The letter was not intended to remember or praise the dead, but to focus on advising the living. Cicero used the following arguments: men are born to die; the dead are not suffering so should not be pitied; to grieve excessively is unworthy of a sensible and responsible man; and as grief passes, 'we should not wait for time to provide the medicine that our intelligence has ready supply of'. Cicero placed this advice against the current political backdrop, even arguing that the dead were better off in such unfortunate times: 'I believe that whoever has left behind the current political turmoil, and all that may happen ahead of us, has been cheated of nothing.'[13]

The following year Cicero's adult daughter, Tullia, died. Cicero was devastated and struggled to maintain the decorum and sense of duty required of a man in his position. He received several letters offering him consolation. Of the letter sent by Brutus, Cicero said, 'There was much good sense in it, but nothing that could help me.' Two of the consolation letters received by Cicero survive, and these employed some of the standard arguments: all men are born to die, grieving is of little benefit and time does heal. The letters also had a brisk, almost admonishing tone: Cicero must pull himself together. Servius Sulpicius wrote, 'Do not copy bad doctors, who claim to know how to heal sickness in others but are unable to heal themselves.' Lucceius, remonstrating about Cicero's absence from

Rome, said, 'I will criticize you . . . complaining gains nothing.' In his letters
of reply Cicero justified his grief because many of the standard remedies
available to men were gone. His friends were dead, his political career was
over and the Republic was on the point of collapse: 'I am mortally weary of
times and men, of Forum and senate house.' If there was therapy in public
duty, it was failing Cicero. With his faltering public role, Cicero lacked the
usual and expected therapy of a leading politician.[14]

Letters of consolation often had an abrasive and direct style. These
letters were not about offering sympathy, succour and support, but about
exhorting the bereaved to fight their grief. The genre was perhaps taken
to its extreme in the letter written by Seneca the Younger to a certain
Marullus on the death of his son. In this letter Seneca does not beat about
the bush: grief is useless, thankless and madness; life is short, and since
all men will die, grieving for a young child is pointless; such a loss is a
sting, not real pain; it is human to cry, but tears in excess are indulgent
and dishonourable; the boy is not suffering, so 'continue to remember
but cease to mourn'. We can question whether this letter was ever sent. It
is presented as a letter within a letter, with Seneca claiming that he sent it
to a philosopher friend who 'deserved criticism rather than consolation'.
The letter is a rhetorical and philosophical exercise that allows Seneca to
display Stoic principles.[15]

Seneca also wrote two essays centred on the consolation of grief. A
consolatio was an essay, often addressed to a named individual, offering
the bereaved support through philosophical example. These consolations
can appear like extended letters, lecturing the bereaved to 'cure' their grief.
In origin they were probably inspired by the work of Crantor. They were
taken up by authors of the Roman period such as Cicero – who wrote a
consolation for himself at Tullia's death, which does not survive – and
the Platonic author Plutarch. Seneca's consolations to the bereaved are
addressed to Marcia, three years after the death of her son, and to Polybius,
an Imperial freed slave of the emperor Claudius, on the death of his
brother. The recipients are not fellow philosophers, and although Seneca
takes a firm line, his tone is often consolatory. The standard arguments are

voiced: death is inevitable, death is not an evil and time heals. However, Seneca also acknowledges that it is human to mourn for the dead: 'But never will I demand of you that you should not grieve at all'; and he offers hope that the souls of the departed have been released to be 'welcomed by a saintly band'. Nevertheless, Seneca's purpose is clear: to council against excessive and prolonged mourning. 'If no wailing can recall the dead, if no distress can alter destiny that is unchangeable and fixed for all eternity, and if death holds fast whatever it has carried off, then let grief, which is futile, cease.' There is a difference in tone between the two consolations that is related to the identities of the recipients, reflecting male and female and also high and low birth. Marcia is a woman of high status, and Polybius is a man of low birth who has gained a prominent position. Marcia must find comfort in her family reputation and her surviving family; Polybius must find comfort in service to the emperor and his literary pursuits. It would be better for Polybius to write than to weep. Both must think of their reputations and their virtue, but this has a particular resonance for Polybius; his learning, education and eminence must make him rise above any base inclinations associated with his birth. Polybius lives in the public gaze, and all aspects of his behaviour are open to scrutiny. When it comes to grief, 'nothing vulgar, nothing base befits you.'[16]

Seneca was a philosopher through and through. He might tailor his voice and the nature of his works to fit the apparent needs of the recipient, but the overall messages about the nature of virtue, especially male virtue, and the importance of self-control remained clear. The letters received and written by Cicero show philosophy in action in a more workaday but still idealized form; revealing how arguments were used and how individuals struggled with the ideals. We also see this compromise between élite ideals and the reality of grief in some of the letters of Pliny the Younger. These letters were composed at the end of the first century AD, and they perhaps reflect a softening of the élite ideals and more open acknowledgement of the need of the bereaved to mourn the dead (see p. 130–131).

The letters of Pliny the Younger that explore death, loss and grief were not consolation letters as such. These letters were written not to the bereaved relatives but to other friends and acquaintances of Pliny's, telling them of a death and often commenting on how the bereaved were coping. The letters contained sensitive acknowledgments of the value and worth of the deceased and thus how their death had impacted upon the bereaved. The philosophical arguments were present, but they were underpinned by a greater sense of loss, suffering and sympathy: 'Nothing can heal his wound but acceptance of the inevitable, lapse of time, and a surfeit of grief.' In another letter Pliny advised his correspondent that, in writing to the bereaved, he should avoid the common critical consolations: 'be gentle and sympathetic'. The letters were artfully composed to suggest Pliny's compassion and humanity; they were a showcase for him as a thoughtful Roman gentleman. Indeed for us this is the difficulty with all the surviving consolatory letters and treatises – they were written not as personal informal correspondence but as edited and published literary showpieces. Seneca's consolations may be addressed to Marcia and Polybius, but they were intended for a much wider audience. Even Cicero's correspondence was edited and selected for publication. The works reveal more about the authors' beliefs and philosophical leanings than about how people actually mourned and sought to heal the pain of grief.[17]

Some of this discourse underpinned by philosophy can be difficult for a modern reader to stomach. The clichéd arguments and exhortations to be strong can seem impersonal, harsh and unfeeling, but this evidence needs to be seen in the context of an élite world where modes of behaviour were idealized. It was largely a public world, and the advice offered is about how to behave and to negotiate one's position in that world. It was not all tough love: the need for tears and the reality of human emotions were acknowledged, but they were tempered by the hard practical reality that life was short and grief of little benefit. We may be cynical about the intentions of the letter writers and shocked by the hard-hearted words, but these genres had an accepted place in society. Cicero, as we have seen, appears to have genuinely suffered in the loss of his daughter; he underwent a sharp realization that offering advice was easier than taking it. Nevertheless, Cicero persevered. He battled with his grief, and his main weapon in this battle was the available scholarship. Cicero read everything that had been written on grief, looking to those who coped with it well, and in the end he found solace in writing his own words. Cicero may have been far from the norm, but in his own élite circles, which for us are better represented than any other, insights survive into how philosophy, for all its hackneyed arguments, helped people to cope. It was not easy, but life did go on.

THE LOSS OF A CHILD

How the Romans mourned for their children becomes an interesting case study of the interaction between ideals and realities. On the one hand children, infants in particular, were expendable; their risk of death was so great that it was impractical to weep for every baby. On the other hand there is plenty of evidence that parents often did mourn for their children, including babies, intensely. Once more we see a divide between élite, philosophically driven ideals and the lived realities of the majority of the population; but here in particular it was often tempered by some harsh economic factors.

The philosophical viewpoint was that an infant should not be mourned for, since 'these children have no part on earth or earthly things'. Instead the death should be accepted as Nature's choice, and parents should focus on other children and future babies. This attitude was enforced by the practical treatment afforded the bodies of the young. Babies were not given full funeral rites, and those who had not teethed could not be cremated. Children's funerals could be held at night, as if 'out of sight, out of mind'. This is not to say, however, that the bodies of young children were disrespected; infant inhumation and cremation remains are fairly common discoveries in Roman cemeteries. Some infant remains have also been found placed in the foundations of new buildings, which may suggest marginal treatment for the young but also that these were careful and considered choices.[18]

It is hard to dispute that repeated infant deaths may have hardened mothers and fathers against loss. Some parents may have even deliberately distanced themselves from their very young children. The employment of wet nurses and other carers could cushion more affluent parents against infant bereavement. For the poor, there may have been little time and money available to mark or mourn the deaths of the vulnerable young. This was an environment in which infant exposure could be practised. We do not know how frequently it was used, and economics was not the only driving factor, but some babies were not wanted and the early death of a child may have been a blessing for some parents.[19]

This perspective can be countered by plenty of contrasting evidence that suggests young children, including babes in arms, were desperately wanted and dearly loved. The emperor Nero was said to be devastated when his infant daughter died. Marullus, the recipient of a consolation letter from Seneca, was apparently struggling to come to terms with the death of his young son (above p. 134). Admittedly in both these cases the grief was portrayed as a bad thing; it was a negative character trait, especially in a man, to cry for an infant. Yet as Fronto, who lost five children and a grandchild, pointed out, all the standard arguments of philosophers are well and good but they cannot 'heal the yearning of a parent'. Fronto was writing of the death of his 3-year-old grandson, and in an earlier letter he had spoken touchingly of the boy's childish characteristics, his love of grapes and fondness for little birds. We see a similar love of baby prattle and childish play, and also the pain brought by the loss of children, in some of the epigrams of Martial:[20]

> Here I lie, to Bassus' sorrow, the infant Urbicus, to whom the mighty city of Rome gave birth and name. Six months were needed to complete my first three years, when the stern goddesses unkindly broke my threads. What help were my beauty, my talk, my tender years? You, who read these lines, shed tears on my tomb. So that the one whom you wish to survive you does not go down to the waters of Lethe until he has reached the great age of Nestor.[21]

Most evocative of the frequency of infant death and the pain of bereaved parents are the surviving epitaphs that record these deaths. It is notable that babies and very young children were actually under-represented in the epigraphic record. This is to say that, given the high rate of infant mortality, comparatively few epitaphs were set up to babies and toddlers. This may suggest that the remains of the very young were rarely marked by tombstones, emphasizing once more their marginal treatment at death. Nevertheless, the surviving exceptions to this general pattern remain striking. The language may have been conventional and sentimental, but it gave public expression to a grief that many others had experienced or would experience.

> To Aemilia Cornelia, daughter of Gaius. Scribonia Maxima set this up to a very distinguished girl, who lived 45 days.
>
> To the spirits of the departed Aemilia Donativa who lived one year, three months and 13 days. She lies here. Her father Turbo and mother Designata made this for their daughter, who lived as sweet as a rose.
>
> Secundus and Concordia made this for their son Felix who lived two years, six months and 26 days.
>
> To Tiberius Claudius Soterichus, son of Tiberius, of the Camilia voting tribe, who lived two years, 11 months, ten days and four hours. Tiberius Claudius Soterichus made this, a most unhappy father tortured by eternal sorrow.
>
> Nicodromus lived six years. Euphemus lived two years and seven months. There was just 30 days between the sorrow of them being snatched away.
>
> To Successus who lived four years, eight months and five days. Made by Gargillia Flora to a very sweet home-born slave.[22]

To grieve for an older child, a child who had passed the dangerous years of infancy, a child in whom time and money had been invested, a child who was on the point of attaining adulthood, was more acceptable. This is reflected in epitaphs, many more of which were set up to children and teenagers than to infants and toddlers. It is notable that more boys were commemorated than girls, indicating the harsh reality that a boy was more prized than a girl.

To Euvagrius a very sweet child who lived eight years, two months and 20 days. Urbana an unhappy mother made this despite all her prayers.

Olus aged 12 and Fuscinus aged 16. Fuscus to his sons. They lie here.

To the spirits of the departed Lollia Attica died aged 12 years. Lollia Onesime made this for a very dutiful daughter.

To Capito, son of Avitus, aged 14 years, Avita daughter of Avitus aged 10 years, and Avitus, son of Capito, aged 40 years. They lie here. May the earth lie lightly upon them. Fusca, daughter of Capito made this for her son, daughter, husband and herself.

To the spirits of the departed Opinia Neptilia, daughter of Marcus, aged 14 years. A virgin who died just before her wedding. Marcus Opinius Rufus and Gellia Neptilia her parents.

To the spirits of the departed Memmius Vettianus, aged 19 years, a very dutiful son.[23]

Young teenagers were often referred to as very dutiful or devoted (*pientissimus*) in epitaphs, emphasizing the frustrated hopes of parents who had looked forward to filial duty expected from children. Despite the high levels of mortality, it was still felt to be against the order of nature for a child to predecease its parents. The loss of a child removed not just future hopes, but also, for some parents, economic security. Who would now look after them in old age, bury them and tend their graves? Epitaphs could sometimes express this anguish: 'Untimely death made the parent do for the son what the son should have done for his father' said the epitaph of one 6-year-old boy. Elsewhere we find children being given a maturity beyond their years, being viewed as the prospective adults that they would not now become, which emphasizes the dashed hopes of the bereaved and justifies the extent of their grief. In funerary art, children could be depicted as mini adults rather than as small children – as toga-clad, scroll-holding, ideal citizens. In literature, children faced their deaths bravely, having spent a life enjoying their studies and being kind and considerate to others. We can be sceptical of these idealized 'good deaths' for children (*see* p. 51), but at the very least this evidence suggests the interest of adults in these deaths. It indicates that children were not dismissed and forgotten, even if parental grief had to be justified by viewing the dead more as grownups than as children.[24]

Roman childhood could be tough, blighted by high mortality, economic hardship and gender inequality. Childhood was often short, babies and children died, and those who survived might be sent to work or married at an early age. These factors are reflected in the surviving evidence; the death of the young could be simply dismissed and overlooked or viewed only from a self-interested adult perspective. But it would be an exaggeration to say that children, or at least all children, were unloved and little missed at their passing. Roman parents could, and often did, acknowledge the death of their children and their own sense of loss and despair. As so often when viewing the Roman world, we confront conflicting perspectives that reflect the diversity of the experiences of the inhabitants – experiences underpinned by factors such as status, wealth and gender.

WIDOWS AND WIDOWERS

'Nature bids us grieve for our dear ones', acknowledged Seneca the Younger, who was, as we have seen, far from sentimental in his views on death and grief. However, relationships, especially marriage, were primarily driven by economic, political and practical factors. Arranged marriages were the norm among those with money, status and political ambition. Yet the happy marriage underpinned by harmony, concord, respect and love was held up as the ideal. It was an ideal often celebrated at death. Epitaphs could record how long husband and wife had been married, funerary sculpture could picture the happy couple with hands clasped together (Figure 17), and expressions such as the 'best of husbands' and 'the most loving of wives' were used to commemorate the quality of the relationship. Stereotypical traditional qualities, especially modesty and good housekeeping, were associated with wives in particular: Claudia 'kept to the house and made wool', while Postumia Matronilla was 'modest, religious, hard-working, frugal, busy, vigilant and thoughtful'. Clichés characterized epitaphs and monuments, but this does not mean that the sentiments and perspectives expressed were not heartfelt, and the sense of loss was no less acute.[25]

Husbands and wives were supposed to be devoted, and there was no better proof of this than those who chose to die together rather than live apart. Death scenes involving husbands and wives, frequently with suicide by one or both, were a romanticized ideal, the ultimate symbol of love and self-sacrifice. Heroic stories were often associated with disgraced men's wives, who showed not only love but also exemplary honour. The most famous example was Arria, who, after her husband was implicated in a conspiracy against the emperor in AD 42, was said to have stabbed herself. She then inspired her husband to do the same by uttering the famous words, 'Paetus, it doesn't hurt.' Pompeius Labeo and his wife both opened their veins during Tiberius' reign in order to avoid prosecution, humiliation and abuse. Paulina, the wife of Seneca the Younger, wished to die with her husband when he was forced to suicide (AD 65); she slashed her wrists but ultimately survived. Other women chose to die on hearing of the deaths of their husbands. During the proscriptions of 43 BC, the wives of two of the victims starved themselves to death. In 30 BC, Servilia, the wife of the plotter Lepidus, killed herself by allegedly swallowing fire. The most lauded example of a widow determined to die is found in the tale of Porcia, the widow of Brutus, who, despite being carefully watched by her family, managed to seize and swallow live coals from a brazier (42 BC). This is a good illustration of the legendary nature that some of these stories attained, since it seems more likely that Porcia had predeceased her husband, probably through illness.[26]

It is notable that equivalent acts of male self-sacrifice were extremely rare. Women were allowed to mourn, to make dramatic displays and to find honour in self or mutual sacrifice, but this was not the accepted or lauded path for a man. The poet Statius may have said that, 'To love a wife is a joy while she is living and a religion once she is dead', but the hard truth was that a wife was replaceable. Philosophical and poetic consolations were rarely composed to console the bereaved for the loss of a spouse. Most such consolations were addressed to parents on the death of children or to children on the death of parents, and some were for those who had lost siblings. It is for these types of relationships that we find stirring examples of people who bore their grief well and triumphed in the face of such adversity. Such exemplars were rarely associated with husbands who had lost wives. Two poetic consolation poems that did break the mould and sought to console husbands gave the women voice, using the common literary device of the dead speaking to console the living. In these poems the wives urged their husbands to be strong and emphasized their pride in traditional female virtues. Cornelia even imagined her husband remarrying, while Abascantus, the husband of Priscilla, was advised to put his duty to the emperor before his grief and not wish to join her in the grave.[27]

This is not say that a husband was not normally expected to suffer in the loss of his wife. Many a husband did acknowledge deep grief: Quintilian, writing of the death of his 19-year-old wife, said, 'I was so crushed by this one disaster that no good fortune could make me happy.' In the fourth century AD, Ausonius still mourned for his wife 36 years after her death: 'I cannot stop my pain, for it always hurts and even seems new to me.' Pliny the Younger noted that his friend Macrinus had lost his wife of 39 years, 'a terrible blow', and having possessed such a good wife for so long, his sense of loss was all the greater. Some epitaphs also celebrated devoted bonds, wishes for mutual or shared death and hopes for reunion. In the inscribed version of the 'Laudatio Turiae' (see p. 79), the husband wished that, as the elder, he could have died first, and noted how he now found himself overwhelmed by sorrow. In the epitaph to his wife, the husband of Claudia Homonoea stated that he would exchange his life for hers and that he hoped to join her soon, although she was made to counter this in the epitaph, wishing him long life so that he could enjoy all that she had been deprived of. The husband of Claudia Piste announced, 'Nothing is so miserable as to lose everything but to go on living.' In Fano, Italy, Marcus Annidius Ponticus noted that the spirits of he and his wife Sabina would be joined in a shared epitaph and tomb; in Rome Hermodorus noted how the bones of his wife, Euphroysne, would mix with his own in a single sarcophagus.[28]

The sense of extreme grief for a partner was taken to dramatic excess in Latin love poetry, but the object here was often illicit love, and the poets toyed with the idea that the suffering brought by love, and the loss of love, was akin to that brought by dying, death and grief. The love object of Propertius' poetry, Cynthia, made the poet contemplate suicide and imagine Cynthia and himself bound by love, in life and in death. In this poetic world Cynthia predeceased Propertius and, haunted by her ghost, he was reminded of the ties that should bind him:

> Others may possess you now: soon I alone will hold you: you will be with me, and mixed together, my bones will grind against your bones.[29]

The poets played with emotional highs and lows, but they captured the power of love and the impact of grief, even if these were placed at the boundaries of accepted social convention. For others, love and the impact of death existed within those boundaries. Some widows and widowers, especially those of advanced years, would have remained unmarried, but for others remarriage was common and expected. Devotion to a spouse's memory that prevented the dead union being put aside was not greatly admired. Legislation introduced by the emperor Augustus formally encouraged remarriage. Family stability and continuity were the priority, not the memory of a defunct bond. But a handful of epitaphs suggest that previous unions were not always readily forgotten, since they record more than one partner. Marcus Servilius Rufus, for example, commemorated two wives and a concubine who had all predeceased him. Love, or at least duty and remembrance, could survive the grave, as suggested by another epitaph:[30]

> To the spirits of the departed Claudia Laidi, the wife with whom I lived 23 years and to Claudia Helene the wife with whom I have lived for 44 years since her youth [or childhood] without insult. Tiberius Claudius Pannychus inscribed this when 86 years old.[31]

THE LITERATURE OF GRIEF

The philosophical viewpoint was that grief should be controlled, not indulged in or admired. The opposite view was that grief should be expressed in its fullest range, that it was wrong to control natural expressions of loss. The idea that people might even enjoy their suffering was something that philosophers were particularly wary of. Seneca the Younger noted the relationship between sadness and pleasure and that some people almost revelled in their grief. The ancients were aware that there could be a certain beauty and inspiration in grief and loss. Seneca the Elder noted that, 'Grief can sometimes be a great part of genius.' To grieve is human, and such emotional highs and lows are inspiring. It is hard to deny that the artistic products of grief can move like no other, being touching or shocking. Literary and artistic representations of grief encourage the viewer to empathize with the emotions and to enjoy indulging in the pathos of the scene. To evoke grief or to capture the height of mourning is to confront an emotional expression of suffering that, when effectively done, can surpass all other.[32]

Some of most dramatic expressions of grief surviving from the Roman world are found in epic poetry. Building and drawing on the Greek epic tradition, these poems could give voice to despair and anger. In epic poetry, people cry, shout and scream in the face of their loss. Emotion can be raw and uncontrolled:

> Made mad with grief she rushed out, with a woman's wail, and tearing her hair, she made for the front ranks and the walls. With no thought for the men, with no thought of the danger of flying weapons, she stood there and filled heaven with cries of mourning: 'Is this you I see Euryalus? You who were a comfort of my old age, oh cruel one, how could you leave me alone?[33]

Laments provide cathartic relief for the protagonist and entertainment and pleasure for the reader. The reader shares the suffering and perhaps relates it to personal experiences of loss. In epic poetry there can sometimes, however, be a disturbing aspect to the descriptions of the bereaved and the speeches that they make. Laments console the bereaved, but they also entail anger that can be destructive, even fatal. A death often leads to another death through the anger and vengeance stirred up by lament. In Statius' long poem *The Thebaid*, a mythical tale of the battle for Thebes by two feuding brothers, death leads to death, often fuelled by the cries for vengeance coming from the bereaved. The mother of the dead infant Archemorus begs for the death of his neglectful nurse: 'sacrifice her to me and to his ashes'; the mother of Crenaeus provokes her father to avenge the death of her son; and the king of Thebes, Creon, takes revenge on the dead by denying them burial: 'I wish I could put senses in their corpses and chase their guilty souls from heaven and from hell.' Laments in epic poetry are often, although not exclusively, given to women, playing on the stereotype of the bereft and slightly out of control female figure. Yet epic poetry can also challenge gender boundaries in its portrayal of raw grief and the initial shock and paralysis that overwhelms both men and women:[34]

> His mind and eyes were overwhelmed by night, his blood chilled, his limbs fell slack, his weapons dropped, he wept inside his helmet, and his shield fell and hit his greaves. He walked on failing knees and dragged his spear as though injured by a thousand wounds.[35]

Laments for real people, rather than epic heroes and characters, were written as free-standing poems. The lament (*epicedion*) was an acknowledged genre that was, once more, based on the Greek tradition. It was supposed to follow a standard pattern: an address to the mourners, a few comments on fickle fate, a summary of the life of the deceased, an account of the moment of death, a description of the funeral and, lastly, the arrival of the deceased in the underworld. In his poem on the death of the poet Tibullus, for example, Ovid began by noting how even the gods must be mourning the loss and that no man escapes death. Ovid then described the deathbed and funeral, before imagining Tibullus' arrival in Elysium and ending the poem with a prayer that 'the earth lie light on your ashes'.[36]

Other poems known as *consolationes* were written primarily to console the bereaved, either by employing the typical consolatory arguments or by seeking to justify the nature and extent of grief. However, it is not always easy to label poems categorically as either laments or consolations; the poems were not always formally constructed, and consolation could merge with lament. Many poems sought both to console the bereaved and to remember the dead, praising the dead person and celebrating what had been lost in order to explain the extreme grief of the bereaved. Consolatory arguments, such as time heals and grief achieves nothing, were often present, but in a much gentler form than found in prose philosophical consolations. One device was to imagine what the dead would say to the living – how they would urge the living to be strong, to remember but to move on. Propertius had the dead Cornelia remind her husband that death is final, to take consolation from her virtuous life and to shed tears while not being overwhelmed by grief. In the consolation addressed to Livia on the death of her son Drusus, the standard consolatory arguments were also employed, and Drusus spoke, noting that his successful life was not a cause for sorrow. But in these poems, the mourners, as well as being urged to be strong, were also allowed to shed tears and complain at their loss. In poetry, unlike in philosophical consolations and philosophical letters, the bereaved were not lectured or criticized. Mourners were granted permission to weep and wail, to show emotion and to express their suffering. Poetry could even challenge the conventions and ideals surrounding mourning, championing the right of people to express their grief and arguing that it was pointless, patronizing and even insulting to tell the bereaved not to weep. This was perhaps taken to its extreme in the poetry of Statius, who openly condemned philosophy and some mourning traditions: 'You are cruel, whoever you are, who makes distinctions in mourning, and sets boundaries to grief.'[37]

The different literary genres were in dialogue and debate, with poetry and philosophy almost at loggerheads on how to present the bereaved and how to advise people on expressing their grief. The élite code of controlled mourning was not always applicable, and not everyone aspired to philosophical ideals. Statius' poems of lament and consolation, for example, were addressed to, and were possibly read by, a reasonably wide social range, and several of the addressees were former slaves. Poetry was able to push the boundaries of emotional experience, and by the late first century AD (the time of Statius), poetry and freedom of emotional expression seem to be winning over philosophy (*see* p. 130–32). The stiff upper lip may not have been abandoned, but poetry gave a place, even a priority, to tears, and it presented grief, as opposed to formal mourning, as something that was to be embraced, even enjoyed, rather than avoided:

> Daylight faded but the tears did not cease, and the evening did not stop them. Those in misery loved lamentation and enjoyed their sorrow.[38]

CONCLUSION

How people mourned and how they should mourn was an area for debate and comment in Roman society. The perspectives that survive often seem to have polarized and stereotyped behaviour. Mourning, or at least openly showing one's grief and suffering in public, was for women, the plebs, the uncivilized and the uneducated. Weak men and incompetent emperors also cried too much. A real man was in control of his emotions. Simultaneously, evidence survives to show that these ideals and stereotypes were challenged and questioned. Philosophical ideals did not influence everyone; some argued for greater freedom of expression and the rights of the bereaved to express rather than suppress their emotions. There was a conflict in literary genres that may have reflected a real conflict between the traditionalists and the more open-minded, or at least those who realized that traditional ideals of the Republic did not always sit well in an Imperial age. At the very least the genres pushed and pulled against each other, creating stereotypes and then undermining them.

Ultimately, for the élite at least, the tradition of decorous behaviour persisted. People were expected to behave in certain ways, and not to do so was to risk criticism, but there was perhaps some softening, a subtle shift with changing times, about how a Roman gentlemen should reveal his sense of humanity and compassion. We are left with issues of presentation and interpretation rather than real people's experiences. We may sympathize more with Statius than with Seneca the Younger, but both act as a barrier, or at least a filter, for the reality of grief and mourning for the people to whom they addressed their works.

6

Commemorating and Remembering the Dead

Sometime in the mid to late second century AD, a freed slave by the name of Allia Potestas died in Rome. To record her death and remember her life, her former owner set up a lengthy verse inscription. Such detailed epitaphs, perhaps based on eulogies or laments delivered at funerals (*see* p. 79) that recalled the moral character and virtues of the deceased, were not so unusual, but other aspects of Allia's epitaph were less standard. One element that has intrigued scholars is the claim that Allia had lived harmoniously with two lovers, but other features are just as striking: the description of her physical appearance – her ivory complexion, blonde hair, beautiful eyes, long legs, flawless body and perfect breasts – and also a reference to certain items, a gold bracelet inscribed with her name and a portrait, that consoled the bereaved patron.[1]

What was to be remembered about Allia Potestas was shaped by this epitaph. The commemorator chose to remember certain, but by no means all, aspects of her life, presumably reflecting what to him, as her former owner and probable lover, mattered most. Whether Allia would have wished to be remembered primarily for her perfect figure, industrious wool-working and lovemaking we will never know. The epitaph, perhaps set into a monument of some size, would have marked her grave and been to some extent public. The commemorator also hinted at another more private world of memories, of mementos and images that he would treasure. The reference to these personal items is reminiscent of Victorian and Edwardian mourning jewellery – lockets and brooches with portraits and locks of hair taken from the dead. It is unclear whether the patron had these reminders specially made or if they were items that had existed while Allia was still alive and had now taken on a new significance. Nevertheless, the epitaph provides a unique insight into memory promotion at both a personal and domestic level.

Other sources hint at the importance of private portraiture of the dead. Suetonius noted how the emperor Augustus kept an image of a dead favoured grandson in his bedroom, which he would kiss. Seneca the Younger wrote that Octavia (sister to the emperor Augustus) was so distressed at the death of her son Marcellus that she could not stand to see portraits of him or hear his name mentioned, whereas Livia (wife of the emperor Augustus) had her son, Drusus the Elder, pictured in both private and public. Pliny the Younger noted that Regulus commissioned numerous portraits of his dead son in 'wax, bronze, silver, gold, ivory and marble' (see p. 1). Masks taken at death may have been used to create such likenesses if portraits had not already been produced (see p. 71). We know less about the production and significance of memorial jewellery and other more portable keepsakes. It is possible that these were more often connected to remembering women, who were less likely than men to receive memorials outside the home, at least among the élite. Jewellery and precious domestic items may have been particularly potent reminders of their former owner(s), and expensive goods were expected to he handed down to the next generation. Suetonius observed that the emperor Vespasian, on special festivals, drank from a small silver cup that had belonged to his grandmother, 'so dear was her memory to him'. In general it is the more public forms of memory preservation that we can access. In Chapter One we saw the scale this memory promotion could take on – how being remembered exercised the imagination of testators and the living in general. People could build their own tombs or order tombs through their will. They could also establish foundations, make philanthropic gestures, set up statues and commission or even write great works of literature. The epitaph of Allia Potestas adds another dimension. This woman was not a well-known public figure, nor was she particularly wealthy. There was no statue to her in the forum, no foundation in her memory; she was simply to be remembered by those who loved her, who employed varied methods, private and public, to cherish that memory.[2]

The epitaph of Allia Potestas is unusual for its content, but it is among thousands of epitaphs that survive from the Roman world, all united by the aim of preserving and promoting the name of the deceased. For most people there was no other public option to keep a name alive. Simple inscribed memorials were the only affordable statement of memory which could be directed at a wide audience. Most people did not commission or receive public statues, poetic laments or grand buildings or set up foundations in their name or the names of their loved ones. The majority of the inhabitants of Rome and its empire are unknown to us, and the names of even fewer would survive without epitaphs. We access most people, or at least their projected identities, through the cemetery, through their deaths and through the surviving indicators of those deaths rather than through their lives.

The cemeteries of Rome stood outside the city gates. Lining the roads, the varied tombs, altars, temples and house-tombs, with their sculpted décor and epitaphs, competed to gain the attention of the passers-by. This city of the dead paralleled the city of the living, with all its social distortions and aspirations. Little now survives of the cemeteries of ancient Rome. Only stretches of the graveyard that faced the Via Appia and a few other scattered groups of memorials recall the former grandeur of these cities of the dead. For a more evocative impression of a Roman cemetery we need to look beyond Rome. Pompeii, buried for hundreds of years following the AD 79 eruption of Vesuvius, provides one of the few available insights into how a Roman cemetery looked and operated. At a site such as Pompeii we can walk along the ancient road, look at the monuments, read the epitaphs and wonder at past lives (Figures 14 and 15). Most surviving funerary monuments are now removed from their original cemetery context. Epitaphs, small monuments and bits of sculpted stone litter museums across the former Roman Empire, but rarely do we gain detailed insights into how the different elements of these monuments came together in the environment of the cemetery. Nevertheless, the grandeur of the cemeteries of Pompeii may mislead us: not all Romans were commemorated by a stone monument; not all the cemeteries across the empire would have appeared as this.

The cemeteries of the Roman period, or what remains of them, have the potential to provide fascinating insights into the world of the living. The tombs commemorated the dead but were the products of the living. In the cemetery, people reflected and constructed their social identity, their familial role, their work or their standing in the community. The cemetery was where the dead were stored, removed from the world of the living but still at its edge and demanding attention. Cemeteries could be neglected and, as individuals, the dead could be forgotten, but collectively the graves, epitaphs and monuments begged that the dead be remembered and promoted their continuing presence.

CEMETERY LOCATION AND ORGANIZATION

It was illegal to bury or cremate a body within a town or city in the Roman world. This law was in place in Rome from an early date. Cicero noted it as one of the provisions of the laws of the Twelve Tables (c. 450 BC). The law may have sprung from religious scruples about the polluting presence of the dead, but it was also a product of practical considerations; Cicero observed the potential fire risk from cremation. The importance of the policy was made clear by its inclusion in provincial town charters. One of the characteristics of a Roman settlement, one of the rules that needed to be observed for the community to run safely and appropriately on Roman lines, was extramural burial. The dead needed to be separated from the living.[3]

Exceptions to the law were rare. In some areas of the eastern Roman Empire, monumental tombs were built within the city walls. This represented the continuation of a local tradition of honouring exceptional and well-deserving citizens with special burial. This tradition did have some impact on the western empire, but here burial within the town remained extremely unusual. Cicero noted that a few notable citizens were buried within Rome's walls at an early date, but this honour was far from the norm. A more common honour was burial in or close to the *pomerium*, a narrow strip of land that could ring the walls of a settlement. No building or burial was allowed in the *pomerium* without special permission, and it acted as a sacred and practical buffer zone.[4]

The majority of burials took place beyond this *pomerium* (and the walls), making burial monuments and graveyards a characteristic feature of the Roman suburbs. Burial areas were not publicly owned, laid out or organized, nor were they managed or segregated by religious authorities, although there was nothing to prevent a religious group or sect establishing a separate burial area if it so wished. But in general, burial areas were not formalized and delimited, and funerary monuments and graves could coexist with other suburban buildings, businesses and activities. Tombs could be interspersed with villas, gardens, inns and shops, making us question the appropriateness of the word cemetery – that is, a separate place or area set aside for burial – in the Roman context. Indeed the Romans did not use the word cemetery, which is derived from a Greek term meaning 'sleeping place'. The Latin equivalent, *coemeterium*, was not applied to burial places until the Christians began to use it in the third century AD. The word 'necropolis' (from the Greek 'city of the dead') was more often used in the Roman world, while graves and single burials were referred to by words such as *tumulus* (mound), *sepulcrum* (grave), *monumentum* (monument) and *bustum* (pyre and grave).[5]

The roads that led to the town gates became a focal point for burials. Roman cemetery areas often had an elongated appearance, stretched out along the main access routes. The association between road and burial allowed maximum visibility and access to tombs for casual passers-by, travellers and more regular, purposeful visitors. The cemetery was part of a pathway of movement and activity in the suburbs; tombs may have acted as local landmarks or even meeting places (not always for the good, *see* p. 176–7). Some tombs were designed as benches or incorporated seating for the weary traveller or visitor. The association between burial and road was probably also a result of how land was sold and developed. The Roman suburb could be a busy place with high demand for land. People bought

up patches of ground for individual tombs, and the road allowed ready
access to these without precluding the use of the land lying beyond for
other purposes. Entrepreneurs probably also played their part in cemetery
development, selling off areas of land divided into convenient-sized grave
plots. The standardization in size of some burial plots and the fact that
those setting up memorials could be eager to state the exact dimensions of
their plot (or tomb) indicate such transactions. The need to state the tomb
area also suggests that tombs might be encroached upon. When given, the
dimensions recorded were normally the road frontage and the depth into
the field, which were often inscribed at the end of the titular epitaph or on
a separate plot marker. Most recorded dimensions were modest, between
10 and 15 Roman feet, but a few plots were of exceptional size. Trimalchio,
with seeming exaggeration, demanded that his tomb plot should be
100 feet by 200 feet. Yet a few epitaphs match or surpass Trimalchio's
demands. In Lanuvium (Lanuvio, Italy), for example, the plot for a certain
Aquilia's tomb was 330 by 98 feet. In such cases the dimensions reflect not
the size of the actual tomb but the area in which the tomb would sit, often
surrounded by gardens, orchards or even vineyards.[6]

Once the land was secured, a tomb or enclosure could be built to house
the remains of the owner and others. Many owners, especially from the
early first century AD onwards, built family tombs or grave enclosures to
house the remains of relatives, slaves and freed slaves. These individuals
acted as patrons, recreating in death the hierarchy of the household of
the living. Epitaphs from the house tombs of the Isola Sacra necropolis
(Figure 9), near Portus in Italy, declared the name of the tomb founder
and stipulated who could be buried there. For example:

> To the spirits of the departed. Tiberius Claudius Eutychus built this for his well-
> deserving wife, Claudia Memnonis, for himself and their children and for their
> freedmen and freedwomen and their descendants. There will be a right of approach
> to move around the tomb. The tomb does not go to the heir. In front 15 feet, into
> the field 15 feet.[7]

In such communal settings many individual graves or spaces for urns may
have not been marked in a permanent manner; the deceased person was

part of a group commemoration but individually anonymous. In large tombs and enclosure burials, space might be gifted to people outside the immediate family or even sold on. Tomb 94 of the Isola Sacra necropolis, a tomb originally built by a certain Valeria Trophime, saw the sale and gift of numerous burial spaces. In the columbaria of Rome, the walls of which were lined with numerous niches (Figure 10), spaces (*ollae*) for urns could be sold. In a columbarium found between the Via Appia and Via Latina, for example, the epitaph of Marcus Valerius Polyclitus stated that he bought an *olla* from Cacurius Pamphilius.[8]

In some settlements, generous benefactors may have given land for the burial of the local inhabitants. In Sassina (Sarsina, Italy), a certain Horatius Balbus left land that was to be divided into plots sized 10 by 10 Roman feet for the burial of his fellow citizens. In Tolentinum (Tolentino, Italy), Gaius Veienus Trophimus gave a plot of land measuring 200 by 282 feet to the town for burial, although how the land was to be allocated was not specified. These examples are unusual and raise issues as to how and by whom the bequests would have been administered. Where such benefactors and patrons were not to be found, some people might have struggled to find a burial space. There were no publicly funded or state cemeteries. One option was for like-minded people to pool their resources and form burial clubs (*collegia*). The burial clubs might be organized by people working in the same trade or living as slaves in a large household. The members paid regular contributions, which could be drawn on for their own funeral and commemoration (*see* p. 68). The columbaria of Rome, dating to the early Imperial period, were often associated with burial clubs or large slave households. These were substantial, often subterranean structures with walls lined with niches to hold small urns containing the cremated remains of the deceased (Figure 10).[9]

For the destitute, the basic cost of the funeral and burial may have been too much. There were laws to prevent the dumping of corpses, and the regulations for undertakers at Puteoli suggest that those abandoning bodies should be fined (*see* p. 69–70). The fact that bodies and body parts did turn up in places where they were not expected or wanted suggests that some corpses were left unburied or were disposed of inadequately. When the emperor Nero was fleeing Rome, for example, his horse took fright at the smell of a dead body left abandoned close to the road. The homeless and the poverty-stricken may have had no one, or at least no one with sufficient money, to dispose of them properly. John Bodel has estimated that perhaps 30,000 people died in Rome each year, and that one in 20 (that is, 1,500 corpses annually) may have been unclaimed and unwanted. Paupers' graves, which may have been mass graves, may well have been a feature of many of the cemeteries of the empire. Varro, writing in the first century BC, described *puticuli* ('little pits') into which corpses were thrown. In Republican Rome these open pits were probably located outside the Esquiline Gate. Excavations in this area during the nineteenth century apparently uncovered pits that had been filled with human and animal remains, although the exact nature of the find and whether these were the *puticuli* can be questioned. We do know that during the late Republic there were efforts to improve the unsanitary nature of the Esquiline area, and gardens came to cover much of the region, which allegedly had once seen bones lying on the ground. Whether the *puticuli* or an equivalent continued in Rome during the Imperial period is unclear. Mass inhumation graves may have been replaced by mass crematoria.[10]

Simple burials of cremated and inhumed remains and simple grave markers suggest that many among the poorer elements of Roman society were buried with a level of decency (although note that lack of memorials and modest memorials were not an automatic sign of poverty, see p. 163). At Pompeii names have been found scratched onto the town walls, and cremation urns found nearby suggest that these basic inscriptions may have functioned as grave markers. In the busy suburban environment, modest burials were slotted into available spaces between, in front of and behind more grandiose monuments. This is best illustrated by the Isola Sacra necropolis, near Portus, where small tombs and cremations placed in pottery amphorae were dotted between and around the larger monuments (Figure 11). Nevertheless, many people must have struggled with the associated costs of even the most simple funeral, cremation and interment. A burial allowance introduced by the emperor Nerva (*see* p. 69) suggests that burial, its cost and how to dispose of the bodies of the poor could become a political issue, although the allowance was short-lived and may have applied to only limited groups of people. In general paying for the burial of the dead was a private, not public, matter, and individuals of insufficient means must have looked to the wealthier members of society for aid and support.[11]

MONUMENTS

Types of grave markers varied greatly, from simple earth mounds to grand architectural flights of fancy. Many graves may have been unmarked or marked simply with earthen, wooden or pottery indicators that perished rapidly. In the Isola Sacra necropolis, for example, amphorae or terracotta jars have been excavated that had been reused as both simple markers and receptacles for cremated remains (Figure 11). Many individuals were buried in communal tombs or enclosures that allowed little opportunity for individuality, even if individual gravesites or urns were respected. The majority of stone markers were also relatively modest. Stelae (Figures 2 and 3) were slabs of stone that marked a grave, cremation or inhumation; they were not dissimilar in appearance to modern headstones found in many British and European cemeteries. The stone would have stood above or in front of the place of burial, with any inscribed text or images facing the road. A stone from Asisium (Assisi, Italy) summarizes the marking and commemorative role of such stones: 'Caius Vesprius Eros set this up for himself and his wife Leria, and behind this *cippus* [stone] is a place for their bones.' Many stelae were small and undecorated or only basically decorated, inscribed with little more than the name of the deceased. An alternative marker was the funerary altar, a rectangular block of stone with mouldings made to resemble a sacrificial altar. Such altars could mark a gravesite or sometimes serve as receptacles for cremated remains (then being known as ossuary altars). Funerary altars were sometimes placed

within tombs or enclosures (Figure 15), as were carved stone ossuary or
ash containers (Figure 12) and sarcophagi (Figures 4 and 8). Ossuary
containers and later sarcophagi could be highly sculpted, but when placed
in poorly lit and closed tombs, they would have only been visible to a few
people on limited occasions. This serves to remind us that memorials
and epitaphs can be difficult to read and understand when removed from
context. A now isolated stele, altar, urn, sarcophagus or inscribed plaque
may have once been associated with an enclosure or tomb, displayed
in a niche-lined wall or grouped with other similar memorials. These
contexts could have created connections between individuals or asserted
familial, work or other identities, mediated by aspects such as visibility
and access.[12]

For those with extensive funds and the inclination, tomb possibilities
were near endless. The mausoleum of the emperor Augustus was an
eye-catching landmark on Rome's skyline, visible from both the road and
the river Tiber. It survives today as a circular concrete ruin with an outer
diameter of 89 metres (Figure 13). This base was originally faced in white
limestone and was covered with a substantial earth mound, topped by
a bronze statue of the emperor. Such round tombs were popular at this
time, although Augustus' outstripped all the competition in terms of sheer
scale. Other tombs took the form of enclosures, houses, towers, temples
(or aedicule tombs), large altars and even pyramids.

The excavated cemeteries of Pompeii display a wide variety of tomb
types dating from the late Republic through to AD 79. Figure 14 shows a
small stretch of the Pompeian necropolis that faced the road close to the
Porta Nocera. To the left is a large altar-shaped tomb, behind which is a
smaller round tomb that may have originally been topped by a mound.
Next is a small enclosure tomb sandwiched into the available space between
the two adjacent tombs. This enclosure tomb had a rear wall lined with
niches and a small inscribed panel placed high in the gable of the back wall.
Adjacent to this is a substantial chamber tomb with an impressive façade
lined with niches, the top row of which originally displayed portrait busts
and the bottom row of which displayed stones roughly shaped as human

heads. These stones, known as *columellae*, were a distinctive feature of Pompeian commemoration (*see* p. 165). Finally, to the far right of Figure 14 is temple-style tomb; a high base with a columned canopy shelters seated statues of those commemorated. Figure 15 shows an area of the cemetery running alongside the road that led to the Herculaneum Gate of Pompeii. The tombs here are slightly later in date than those at the Nocera Gate, and they consist of enclosures, several of which had large marble altars, inscribed and carved, raised on high podiums to make them visible. Indeed it should be noted that tombs could be stuccoed and painted to give the impression of coloured marbles. In Figure 14 traces of the covering are still visible on the large altar tomb to the left of the picture. Portraits and sculpted décor may have also been brightly painted, with letters of inscriptions highlighted in red paint. In its heyday a Roman cemetery may have been far removed from the sedate monochrome impression now created by the surviving stone, marble and brick memorials.[13]

Smaller monuments may also have employed colour to highlight sculptural details. Many modest markers were only roughly hewn and inscribed with simple information (for example, Figure 3), at most accompanied by floral motifs. Certain sculptural designs were, however, popular on altars, stelae and sarcophagi, frequently complementing information contained in the epitaph. Portraiture was often favoured, showing a likeness of the deceased in bust or full figure form. Sculpture could also reinforce the occupation of the deceased, depicting people at work or displaying symbols of their trade. Other designs, such as dining reliefs, provided an idealized perspective that suggested the deceased had and would continue to enjoy the pleasures of life such as the feast (Figure 2). Far removed from the daily grind were mythological scenes, allegories that suggested comparisons between the human and the divine (see Figure 8 and p. 110). In short, by using inscriptions, sculpture, colour and sometimes sheer scale and visibility, monuments provided a snapshot of the life of the deceased, though often an edited or idealized one, that served to sum up aspects of his or her life, such as work, family and, if appropriate, achievements and even aspirations.

The choice of shape, size and décor for a tomb must have been affected by numerous factors. The skills of the available craftsmen and personal wealth must have played a substantial role, but aspects such as social status, social competition and chronological era also came into play. Different types of monument went in and out of fashion. Before the late Republic, evidence for monumental tombs in the city of Rome is limited. The wealthy élite families did build some striking edifices to their dead, but the graves of other social groups appear to have rarely been marked in lasting form. In a town such as Pompeii, grave markers were rare until the late Republic. In the final decades of the Republic and in the early Augustan age, tombs seem to have caught on in a big way, first in Rome and then across the empire. Modest stone markers, initially stelae and then altars, began to appear, and these increased in popularity throughout the first century AD. For the more wealthy, novel grand designs seem to have peaked in the Augustan era. We can note some particularly unusual and striking examples that appeared in Rome and have probably survived for that very reason. The tomb of Caius Cestius was built in the shape of a pyramid, standing more than 36 metres high; that of Eurysaces the baker incorporated an unusual design of cylinders that have been interpreted as bread ovens or kneading machines related to his trade (Figure 16). By the mid first century AD, larger tombs were becoming more communal in nature, being designed to accommodate the remains of many people rather than being focused on individuals or small family groups. We can, for example, contrast the cemeteries of Pompeii (Figures 14 and 15), buried in the AD 79 eruption of Vesuvius, with that of the Isola Sacra necropolis (at Portus, near Ostia, Italy), which dates predominantly to the second century AD. Pompeii has an eclectic mix of large altars, round tombs, temple tombs and so forth, while the Isola Sacra necropolis is characterized by rows of similar house tombs, which incorporated niches for the interment of the remains of many people (Figure 9). By the late second century the production of stone funerary monuments seems to have gone into decline. Stone sarcophagi were in vogue for some, but many other people from this time on seem to have been interred without markers, or at least without markers that have lasted. Ultimately, underground *hypogea* and catacombs developed, but above-ground stone monuments, sculpted and inscribed, seem to have had their day. This is not to say that the graves of late antique Rome and its empire were unmarked, abandoned and uncared for, but the role of the cemetery and its importance as an area for display had shifted and changed.[14]

This chronological outline, needless to say, gives a useful overview but simplifies an often complex situation. Not all parts of the empire followed the same pattern of adoption, proliferation, simplification and abandonment in tomb and monument design (*see* p. 165–6). For this reason it may be misleading to view the differences between the cemeteries of Pompeii and the Isola Sacra only in chronological terms. Besides, if there was change, what was driving it? One model is that of social competition and emulation. Who you were affected the type of monument selected. However, the choice of funerary monument was not a simple case of reflecting social status but more a case of constructing it. Élite competition may have created the showy funerary monuments of the late Republic, but the huge tomb built by the first emperor, Augustus, seems to have put an end to that (*see* p. 160). In the city of Rome, at least, the emperor was not to be outdone. In the first century AD we see some discussion among the élite of the value of funerary monuments; the impermanent nature of stone memorials was often noted by writers who believed that only literature would last (*see* p. 35–36). Frontinus, a one-time consul of the late first century AD, apparently forbade a funerary monument, declaring that 'My memory will endure if my life has deserved it.' This perspective was countered by Pliny the Younger, who defended the choice of his mentor, Verginius Rufus, to design his own tomb – not to be built in Rome, it should be noted, but at his country estate. We can hypothesize that such differences in opinion reflect a real debate about how people should be commemorated and remembered, just as there were tensions at this time in how expressive public mourning should be (*see* p. 130–131). By the end of the first century AD, Rome was no longer a Republic, or pretending to be, and how the élite buried, mourned for and commemorated the dead was being renegotiated.[15]

As the aristocratic élite moved toward and celebrated a certain under-statement in funerary commemoration, at least in terms of suburban cemetery display, other social groups may have found funerary monu-ments a useful medium for constructing and celebrating their identity. One such group was freed slaves. Ex-slaves had a somewhat mixed and confused social position. An ex-slave became a Roman citizen, with the many advantages that this conveyed for him or her and for any subsequent children, but simultaneously the ex-slave was in some respects a second-class citizen who could not hold high office, however wealthy and successful he became. In death, freed slaves may have been inclined to celebrate their successes and even compensate for the stigma of their social position. Certain types of tomb design and décor appear to have appealed to them. In the late Republic and early Imperial period, for example, freed slaves preferred portraits that showed them wearing the toga, as if proclaiming their citizenship; and they were often pictured with spouses and children, celebrating relationships that were legally denied to the slave (Figure 17). Ex-slaves may have had an understandable pride in their achievements, integration and new identity and marked this at death. However, as lesser social groups such as freed slaves gained access to the cemetery and funerary display, their attraction for the élite may have further declined. Frontinus' dismissal of tombs and Petronius' mockery of the grandiose tomb plans of the fictional ex-slave Trimalchio may represent a sort of inverse snobbery. Once everyone wanted a tomb and more people could afford them, thereby blurring social distinctions, the perceived value of tombs and stone markers may have declined (at least for some). Eventually the bottom fell out of the market.[16]

Such a model of social emulation followed by decline is attractive and fits the principle of a hierarchical Roman society. However, it may be an exaggeration to say that all ex-slaves had a huge chip on their shoulder that they were eager to remove. Some would have been important and respected members of the community, not shunned or despised, and they may have been creating their own hierarchy and means of display rather than just emulating social betters. Equally, Rome's traditional élite did not completely reject funerary monuments or overt display. Some may have talked down funerary extravagance, but in the privacy of their rural estates they were hardly going to paupers' graves. In addition, beyond Rome and Italy there were often few slaves or freed slaves and rarely any senators or literati. If social emulation, or at least the use of funerary monuments to compensate for social stigmas or express social mobility, was a factor elsewhere in the empire, it was related to facets of identity other than just slavery versus freedom or senatorial versus non-senatorial status. Across the empire, regional, as well as social and chronological, factors impacted upon monument design. Many areas of the empire had existing traditions, most notably in the Greek East and in Egypt, aspects of which continued into the Roman period. In some areas of the empire we can see cultural fusions, with markers and monuments that employed local sculptural motifs, and sometimes local languages, creating hybrid monuments. In North Africa, for example, some early monuments of the Roman period were inscribed in the Punic language rather than in Latin, and during the second and third centuries AD, large tower tombs, several storeys high and crowned by distinctive pyramidal roofs, peppered the rural African landscape. These tower tombs represented a renaissance, and to some extent reinvention, of a local pre-Roman monument type. [17]

In other parts of the empire, funerary monuments, whether grand stone structures or simple stelae, were largely unknown before the arrival of the Romans, and the adoption of some or all of these forms can be viewed as a sign that the community did become Romanized, accepting and embracing Roman culture. However, even where this can appear to be the case, funerary monuments and cemeteries often exhibit local characteristics. In Pompeii and parts of Campania, for example, *columellae* are found; these are small stones shaped into the form of heads, sometimes inscribed with the name of the deceased, which were used to mark the sites of interred ashes (Figure 14 – bottom right). *Columellae* were placed in enclosures or at the base of tombs, and they were a distinctive feature of this one area of the empire. Another striking example is the stone funerary markers shaped, and sometimes decorated, to take the form of barrels, which were particularly favoured by slaves in some parts of Spain. In yet other regions of the empire, funerary monuments constructed from stone and inscribed with Latin were rarely found. In Britain, for example, comparatively few stone funerary markers of the Roman period have been recovered. This may reflect the lack of suitable materials for carving, but it could also suggest that the fashion for inscribed funerary monuments just did not catch on. This is not to say that the local population in these areas was rejecting Roman culture, only that funerary monuments (which, as we have already seen, went in and out of popularity) just did not appeal to large enough sections of that population. The impact of social emulation and changes in fashion (some driven by the élite) did then affect the appearance and level of monumentalization in the cemetery, but there were other factors at play. At the end of the day, the dead, whether in a fancy tomb, a suburban cemetery or on a rural estate, were still buried.[18]

EPITAPHS

One of the most striking features of the thousands of funerary monuments that survive is the Latin (and Greek) words with which they were inscribed. These epitaphs help us to repopulate, as it were, the Roman world like no other source; the vast majority of surviving literary texts were the products of an élite, educated, male minority. This is not to say that epitaphs, by contrast, represent the full social range of Roman society, but often they do give us the names, and to some extent the voices, of a wide spectrum of people who would otherwise be anonymous and completely lost from view. Most epitaphs were very short, stating little more than the name of the deceased and that of the person setting up the inscription. Names were important and could reveal a great deal about gender, legal status and family connections. Names were central to how people were remembered.

Cicero said that by reading epitaphs, especially the names, he remembered the dead. In addition to names, sometimes an age at death or an indication of career or social status was also provided. A handful of epitaphs were long and detailed, providing full career structures, life stories, poems on grief or thoughts on the afterlife. These long inscriptions, occasionally composed in verse, are now a valuable source. The detailed epitaph of Allia Potestas with which this chapter began provides an example. But it needs to be emphasized that long epitaphs were the exception rather than the rule.[19]

Despite their frequent simplicity and repetitive content, epitaphs are rich sources both collectively and individually. A single simple epitaph can be packed full of insights into the Roman world and society. Take the epitaph to the young Flavia Helpis, which is inscribed on an urn that would have originally been placed in a niche within a columbarium. The columbarium would have been filled with hundreds of similar brief inscriptions. Here the epitaph is presented first as the letters were inscribed, then with the Latin abbreviations expanded and finally in translation:

DIIS MANIB FLAVIAE
HELPIDIS VIX ANN XIII M VII
D XVI
T FLAV AUG L EPAPHRODITUS
F ET SIBI

Diis(!) Manib(us) Flaviae / Helpidis vix(it) ann(os) XIII m(enses) VII / d(ies) XVI / T(itus) Flav(ius) Aug(usti) l(ibertus) Epaphroditus / f(iliae) et sibi

To the spirits of the departed Flavia Helpis, who lived 13 years, seven months and 16 days. Titus Flavius Epaphroditus, a freed slave of the emperor, made this for his daughter and himself.[20]

This epitaph is a good illustration of the various issues and insights that surround reading epitaphs and of their role in understanding Roman society. The content is simple: the name of the child, the age of the child, the name of the commemorator and their relationship. But all these basic pieces of information, standard as they are, can be revealing. The father has three names (the *tria nomina*), demonstrating that he was a Roman citizen. However, he had not been born to this status, since his name also indicates that he was an ex-slave (*libertus*) who had belonged to the emperor (*libertus Augusti*). The epitaph does not explicitly state which emperor he had served or what his role was. Had he been close to the seat of power as an adviser or secretary, or had he played a more humble role as cook, cleaner or gardener? The name of Flavius was associated with the Flavian dynasty of emperors (Vespasian, Titus and Domitian), and as ex-slaves adopted their former owners' names, it suggests that Titus Flavius Epaphroditus lived during the late first century AD. The daughter had also inherited this name, taking Flavia, the female form of Flavius. This serves to remind how names were passed down across the generations, and not all people with the name Flavius or Flavia were direct former slaves of the Flavian dynasty. Flavia Helpis is not described as a slave or ex-slave, and her two names (the female equivalent of the *tria nomina*) suggest she was a citizen too. Had she been born after her father's manumission or granted freedom at the same time? And what of her mother – had she too been a slave? And why is the mother not mentioned in the epitaph? It was presumably the case that she had predeceased her daughter; if so, was she buried nearby? The relationship between father and daughter is symbolized by a single letter in the epitaph: F for *filia*. It was the father's responsibility to bury and commemorate his daughter, and in doing so he advertised his own name and status. This was particularly relevant because the epitaph was also for him; when his time came, Titus Flavius Epaphroditus hoped his ashes would be buried with those of his daughter. The epitaph contains no expressions of grief and no sentimental words to describe the child or the relationship. The only additional information is the girl's age, given in exacting detail, which is a powerful suggestion that the life of this child had been carefully measured and valued. There are also no expressions of faith or belief in the afterlife, although the opening expression, common and formulaic as it was (*see* p. 115), did address the spirits of the deceased.

The content of this epitaph represents the basic relationship between parent and child, and the desire of the former to commemorate the latter, but in doing so it reveals insights into the social background and milieu of those involved, while also raising now unanswerable questions, especially about the wider family. Due to the reuse of stone and loss of the original evidence, we often know little about where epitaphs were originally placed. The text of this epitaph raises issues about its visibility and accessibility. Who would have seen and been interested in it? The epitaph is succinct and full of abbreviations. Understanding it must have been a bit like cracking a code. How many people could do this? How many people could read and write in the Roman world? Understanding ancient levels of literacy is a complex process, but the frequent creation of epitaphs suggests that many people would have at least understood these simple texts. Petronius has one of Trimalchio's guests explain that he can read stonecutters' capitals, implying that he may have struggled with more complex texts. Epitaphs were highly standard and formulaic, and some letters and groups of letters may have functioned almost as pictograms; it was not that difficult to spot the names and age statements and thus get the gist of the content.[21]

Thousands upon thousands of inscriptions survive from the Roman world. It has been estimated, for example, that 100,000 inscriptions have been found and recorded from the city of Rome and 60,000 from North Africa. The majority of these inscriptions – probably more than two-thirds – are epitaphs, and such vast numbers of epitaphs have lent themselves to statistical analysis. Scholars have used epitaphs in demographic studies of the Roman population in order to gain insights into life expectancy, social status and family structure. When used in this fashion, epitaphs can be a vital and exciting source that can make us rethink assumptions about Roman life. One striking example is the use of epitaphs in the study of family structure. Legal texts and some other sources emphasize the importance of the father (*pater*) in the Roman family and his influence across the generations. In short, the father had legal power (*potestas*) and authority over his sons and their offspring, which creates the impression that the Roman family was a multi-generational extended unit. However, statistical studies of epitaphs give a different impression. Epitaphs often contain statements of relationships, especially between the commemorated person and the commemorator. Detailed analysis of these relationships suggests that the majority of them refer to the nuclear family – that is, parents, children and spouses. Further analysis of relationships alongside statements of age of death and length of marriages also suggests a pattern of early female marriage and comparatively late male marriage. In many families this would have meant that fathers did not live to see their sons reach adulthood, let alone the birth of their grandchildren. In theory a father might dominate the lives of his sons and grandsons, but the reality was probably somewhat different. Epitaphs would then seem to undermine the myth of a multi-generational Roman family.[22]

Arguments about family structure that are based on epigraphic evidence may be persuasive and may complement other evidence, but the statistical analysis of epitaphs can be a minefield. The debunking of figures and statistics on life expectancy drawn from epitaphs is a well-known cautionary tale. It might be thought that epitaphs, with their numerous statements of age at death, could be used to calculate average life expectancy. However, the vagaries of the evidence have long been identified. Age statements were rarely accurate; ages were often rounded up or down; ages were more frequently given for the young and the very old; and ages were given more often for males than for females (*see* p. 42–43). In other words, the commemorated population with ages given is not necessarily a representative one. Statistics derived from epitaphs all too easily overlook the fuller context and content of the inscription. An age statement, for example, only makes sense or has a value, now and in the Roman era, when considered with the rest of the epitaph, such as information on who was commemorated, their gender and their relationship to the commemorator.[23]

Chronology is another factor that impacts on the way in which epitaphs are studied. Dates in epitaphs are extremely rare, and dating epitaphs (generally by comparison with the few examples that can be dated) is a complex process. Nevertheless it has been noted that the use of epitaphs was far from chronologically static. Production increased across the first two centuries AD and then declined. Such a basic summary conceals many regional and social differences and anomalies, but the broad pattern, in line with the chronological production of funerary monuments (*see* p. 162–4), is of a peak and then declining interest from the late second century AD. Epitaphs went in and out of fashion, and these changes have been linked to the display of Roman citizenship, personal identity and social mobility. Once more, explanations for this pattern are contentious, as is proving the universal accuracy and applicability of such theories, but the existence of this pattern does underline that any statistics derived from epitaphs may not apply to all periods equally.[24]

Epitaphs, especially when used to create statistics, become disembodied texts, removed from their original role as part of a grave marker serving to commemorate the dead. The words of inscriptions appeal to scholars because they can be read, deciphered and tabulated; it can be tempting to prioritize texts over other sources such as images, material and skeletal evidence. Inscriptions are often now recorded primarily as texts in vast epigraphic volumes, with little acknowledgement of their appearance and original location. Getting all these epitaphs back into the cemetery, that is, understanding all aspects of their spatial and visual context, would be an impossible task, but as sources epitaphs do need to be handled with care.[25]

PRESERVING TOMB AND MEMORY

When someone built a tomb or set up a tombstone, whether in preparation for their own death or as a result of the death of a loved one, they made careful choices, even if guided by convention and the stonemason, about what to inscribe and what to depict. The ideal was to set up a monument that would last – maybe not forever, but for a substantial length of time. However, such monuments would only endure through the care and interest of the living, and the living were fickle and unreliable.

Testators and tomb founders often realized this and looked for ways to maintain and preserve the monument and keep other parties interested in the physical structure.

In the first place an individual might decide to build their own tomb or memorial rather than relying on the heir to carry out their wishes (*see* p. 36). However, if a tomb was constructed prior to death, once the founder was dead and buried and their influence was gone, the only option to maintain such a tomb was to give others a vested interest in the structure. Communal tombs often primarily commemorated only one or two people, at least in the titular epitaph, but provided space for the burial of many others. These often anonymous 'others' would benefit from maintaining the tomb. Tombs may have provided spaces for children and future generations, creating a dynastic interest in and dimension to the building. However, families died out or moved away, or the next generation might decide to build something bigger, better or more fashionable. Thus the wider family, consisting of ex-slaves and their descendants who on achieving freedom adopted the family name, were often also given permission to use the tomb. A common formula in epitaphs was *libertis libertabusque posterisque eorum*, meaning 'for their freedmen and freedwomen and their descendants'. This was an effective way of tying dependants to the tomb and creating an extended network to maintain the tomb and continue to promote the memory of its founders. The freed slaves and their families gained a place for burial, and their economic circumstances may have made them more reliable than an independent heir.

Some founders of communal tombs had concerns about the reliability of their heirs and what might happen to the tomb if it was inherited by others. The formula HMHNS (*hoc monumentum heredes non sequetur* – this monument does not go to the heirs) was inscribed on some epitaphs, especially in Italy and southern Gaul, in an attempt to stop the tomb passing to the heirs who might sell, reorganize or abandon it. At the Isola Sacra necropolis we find examples of tombs being subdivided and land and burial places being sold. Tombs 75 and 76 were originally one tomb built by Marcus Cocceius Daphnus, intended for his family and those of two named male heirs. Following his death one of these men built a dividing wall, creating his own separate tomb complete with entrance and epitaph. Tomb 89 was built between two pre-existing tombs, and the epitaph makes clear that the owner, Messia Candida, had bought the land from people who owned the tombs on either side. The names of the owners from whom she had made the purchase, however, do not match the names found in the titular epitaphs of the two tombs, although they may well be descendants, suggesting that these structures had passed to new owners or to the next or subsequent generations. Such changes show that the Isola Sacra necropolis was an evolving space. The next generation did not necessarily respect the wishes of their predecessors. Marcus Cocceius Daphnus may have been turning in his grave at the alterations made to his tomb by his heir, but at least these changes were formally recorded in a new inscription, thus avoiding any future disputes about ownership.[26]

Testators and tomb founders could also plan ahead by furnishing the tomb with certain facilities and assets. Money could be left for maintaining the tomb and even for guards to protect it. Petronius' Trimalchio planned to have a guard outside his tomb to prevent people 'shitting there'. Abascantus of Misenum left money not only for the local community to celebrate his memory (*see* p. 33 and 100) but also for the repair and maintenance of his tomb. Property such as gardens could be attached to or surround the tomb, and the produce from such a garden tomb (*cepotaphium*) could be used in tomb cult or sold to help maintain the tomb, as well as providing a pleasant environment for those visiting. A testator from Langres who left detailed requests for the design and furnishing of his tomb also provided money for the repair of the monument and the upkeep of the gardens, including funds to employ three gardeners and their apprentices. Some of Trimalchio's vast tomb plot may have been intended for gardens. The epitaph of Claudia Semne noted that within a walled enclosure there would be a garden, vineyard, water supply, temple tomb and statues. Other epitaphs also refer to tomb gardens, occasionally specifying how the produce was to be used. The freedman Titus Vettius Hermes from

Vardacate (Casale Monferrato, Italy), for example, stated in his epitaph that the roses grown in the tomb garden were to be offered to him on the anniversary of his birthday forever, and the garden was not to be divided up or sold. Two plans of tomb gardens survive. These unusual finds were incised onto marble slabs and must originally have been displayed on the tomb or somewhere in the garden enclosure. One of these, from the Via Labicana near Rome, appears to show a tower tomb monument, with an area, largely behind this, filled with dots, presumably representing trees, interspersed with rectangular areas denoting lawns or flowerbeds.[27]

An additional way of perpetuating memory was to encourage people to visit the memorial through leaving money to fund feasts and celebrations or even through paying people directly to celebrate annual rites (*see* p. 33 and 100). Tomb founders might provide facilities specifically for tomb cult. The testator of Langres richly furnished his tomb with items such as cushions and rugs that were aimed at the comfort of the living more than that of the dead. Epitaphs sometimes refer to the spaces and rooms provided at the tomb, such as dining rooms, sun rooms and porticos. Wells, ovens, seating areas and dining rooms at tombs are attested archaeologically. At the Isola Sacra necropolis, tombs often had wells and areas for the preparation and cooking of food. Some tombs had second storeys that could be used as sun terraces or dining spaces, while other tombs had dining couches (*biclinia*) flanking the entrance of the tomb.[28]

Some tombs did survive and were respected for extended periods of time. More than two centuries after the death of Atilius Calatinus (a politician of the third century BC), Cicero was still able to read his epitaph. The tomb of the Scipios was used for several centuries (*see* p. 177), and that of Licinii Crassi (near the Porta Salaria), a family to whom Pompey the Great was related, continued in use under the emperors, at times reflecting the chequered history of the family but also the continuing potency of the family name. A century after the death of Rome's great poet Virgil, his tomb was still visited and treated almost as a temple. However, despite the grand designs and aspirations of tomb founders and testators, many tombs fell into disrepair or were reused, robbed or demolished. Some people, and probably then only a minority, might seek to protect their tombs, but ultimately such provisions could not last. Once personal interest fell away and those who actually remembered the dead were dead and buried themselves, who would take care of a tomb? Foundations and money left in trust might not last or might be neglected. For how long did the people of Misenum party at and maintain Abascantus' tomb? Tombs could struggle to withstand the ravages of time and man's disrespectful nature, and this may have been particularly the case with modest, relatively isolated markers such as stelae. At Pompeii election notices and advertisements were painted onto the exterior walls of tombs; such graffiti showed little respect for the dead or for their survivors. In the longer term, cemeteries were plundered for building materials. The late defensive walls of Roman Chester contained many old tombstones, and in Ostia a tombstone was even reused as a toilet seat in the public latrines. Grave sites marked by earth mounds or perishable or temporary markers may have been easily disturbed, as the cross-cutting of graves in many excavated inhumation cemeteries so well illustrates. A late source, Sidonius Apollinaris, tells of how his grandfather's grave, presumably unmarked beyond a mound, was disturbed by thoughtless gravediggers. The lack of permanency and the vulnerability of grave markers was a common motif for poets and writers; only great works of literature would last forever (*see* p. 33–36).[29]

Tombs were, in theory, sacred. A tomb was a religious place protected by the law, and the law could punish grave violation as sacrilege. Those who removed bodies or scattered bones could be exiled or even executed. Those who wished to move a body or human remains, even for legitimate reasons, needed to ask for permission. If someone buried a body or interred ashes on someone else's land or in someone else's tomb without permission, the owner could only remove the remains once agreement had been received from the pontiff or emperor. An inscription set up in Rome, presumably attached to a tomb as proof of sanctioned action, recorded that in AD 155 Arrius Alphius was granted permission to move the bodies of his wife and

son to a new tomb. Arrius Alphius had buried these relatives temporarily
in clay coffins at another tomb until he was able to afford a tomb of his
own, which was to have a marble sarcophagus for their remains and his,
'so that when I die I can be laid there next to them'. The law might be
strict, but when tomb owners died and family interest fell away, who
would monitor or report any damage or abuse to a tomb or a grave
marked by an amphora or small stele? From the second century AD the
phrase *sub ascia dedicavit* (dedicated while under the hammer) became
common in epitaphs in parts of Gaul and Italy, sometimes accompanied
by the image of a hammer carved onto the tombstone. These words and
the accompanying image may have been intended to signify symbolically
that the grave was a religious and protected place. Epitaphs could also seek
to reinforce the law by including their own threats and warnings against
would-be violators: fines that were to be paid to the town council; spiritual
or emotional threats; and curses that evoked the gods and threatened
physical and spiritual suffering. One bereaved mother in Rome summed
up the fears: 'If anyone should disturb his bones, may he suffer the same
torment as me.' The commemorator of Allia Potestas emphasized that
trespassers would be guilty of offending the gods. The parents of Quintus
Iulius Hermes, from Portus, had inscribed on his epitaph, 'If anyone
defaces, damages or sells this inscription, monument or tomb he shall pay
200,000 sesterces to the treasury of the Roman people.'[30]

The tombs of the cemetery were vulnerable due to their location. The
suburb could act as an extension of the town, but this was still a marginal
zone lacking the real hubbub of the centre, especially after dark. Tombs
could become the haunts of undesirable characters such as tramps, thieves
and prostitutes. The poet Martial pictured whores using tombs, and tombs
could provide a shelter for the homeless or a quiet stash for robbers. The
cemetery was also regarded as a superstitious or even ill-omened place.
Petronius set a story of a werewolf in a cemetery, and witches were often
thought to live in cemeteries, exploiting the graves and the dead. Lucan's
Thessalian witch Erictho was a frequenter of cemeteries, living in a tomb
and seizing corpses (*see* p. 118). For some people the cemetery may have

held a real fascination and the bodies (and spirits) of the dead special powers. Curse tablets (*defixiones*) have been found in graves; these sought to harness the powers of the dead to perform special tasks for the living (*see* p. 117). Pliny the Elder lists, in a sceptical fashion, some of the cures that were purportedly to be obtained from corpses, especially from the corpses of those who suffered violent or premature death: the blood of gladiators was thought to cure epilepsy, a touch from the hand of the dead could cure sore glands and throats, and earth taken from skulls was useful for thinning eyelashes. Such anecdotes were meant to sound faintly ridiculous and suggest man's gullibility, but they also served to highlight the vulnerability of the dead and, simultaneously, a sense of interaction between the dead and the living. Not all bodies and not all graves were honoured and respected, and even those that were could not be protected for all time. It was a duty to remember the dead, but tombs, monuments and graves could also become a burden for the living.[31]

HONOUR AND DISHONOUR

The cemetery was underpinned by ideals: honour, memory and respect for the dead, but it also could represent dishonour, forgetfulness and disrespect. Social status and success found their place there, even if the cemetery and its monuments went in and out of fashion. There was a persistence of Republican ideals that the best citizens got the best burial and that a distinguished life (or death) deserved a distinguished burial and commemoration. Aristocratic families of the Republic had their own traditional burial spaces, often in locations where the family owned property. The monuments of the Claudii Marcellii, the Servilli, the Metelli and the Scipios were clustered together in an area between the Via Appia and the Via Latina, not far from the Porta Capena. The tomb of the Scipios, which was excavated in the eighteenth century, contained a series of sarcophagi dating from 298 BC onwards. The façade of the tomb was originally modest, although it was later remodelled in more grandiose style, but the interior, with its sarcophagi and eulogizing epitaphs, told a family success story. During the mid to late Republic, distinguished individuals could be buried at public expense in certain key locations. One such location was the Campus Esquilinus, and Cicero proposed this site when he requested a public funeral and tomb for Servius Sulpicius Rufus, who had died while part of an embassy to Mark Antony. The most favoured location was the Campus Martius. The dictator Sulla's grave was located here, as were the monuments to the consuls Aulus Hirtius and Caius Vibius Pansa, who died at the battle of Mutina in 43 BC. It was also on the Campus Martius that Augustus built his huge mausoleum, curtailing the use of this area for the burial of other distinguished citizens and in general dissuading other leading families from being too showy in their tomb construction. The élite often now associated their tombs with family estates at a distance from the centre of Rome, villa and tomb operating together to promote the honour and dignity of the family. The importance attached to reflecting honour and public service in the cemetery continued in the towns and cities of the provinces, where local magistrates, councillors and benefactors might be given distinguished burial spaces, sometimes even in the *pomerium*. These might only be small-town big men, rather than the senatorial élite of Rome, but in their local communities the suburban cemetery could still echo the hierarchy of inner-town life.[32]

Alongside honour went dishonour. Some people struggled to gain admission to the cemetery or any sort of decency in death. The grand tombs of the rich and famous were contrasted with the communal pits of the poor. Those who committed suicide and people of a dubious profession might find themselves, if not excluded, placed in separate zones; no one wanted to be buried, or have their loved-ones buried, next to a prostitute, beggar or undertaker. When Horatius Balbus donated a burial ground to the people of Sassina (*see* p. 157), he excluded 'contract gladiators, those who hanged themselves and those who made a dirty living'. In general, evidence for which groups were 'dirty' and stigmatized and how people were marginalized in death is limited, but the treatment received by dead gladiators may be revealing. Gladiators were often recruited from slaves and criminals, although free men could choose to become gladiators. Those who fell in gladiatorial combats were unceremoniously dragged from the arena, and their bodies were disposed of rapidly and basically. However, the survival of tombstones set up to gladiators indicates that at least some gladiators were buried with a degree of respect and were remembered by others (Figure 3). Gladiators may have formed *collegia* that assisted with burial (*see* p. 68), and this is perhaps supported by the fact that gladiatorial tombstones have often been found grouped together. However, the grouping of gladiators' tombstones may also suggest a degree of separation from the wider community. It is possible that, just as these men were forced to live on the edge of society and acceptability, so they were also buried on the fringes of the cemetery, isolated from others.[33]

Some individuals were denied burial altogether. The bodies of criminals and traitors could be dumped in the river Tiber or be left to rot in a gruesome display. Even great men, such as former leaders who fell from grace and power, could suffer insults to their bodies and the denial of burial. During the early Imperial period, bodies could be exposed on the Gemonian Steps or Stairs of Mourning (*Scalae Gemoniae*). These steps were in full view of the Forum, and it was here, for example, that the body of Sejanus was thrown and abused by the mob for three days prior to being thrown into the river Tiber (*see* p. 62). For those in authority, including the emperors, controlling the fate of the dead – their bodies, their burial and how they were subsequently remembered – was a means of exerting power and authority. A regime or an individual ruler could choose not only to honour or dishonour a corpse but also seek to control whether and how the dead were memorialized. Just as funerals, statues and literature could promote memory (*see* p. 34–37), the denial or destruction of these things could seek to obliterate memory or at least tarnish it. The ultimate sanction was to damn the dead. There was a repertoire of penalties used for destroying the memory of a public enemy; although these were not fully legally recognized, they are often now known as *damnatio memoriae*. Statues could be defaced and toppled, *imagines* (*see* p. 89) could be banned from public display, names could be chiselled out of inscriptions and property could be confiscated. One of the most famous cases involved Cnaeus Calpurnius Piso, who was posthumously condemned by the Senate on 10 December AD 20. Piso, the governor of Syria, had quarrelled with the emperor Tiberius' nephew, Germanicus, and had been implicated in the death of the latter. Piso was put on trial for treason, but he committed suicide before a verdict was reached. The posthumous condemnation of Piso stood in stark contrast to the posthumous honours that were voted to his rival, Germanicus. The senatorial decree concerning Piso was widely published, and copies have been found in Spain listing the details of his posthumous punishment: Piso was not to be mourned by his family, his statues and portraits were to be removed, his funerary mask was not to be displayed at future family funerals, his name was to be erased from an inscription honouring Germanicus and his property was to be confiscated. The decree aimed to suppress the name and memory of Piso and condemn him to oblivion, thus reversing the senatorial ideal of leaving a reputation worthy of remembrance by posterity. However, thanks to the trial, the decree and his suicide, Piso is well remembered. It may not be a positive memory, but Piso is far from forgotten. A political regime might seek to control public memory, to destroy or promote public monuments, but ultimately it could not control what people actually remembered or how different groups characterized the dead.[34]

CONCLUSION

In the Roman world, the dead were everywhere and memories of the past were integrated into daily life. Statues in the Forum, commemorative arches, building dedications, tombs and foundations were some of the many public ways of remembering the dead. There were also more private and personal mementos of the dead, as the epitaph of Allia Potestas suggests; these included jewellery, portraits and presumably other keepsakes and heirlooms. Remembering the dead was a public duty

9. House tombs at the Isola Sacra necropolis, Portus (near Ostia, Italy). Second century AD.

10. Niches, some with inscribed panels beneath, lining the walls of a columbarium. Vigna Codini, Rome. First century AD.

11. Amphorae burials at the Isola Sacra necropolis, Portus.

12. A container for cremated remains carved to appear as a wicker basket. Aquileia. First century AD.

13. Mausoleum of Augustus. Campus Martius, Rome. Late first century BC.

14. Porta Nocera necropolis, Pompeii. Late first century BC and early first century AD.

15. Herculaneum Gate necropolis, Pompeii. First century AD.

16. Tomb of the baker Eurysaces. Porta Maggiore, Rome. Late first century BC.

17. Tombstone of Lucius Vettius Alexander (ex-slave), Vettia Polla (free-born), Vettia Eleutheris (ex-slave) and Vettia Hospita (ex-slave). The Greek letter theta (θ) adjacent to the first two names indicates that they were dead when the epitaph was inscribed (*AE* 1980, 186). A couple are depicted clasping hands, with two portrait busts in the background. The latter presumably represent the other two women named in the epitaph, daughters or fellow freed slaves of the couple (the familial relationships are not stated in the epitaph). Aguzzano, Rome. Late first century BC. Held at Museo Nazionale, Rome.

but also a private one. Rome's present was underpinned, justified and dependent on the past. To look forward was also to look back.

The physical remains of the dead were not isolated in segregated cemeteries. Instead, tombs were an integrated and integral part of the suburbs. The cemetery was a marginal but active zone, serving as a meeting place for the living and the dead, whether a casual encounter of a passer-by or a more structured visit of a relative or friend. Tombs could become landmarks and were an accepted and expected part of the suburban landscape, providing a backdrop for a range of activities such as travel, business, funerals, cult, religious observance, dining and witchcraft. In some of these activities the dead were perceived as participants and in others they were little more than silent spectators.

A successful grave marker or tomb promoted interaction between the living and the dead, drawing the visitor in to look, read, admire, stay awhile and remember. How the cemetery was organized and how it appeared, who chose to use monuments and the shape and style of those monuments did change across time. However, the ideal remained that the dead would not be pushed from sight; they would be seen, honoured and recalled. The reality may have sometimes run counter to this ideal. Despite the best attempts of testators and tomb founders to tie the living to the dead, it was impossible to protect, honour and personally remember so many dead, but collectively the dead, united outside the gates of the town, continued their fight against oblivion.

Epilogue

FROM THE DEATHBED TO THE AFTERLIFE

From the deathbed to the afterlife, this book has chronicled the journey of the dying, the dead and the bereaved in the Roman world. In some respects this has involved a narrative account, with a synopsis of key events and activities such as will-making, the deathbed, the funeral, tomb cult, mourning rituals and tomb construction. Creating such an account can be problematic since it involves the careful assembling of bits and pieces of evidence and the inherent challenge of unravelling the impact of geographical, chronological and social specificity on this evidence (*see* p. 15).

The inhabitants of the Roman world were often forced to confront their mortality. Life expectancy was low, and death, of the self and of others, was a daily concern, but people may not have been overly morbid or fixated on death. Philosophy, divine forces (such as Fortune and Fate) and the common currency of (if not always devoted belief in) religion, the afterlife and spirits gave people a shared language, if not an organized system as such. This shared language allowed them to speak of, anticipate and to some extent accept death.

Death raised practical issues about the transmission of property and the continuing place of the dead in the lives of the living. Last wills and testaments allowed people to express wishes about the destiny of their worldly goods and also about the treatment of their bodies and how they as individuals should be memorialized and remembered. The fate of the dead ultimately lay in the hands of the living. It was the living who organized the funeral and assigned symbolic roles to both the dead and the living participants. The funeral moved the body from this world to the next, disposing of unwanted matter and 'cleansing' the bereaved. It enforced social roles and differences and could even become a public statement of Roman unity. For those in mourning, the end of the funeral rituals did not necessarily mark the end of despair and loss, and there could be tension between societal norms, and between the public and the private sphere, as to accepted behaviour.

The dead were separated, removed to the edges of the world of the living, but their new 'life' in the cemetery gave them a continuing presence. Tombs, epitaphs and festivals for the dead imbued the dead with a role and a voice, and they drew the living to the cemetery. Simultaneously, the memories of the dead, if not their physical presence, remained in the spaces of the living as ancestors. Portraits, statues, heirlooms, inscriptions and buildings were the legacy of the dead, placing them squarely in the sight, touch and hearing of the living. In Rome the dead were always present.

The chapters of this book have each addressed specific aspects of Roman death, but they are cross-cut by shared themes. These connecting strands include the impact of social status and gender, the importance of memory, the interaction between the living and the dead, the significance of tradition and the role of chronological changes and developments.

Who one was and where one stood in the social pecking order affected one's experience of dying or one's role in the funeral and behaviour as a mourner. For the slave, freedman, citizen, non-citizen, senator and emperor, some aspects of death were very different. For example, there were differences in details of the funeral or the type of funerary monument constructed. Yet there was a general awareness that death was the ultimate leveller and that in some basic way all deaths, all funerals and all mourners were united by core rituals, beliefs and behaviours. In theory it cost nothing to close the eyes of the dead, to wash them, to carry them out for burial, to praise them and to weep.

Certain roles and behaviour were dictated by gender. Women often played a pivotal part in funeral ritual and the commemoration of the dead, performing duties that could both demean and elevate them, both shame and empower them. But these roles and even gender itself were not absolute givens. In the funerary sphere men could be womanly, women manly. Death, funerals and mourning entailed emotional and behavioural extremes that could undermine an individual's identity or help to recreate or invent it. Behaviour could be idealized or polarized as good or bad, but this created a spectrum on which both to place one's own behaviour, identity and role and against which to judge and evaluate the behaviour of others.

Remembering the dead, collectively and individually, was a duty. The living, when they imagined themselves dead, wanted to be remembered. Memory strategies pervaded society. Literature, inscriptions, buildings, statues and tombs all shouted aloud the names of the dead. For the living the act of remembering could be hard work, and therefore it was to some extent organized and structured. Annual festivals for the dead and the role of the *imagines* in the funeral, for example, forced the living to acknowledge the dead. The ideal was for interaction between the living and the dead – for the living to speak the names of the dead, to dine with them and to bring them small gifts. This was a one-sided relationship; the last will and testament of the deceased might offer incentives to the living, but for how long would they be honoured?

Roman funeral and commemorative rituals were underpinned by tradition. In reality there was probably little that was static. Many things evolved with time, creating compromise and tension between tradition and change. Things may have remained rooted in the past, but they had to move forward in tandem with changing times and regimes. A particularly fascinating aspect of studying Roman death is the insights into the debates that these changes could occasion, such as disagreements about how people should mourn or whether it was appropriate to build a showy tomb. When Roman death is viewed as a process from pre-death planning to the grave, as has been the purpose of this volume, it is possible to see parallel shifts in areas that are often studied separately, such as mourning rituals, funerals, epitaph production and monument types. The study of Roman death would now benefit from more joined-up thinking in mapping all these changes and their relationship to Roman society. To what extent are there connections between increases and decreases in the 'epigraphic habit'; alterations in the display aspects of the cemetery; changes in the types of funerary monument; shifts in the public and private dimensions of funeral and mourning rituals; and changes in burial practices, such as that from cremation to inhumation? Do some of these shifts coincide? Were the changes interrelated or separate? Did change in one area impact upon another?

These are big questions, and indeed Roman death is a big subject, arguably too big for a single volume. Death impacted on every aspect of life, and what has been covered here can only represent so much of Roman life and death. Nevertheless, I hope to have highlighted the main features of how people died, how they prepared to die, how they accepted death, and how they buried, mourned for, commemorated and remembered the dead. Above all, I hope to have demonstrated the relevance and importance of studying death, dying and the dead in ancient Rome.

Appendix 1

Roman Emperors
(31 BC–AD 211)

31 BC–AD 14	Augustus (Octavian)
14–37	Tiberius
37–41	Gaius (Caligula)
41–54	Claudius
54–68	Nero
68–69	Galba
69	Otho
69	Vitellius
69–79	Vespasian
79–81	Titus
81–96	Domitian
96–98	Nerva
98–117	Trajan
117–138	Hadrian
138–161	Antoninus Pius
161–180	Marcus Aurelius
180–192	Commodus
192–193	Pertinax
193	Didius Julianus
193	Pescennius Niger
193	Clodius Albinus
193–211	Septimius Severus

Appendix 2

Guide to Monetary Values

1 denarius = 4 sesterces
1 sesterce = 4 asses

	Sesterces
The property qualification for Rome's equestrian class	400,000
Local councillors (decurions) had to possess	100,000
Funeral costs for Marcus Aemilius Lepidus (second century BC)	250,000
Tomb costs of Manius Valerius (early first century AD)	50,000
Tomb costs of Lucius Tarquitus Sulpicianus (first century AD)	20
Nerva's funeral grant (late first century AD)	250
Lanuvium funeral club entrance fee (AD 136)	100
Lanuvium funeral club monthly subscription (AD 136)	1.25
Lanuvium funeral club payment at death (AD 136)	300

Note that it is difficult to understand relative values across the Roman period and empire due to factors such as inflation and regional economics. For the Roman economy, see Duncan-Jones 1982, 1990. For the epitaphs of Manius Valerius and Lucius Tarquitus Sulpicianus, see Chapter One, note 26. For the funeral costs of Marcus Aemilius Lepidus, the Lanuvium *Collegium* and Nerva's funeral grant see Chapter Three, notes 2, 3 and 4.

Appendix Three

Glossary of some Funerary Terms

bustum	A place where a corpse was both burned and subsequently buried
captator	A hunter (fisher) for legacies or inheritances
Caristia	A February festival that celebrated the continuity of the family
cena novendialis	A sacrifice and feast held nine days after the funeral (or death)
cepotaphium	A garden tomb
Cerberus	The three headed guard dog of the underworld that prevented the dead from leaving
Charon	The underworld ferryman who helped the dead to cross the river Styx
collegium pl. *collegia*	Clubs, guilds or organizations, some of which served as burial clubs, with members paying regular subscriptions for a lump sum payout at death. *Collegia* had a social function, and they might assist with the funeral and provide a place for burial
columbarium pl. columbaria	A tomb the walls of which are lined with small niches for the interment of cremated remains. The term derives from the Latin for dovecote.
conclamatio	The shouting out of the name of the deceased at the moment of death
consolatio pl. *consolationes*	A treatise, letter or poem written to console the bereaved, often exhorting them to be strong by drawing on philosophical arguments
damnatio memoriae	A range of penalties for destroying the memory of a public enemy
defixiones	Curse tablets or binding spells that could be placed in graves
devotio	Deliberate voluntary suicide of a general or army commander by riding into enemy ranks

dissignator	An undertaker with responsibility for organizing the funeral, especially the procession
Elysium or Elysian Fields	An area of rewards and good living for pure souls, sometimes pictured as part of the underworld and sometimes as a separate kingdom
epicedion	A poetic lament
familia funesta	A family marked by death and obliged to undertake a funeral
Feralia	The last day of the *Parentalia*
feriae denicales	Days of rest and mourning following a funeral
fossor pl. *fossores*	A grave digger
Hades	The underworld or kingdom of the dead, ruled by Hades (Pluto or Dis), brother of Zeus
imagines	Funeral masks displayed in aristocratic family homes and worn by actors or mimes at the funerals of family members
Lapis Manalis	The keystone of the *mundus*
laudatio funebris	The funeral speech
lectus funebris	The funeral couch on which the body was displayed
Lemuria	A festival of the dead held on 9, 11 and 13 May, when the dead were thought to enter the homes of the living
manes	Spirits of the dead
monumentum	Monument
mors acerba	A bitter death
mors immatura	A premature or untimely death
mundus	A chamber or pit thought to represent an opening to the underworld.
olla pl. *ollae*	A niche or space in a communal tomb for the interment of ashes
os resectum	The severing and burying of a bone (a finger) taken from the body prior to cremation
Parentalia	A festival for the dead when offerings were brought to the grave, held between 13 and 21 February
Persephone or Proserpine	Queen of the underworld and the daughter of Demeter (Ceres). She was abducted by Hades

	but allowed to return to her mother and earth for six months of the year
pollinctor pl. *pollinctores*	An undertaker who prepared the corpse, washing and anointing the body
pomerium	A strip of land outside the town walls in which no burials could take place
pompa	Funeral procession
porca praesentanea	Sacrifice of a sow to the goddess Ceres that took place at the grave, making it sacred
praeficae	Hired singers of dirges and laments
puticuli	Communal burial pits
rogus	A funeral pyre
sandapila	A combined stretcher and coffin used in the burial of the poor
sepulcrum	A grave
silicernium	A meal consumed in the course of the funeral, the exact timing and location of which is unclear
stele pl. stelae	A stone slab, generally taller than it is wide, used to mark a grave site. Roman funerary stelae were inscribed with epitaphs and often decorated with sculpture
Styx	A river in the underworld that had to be crossed by the dead
suffitio	Ritual purification of the bereaved by fire and water
Tartarus	Greek term for the underworld
tibicines	Flute players employed for funerals
tubicines	Horn players employed for funerals
tumulus	A burial mound
ustor pl. *ustores*	An undertaker or undertaker's slave responsible for tending the funeral pyre
ustrina or *ustrinum*	A place designated for cremations
vespillones	Undertakers or undertakers' slaves employed to carry corpses and coffins

Notes

Notes to the Introduction

1 Pliny the Younger, *Letters* 4.2 and 4.7.

2 Death as an area for study has burgeoned in many disciplines in recent decades, with historical and cross-cultural studies far too numerous to list here. A fundamental and highly influential study was Ariès' *The Hour of Our Death*, 1981. Ancient history has somewhat lagged behind, with the Greek world perhaps better represented than the Roman, at least in terms of looking at death as a subject rather than focusing only on single aspects of death ritual; see, for example, Vermeule 1979; Morris 1987; Sourvinou-Inwood 1995. For the Roman period Toynbee's 1971 study has remained the fundamental reference point, being the only book that looks at the funeral, afterlife beliefs, the cemetery and monuments, but recent years have seen more detailed studies of some aspects of ritual behaviour and continued analysis of burial remains; see, for example, Hopkins 1983; Hinard 1987; von Hesberg 1992; Hinard 1995; Flower 1996; Bodel 1999b; Davies 1999; Hope and Marshall 2000; Pearce, Millet and Struck 2000; Noy 2000a; Noy 2000b; Hope 2001; Bodel 2004; Carroll 2006; Edwards 2007; and Hope 2007 (further references to recent studies can be found by topic in the chapter notes).

3 For use of funerary material as evidence for cultural dialogue see, for example, Jones 1991: 117–19; Hitchner 1995; Curchin 1997; Cherry 1998; Woolf 1998; Fontana 2001. For studies of material from different areas of the empire see, for example, von Hesberg and Zanker 1987; Pearce, Millet and Struck 2000. There are many published reports of excavations of provincial cemeteries, for example, Barber and Bowsher 2000.

4 For an overview of social status and social mobility in the Roman world, see Hope 2000d.

5 For recent work on Roman death, see note 2 above. This research still tends to remain divided by disciplines, often focuses on single aspects of the whole process and is not overly theoretical. For an attempt to break down some of these boundaries and promote contextual study, Ian Morris's 1992 work deserves

special mention. My own 2007 sourcebook provides a range of primary source material related to all aspects of death, burial and commemoration in Rome, and the present volume in some respects complements this.

Notes to Chapter 1: Facing Mortality

1   For philosophical perspectives on death, the afterlife and the continuity of the soul, see Segal 1990; Poortman 1994; Bremmer 2002: 11–26; Warren 2004. Plato quotation: *Phaedo* 67D.
2   Marcus Aurelius, *Meditations* 9.33.
3   Cicero, *Tusculan Disputations* 1.10. For the soul as a moth or butterfly, and also bees as carriers of pure souls about to be reincarnated, see discussion in Bettini 1991: 197–219.
4   Lucretius, *On the Nature of the Universe* 3.865–869.
5   Quotations: Seneca the Younger, *Letters* 26.7, 93.12, 93.3–4, 61.2. See also *Letters* 1, 49, 66, 82. For Seneca and philosophy, see Griffin 1976; Inwood 2005.
6   Cicero, *Tusculan Disputations* 1.11.25.
7   Juvenal, *Satire* 13, 19–22; Petronius, *Satyricon* 71 and 34.
8   Horace, *Odes* 1.11, 7–8.
9   Virgil, *Copa* 37–8.
10 'Pale death': Horace, *Odes* 1.4, 13. Compare, for example, Lucretius, *On the Nature of the Universe* 3, 1024–50; Cicero, *Letters to his Friends* 4.6 (249); Horace, *Odes* 1.28, 15–20; and Marcus Aurelius, *Meditations* 4.48. 'The very gods can die': Martial: *Epigrams* 5.64.
11 Astrology: Cramer 1954; Potter 1994: 17–20; Beck 2007. Tiberius and astrology: Suetonius, *Tiberius* 14 and 36; Cramer 1954: 99–108; Potter 1994: 158–60. Trimalchio and astrology: Petronius, *Satyricon* 77.
12 For merging of the roles of the Fates see, for example, Catullus 64. Quotations; Ovid, *Metamorphoses* 15, 781; Tibullus, *Elegies* 1.7,1–2; Statius, *Silvae* 3.3, 172; Horace, *Odes* 3.29, 51–2. Epitaph from mother to son: *CIL* 6, 16709. Epitaph of Stephanus: *CIL* 6, 5817. Epitaph of Claudia Secunda: *CIL* 6, 4379. Trimalchio's wall paintings: Petronius, *Satyricon* 29.
13 Seneca the Younger, *Letters* 99. 9.
14 Antony and Cleopatra: Plutarch, *Antony* 71. Trimalchio's feast: Petronius, *Satyricon* 26–78.
15 Lucretius, *On the Nature of the Universe* 3, 912–16.
16 For the interplay between dining, drinking and death, see Grottanelli 1995; Dunbabin 2003. Trimalchio's funeral: Petronius, *Satyricon* 78. For death imagery in Petronius, see Bodel 1994a; Hope 2009. Pacuvius: Seneca the Younger, *Letters* 12.8. Domitian's funereal party: Cassius Dio, *Histories* 67.9.1–3.

17 For Roman wills and testators, see in particular Champlin 1991. Cato: Plutarch, *Cato* 9.9.

18 Cicero's will: Cicero, *Letters to Atticus* 12.18. Petronius' will: Tacitus, *Annals* 16.19. Out-of-date wills: Pliny the Younger, *Letters* 5.5 and 8.18. Note that the emperor Constantine did change the law in the later empire so that a dying person's verbally expressed wishes could be valid without a will: Eusebius, *Life of Constantine* 4.26.

19 Will of Dasumius: *CIL* 6, 10229; Gardner and Wiedemann 1991: 133–9. Will of Gaius Longinus Castor: Hunt and Edgar 1970: 251–5, n. 85.

20 'Mirror of character': Pliny the Younger, *Letters* 8.18.1. Honesty in wills: Lucian, *Nigrinus* 30; Seneca the Younger, *On Benefits* 4.11.4–6. Dead man's words have power: Augustine, *Homily 10 on the First Epistle of John*, 9. Testators defying expectations: Valerius Maximus, *Memorable Deeds and Sayings* 7.8. Dasumius: see note 19.

21 Augustus' attitude toward wills: Suetonius, *Augustus* 66.4. Tiberius and Iunia: Tacitus, *Annals* 3.76. Petronius' will: Tacitus, *Annals* 16.19. Domitian and Agricola: Tacitus, *Agricola* 43.

22 Will of Domitius Tullius: Pliny the Younger, *Letters* 8.18; see also *Letters* 7.24. Will of Murdia: *CIL* 6, 10230 (*ILS* 8394). Mother omits daughter: Valerius Maximus, *Memorable Deeds and Sayings* 7. 8.2. Antony's will: Plutarch, *Antony* 58.4–8.

23 Trimalchio's will: Petronius, *Satyricon* 71. Caesar's will: Suetonius, *Julius Caesar* 83. Martial as heir: Martial, *Epigrams* 12.73.

24 For legacy hunters, see Champlin 1991: 87–102. Plautus, *The Swaggering Soldier* 705–9.

25 Martial, *Epigrams* 5.39. See also Martial, *Epigrams* 11.44, 12.56, 12.90.

26 Seneca's funeral: Tacitus, *Annals* 15.64. Atticus' funeral: Nepos, *Atticus* 22.4. Epitaph of Manius Valerius: *CIL* 6, 2165. Epitaph of Lucius Tarquitus Sulpicianus: *CIL* 6, 1828. Will of Dasumius: see note 19. Tomb of Cestius: *CIL* 6, 1374. Testator from Langres: *CIL* 13, 5708 (*ILS* 8379; Le Bohec 1991).

27 Bequests of Caesar: Suetonius, *Julius Caesar* 83. Bequests of Agrippa: Cassius Dio, *Histories* 54.29.4. Temple: *CIL* 8, 15576. Portico: *CIL* 12, 3157. Pliny's baths: *CIL* 5, 5262. Aqueduct: *CIL* 13, 596. Theatre: Suetonius, *Tiberius* 31.1.

28 Free entry to baths: *CIL* 11, 720. Iunia Libertas: *AE* 1940, 94 (Dixon 1992b). Birthday dinner: *CIL* 11, 4789. Abascantus: D'Arms 2000. Testator from Gythium: *CIG* 6, 1208.

29 Sallust quotation: Sallust, *Jugurtha* 4.6. Titus Manlius Torquatus: Valerius Maximus, *Memorable Deeds and Sayings* 5.8.3. For the role of memory in the Republic and early empire, see in particular Flower 2006; and for the persistence of Republican ideals and memories during the early Imperial period, see Gowing 2005. Note that most memory strategies and celebrated ancestors were focused on

men, but women could also be celebrated and remembered: see Tylawsky 2001; Flower 2002.

30 Seneca the Younger, *Letters* 21.5.

31 Caesar's honours and public works: Suetonius, *Julius Caesar* 28, 44, 76.

32 Horace, *Odes* 3.30.

33 Propertius, *Elegies* 3.2, 18–27.

34 For the relationship between memory and history, see Miles 1995; Jaeger 1997; Gowing 2005. Quotation from Lucan: Lucan, *Civil War* 9, 980–1.Cicero's plans for being remembered: Cicero, *Letters to His Friends* 22 (5.12).

35 Trimalchio's tomb: Petronius, *Satyricon* 71.

36 For Trimalchio and death, see Bodel 1994a; Hope 2009.

37 *CIL* 11, 6435 (Pisaurum – Pesaro, Italy); *ILS* 5150 (Venafrum – Venafro, Italy); *CIL* 14, 356 (Ostia, Italy).

38 Examples of epitaphs advising the living: *CIL* 3, 293 (Antioch, Turkey); *AE* 1947, 31 (Aquinicum, Hungary).

39 Images of skeletons in art and funerary art: Dunbabin 1986; for another example, see Walker 1985: 62. For discussion of banquet scenes, often termed *totenmahl*, see Noelke 1998; Dunbabin 2003: 103–40; Carroll 2005; Roller 2006: 22–45.

Notes to Chapter 2: Death Scenes

1 Ausonius, *Epitaphs*. Pliny the Younger refers to two authors who were writing books about the deaths of famous men in *Letters* 5.5 and 8.12. See also the death stories in Valerius Maximus, *Memorable Deeds and Sayings* 9.12.

2 For the study of Roman demography see Parkin 1992; Frier 2000. For the pitfalls of using epigraphic age statements to reconstruct life expectancy, see Hopkins 1966, 1987; Duncan-Jones 1977, 1990; Revell 2005.

3 For model life tables and Roman society, see Parkin 1992: 67–90. For studies modelling the impact of life expectancy on Roman society, see Saller 1994; Harlow and Laurence 2002. For the limitations of life tables, see Scheidel 2001a, 2001b.

4 Death in festival crowd: *CIL* 6, 29436 (*ILS* 8524). Death of mosaic maker: *CIL* 9, 6281 (*ILS* 7671). Caerleon soldier: *RIB* I 369. Murdered girl: *CIL* 3, 2399 (*ILS* 8514). Murdered wife: *CIL* 13, 2182 (*ILS* 8512). Child drowned at baths: *CIL* 6, 16740 (*ILS* 8518). For causes of death stated in epitaphs, see Lattimore 1962: 151–3; Carroll 2006: 151–62. For living conditions in Rome, see Scobie 1986. For the difficulties of defining poverty and accessing the experiences of the poor, see Atkins and Osborne 2006.

5 For the study of date information in Christian epitaphs, see Shaw 1996. Dangers of the summer: Horace, *Epistle* 1.7, 3–7. Pliny the Younger's villas: *Letters* 5.6,

8.1, 9.20, 9.36. Pliny's sick travelling companion: *Letters* 8.1. For different disease environments, see Scheidel 2001a. Pliny's Umbrian estate: *Letters* 5.6.

6   For diseases in Rome and the occurrence of malaria, see Sallares 2002; Scheidel 2003. For analysis of skeletal evidence from Pompeii and Herculaneum, see Henneberg and Henneberg 1999; Bisel and Bisel 2002. Pregnant girl: Bisel and Bisel 2002: 465. For epigraphic references to death in childbirth, see Carroll 2006: 153–4.

7   Neronian plague: Suetonius, *Nero* 39.1. Plague of AD 189: Cassius Dio, *Histories* 73.14.4.

8   Collapsed amphitheatre: Tacitus, *Annals* 4.62. Eruption of Vesuvius: Pliny, *Letters* 6.16; Suetonius, *Titus* 8. Earthquake: Cassius Dio, *Histories* 68.24. Zama: Polybius, *Histories* 15.14. Cynoscephalae: Livy, 33.10. Defeat of Boudicca: Tacitus, *Annals* 14.37. Jewish War: Josephus, *Jewish War* 3.19.25. Mons Graupius: Tacitus, *Agricola* 37. Breaking of sieges: Polybius, *Histories* 10.15.4–7.

9   Defeat by the Gauls: Livy 6.1; see also Williams 2001. Battle of Cannae: Livy 22.55–6. Varian disaster: Suetonius, *Augustus* 23; Cassius Dio, *Histories* 56, 23–4; Murdoch 2006. For the evils of civil war, see, for example, Lucan, *Civil War*.

10 Sulla's proscriptions: Plutarch, *Sulla* 31. Tally of dead under Claudius: Suetonius, *Claudius* 29.

11 Tacitus, *Annals* 6.16.

12 For crime and punishment, including the death penalty, see Bauman 1996. For arena punishments, see Coleman 1990; Kyle 1998. For gladiators and Roman society, see Wiedemann 1992; Futrell 2006. For gladiatorial tombstones, see Hope 1998, 2000b. Crucifixion of followers of Spartacus: Appian, *Civil War* 1.120.

13 Pliny the Elder, *Natural History* 29.8.18.

14 Death of Verginius Rufus: Pliny, *Letters* 2.1. Man killed by doctors: *ILS* 9441. Suicide due to illness: Pliny, *Letters* 1.12 and 1.22; see also Martial, *Epigrams* 1.78. Sudden death: Pliny the Elder, *Natural History* 7.52.180. Compare Vettius Valens, an astrologer of the second century AD, who noted that those born under certain stars died well, either in their sleep, while eating, from too much wine, during sex or from a stroke. Seneca the Younger also extolled the virtues of a quick rather than a drawn-out death: *Letters* 70.12. For further discussion of the 'good death', see the sections in this chapter on 'The Deathbed' and 'Dying Well'. Death of Pliny the Elder: Pliny, *Letters* 6.16. For doctors at the deathbed, see King 2002.

15 For deathbed ritual and behaviour see, for example, Cicero, *Against Verres* 5, 118 (catching last breath with kiss), *On Divination* 1.30.64 (final words and ability of dying to see the future); Virgil, *Aeneid* 4, 672–86 (calling out of name, last kiss, lament of bereaved), 9, 487 (closing eyes of the deceased); Ovid, *Tristia* 3.3, 37–46 (final words, closing of eyes, tears and cries of bereaved); Pseudo Ovid, *Consolation to Livia* 95–8 (last kiss); Valerius Maximus, *Memorable Deeds and Sayings* 7.1.1 (embracing and kissing of body); Seneca, *Consolation to Marcia* 3.2

(last kiss); Seneca the Younger, *On Tranquillity* 11.7 (*conclamatio*); Lucan, *Civil War* 2, 21–8 (cries and shouts of bereaved), 3, 737–40 (last kiss and closing of eyes); Petronius, *Satyricon* 74 (last kiss); Statius, *Silvae* 2.1.150–5 (last words), 3.3, 17–20 (embracing the body and catching last breath), 5.1, 170 (final words, embrace, kiss, closing of eyes and shouts of bereaved); Suetonius, *Augustus* 99 (final words and last kiss); Servius, *On Virgil's Aeneid* 6, 218 (*conclamatio*). Importance attached to how a life ends: Valerius Maximus, *Memorable Deeds and Sayings* 9.12.

16 Suetonius, *Augustus* 99. See also Tacitus, *Annals* 1.9.1. For deaths of emperors, see Van Hooff 2003, which notes that of 80 emperors for whom the cause of death is known, only 29 died of natural causes, 38 were murdered or executed, while 13 died in battle, civil unrest or at the hands of a foreign enemy.

17 Fundanus' daughter: Pliny the Younger, *Letters* 5.16. Son of Quintilian: Quintilian 6, *Prologue* 11–12. Death of Priscilla: Statius, *Silvae* 5.1, 155–98. For discussion of Fundanus' daughter, see Bodel 1995. Augustus' deathbed: see note 16. Germanicus' deathbed: Tacitus, *Annals* 2.71. For doctors at the deathbed, see King 2002, and note that deathbed scenes in Greek medical treatises tended to be more graphic and less idealized.

18 Epitaphs: *CIL* 6, 1975 (aged 22 years) and *CIL* 6, 29265 (aged 55 years). Sarcophagus relief: Walker 1990: n.6. For other reliefs showing children's deathbeds, see Huskinson 1996: figure 3. Note that mythological scenes on sarcophagi can also depict the moment of death, but once more the dying are generally shown looking peaceful or as if asleep.

19 Ovid, *Tristia* 3.3. For cenotaphs and transporting bodies home, see Carroll 2006: 163–8; Noy forthcoming. Livia's absence at Drusus' death: Seneca the Younger, *Consolation to Marcia* 3.2; Pseudo Ovid, *Consolation to Livia* 95–8.

20 Tacitus, *Agricola* 45.

21 *Devotio*: Livy 10.28. Suicide of Varus: Tacitus, *Annals* 1.61; Velleius Paterculus 119.5. For ideals associated with death in battle, see Edwards 2007: 19–28; Hope forthcoming.

22 Soldier's glorious death: Cicero, *Philippics* 14.12.32. Soldier's soul: Josephus, *Jewish War* 6.46–9. For death in battle and treatment of soldiers' bodies, see Hope 2003 and forthcoming; Cooley forthcoming. For bravery of gladiators, see, for example, Cicero, *Tusculan Disputations* 2.17.41; Seneca the Younger, *On Tranquillity* 11.5–6.

23 Death of Cicero: Plutarch, *Cicero* 48. Assassination of Julius Caesar: Suetonius, *Julius Caesar* 82 and 87. Execution of officer of the guard: Tacitus, *Annals* 15.67. Suicide of Arria: Pliny, *Letters* 3.16. 'dying well or ill': Seneca the Younger, *Letters* 70.6. Bravery in sickness: Seneca the Younger, *Letters* 78.21. Seneca's suicide: see note 29.

24 For different definitions of the 'good death', see Van Hooff 2004.

25 For suicide, its role and its presentation in Roman society, see Van Hooff 1990; Plass 1995; Hill 2004; Edwards 2007.

26 Suicides in the afterlife: Virgil, *Aeneid* 6.434–40. Legal perspective: *Digest* (Ulpian) 3.2.11.3. *Collegium*: *CIL* 14, 2112. Hanged excluded from burial: *CIL* 11, 6528 (*ILS* 7846). Instructions for undertakers: *AE* 1971, n.88. For hanging as a cowardly exit, see Van Hooff 1990: 67.

27 Criticism of suicide: Josephus, *Jewish War* 3.8.5; Seneca, *Letters* 70.14. Path to freedom: Seneca, *Letters* 70.14–16.

28 Suicide of Cato: Plutarch, *Cato* 66–73; for potency of his example, see Edwards 2007: 1–5. Suicide of Brutus: Plutarch, *Brutus* 52–3. For discussion of the presentation of aristocratic suicides, see Plass 1995; Hill 2004; Edwards 2007.

29 Seneca's suicide: Tacitus, *Annals* 15.63–4; Cassius Dio, *Histories* 62.25. Suicide of Petronius: Tacitus, *Annals* 16.19.

30 Suicide of prisoners: Seneca the Younger, *Letters* 70.20–3. Suicide of couple: Pliny the Younger, *Letters* 6.24. Suicide of murderer: *CIL* 13, 7070 (Courtney 1995: n.193).

31 For post-mortem punishment of bodies, see Kyle 1998; Hope 2000a. Lost at sea: Cicero, *Laws* 2.22.57; Virgil, *Aeneid* 6, 338–84, and see also 6, 150–60; Propertius, *Elegies* 3.9.64; Petronius, *Satyricon* 114; Horace, *Odes* 1.28. For discussion of poetic shipwrecks, see Houghton 2007.

32 Epitaphs: *CIL* 10, 4915 (*ILS* 5150, from Venafrum); *CIL* 6, 10097. Suicide of father: Lucan, *Civil War* 747. For epitaphs in which parents complain of reversal of laws of nature, see Lattimore 1962: 187–92; Hope 2007: 188–9. Death of Verginius Rufus: Pliny the Younger, *Letters* 2.1. For the daughter of Fundanus and Quintilian's son, see note 17.

33 For the contrast between good deaths and bad deaths, see Hope 2007: 39–45. Execution of Messalina: Tacitus, *Annals* 11.37–8. Suicide of Nero: Suetonius, *Nero* 49. Fall of Sejanus: Cassius Dio, *Histories* 58.11.1–6. Death of Galba: Tacitus, *Histories* 1.41; Suetonius, *Galba* 19–20. Execution of Vitellius: Suetonius, *Vitellius* 17. Decapitation and the display of the heads of traitors were highly symbolic – see Voisin 1984; Richlin 1999.

34 Galba's death: Tacitus, *Histories* 1.41. Quotation from Seneca the Younger: *Letters* 70.13. Death of Otho: Tacitus, *Histories* 2.47–9; Suetonius, *Otho* 10–11; Martial, *Epigrams* 6.32. Murder of Pompey: Plutarch, *Pompey* 79; Lucan, *Civil War* 8, 610–872. Death of Cicero: Plutarch, *Antony* 20 and *Cicero* 48–9; Velleius Paterculus 2.66.1–5.

35 Caesar's anti-Cato: Tacitus, *Annals* 4.34. Death of Domitius: Julius Caesar, *Civil War* 3.99.5; Lucan, *Civil War* 7, 599–604.

Notes to Chapter 3: Funerals and Feasts

1   Funeral of Drusus: Tacitus, *Annals* 3.5; Suetonius, *Tiberius* 7; Cassius Dio, *Histories* 55.52; Pseudo Ovid, *Consolation to Livia* 170–270. On Tiberius rushing to be with his brother: Pliny the Elder, *Natural History* 7.20.

2   For funeral instructions left in wills, see Champlin 1991: 169–73. Marcus Aemilius Lepidus: Livy, *Summaries* 48; see also Walker 1985: 12. Legal stipulations for funeral costs: *Digest* (Ulpian) 11.7.12.2–4 and 11.7.14.6.

3   For *collegia*, see Patterson 1992; van Nijf 1997. Lanuvium *collegium*: *CIL* 14, 2112 (*ILS* 7212; Friggeri 2001: 175–6). Inscriptions of other *collegia*: *CIL* 6, 10251–423, *CIL* 6, 10234 (*ILS* 7213); *AE* 1929: 16 (Friggeri 2001: 173–4); *CIL* 3, 924–7.

4   Hopkins 1983: 208; Justinian, *Novel* 43. For difficulties of defining poverty and identifying the poor of Rome, see the papers in Atkins and Osborne 2006.

5   For undertakers, see Bodel 1994b, 2000, 2004; Lindsay 2000: 157–60; Hope 2007: 90–3.

6   Cumae and Puteoli inscriptions regulating undertakers: *AE* 1971, n.88; Gardner and Wiedemann 1991: 25; Hinard and Dumont 2004. Insulting comments about undertakers: Horace, *Epistles* 1.7, 3–7; Martial, *Epigrams* 1.47; Valerius Maximus, *Memorable Deeds and Sayings* 5.2.10.

7   For increasing use of undertakers, see Bodel 2004.

8   For the moment of death, see Chapter Two: The Deathbed. Dying person carried from the house and placed on the ground: Artemidorus, *The Interpretation of Dreams* 1.13; see also Varro, *On the Latin Language* 5.64; Servius, *On Virgil's Aeneid* 12, 395. Note recent discussions of parallels between funeral and birth rituals: Corbeill 2004: 67–106. For washing and dressing the corpse, see Virgil, *Aeneid* 6, 218–20, 9, 485–90; Seneca, *Letters* 99.22; Lucian, *On Funerals* 11–12, 19 (binding of jaws); Artemidorus, *The Interpretation of Dreams* 1.13 (wrapping body in strips of cloth). Charon's coin: Propertius, *Elegies* 4.11, 7–8; Strabo, *Geography* 8.6.12; Juvenal, *Satire* 3, 267; Apuleius, *Metamorphoses* 6.18.4–5; Lucian, *On Funerals* 10, *Charon* 11. For discussion of coins in burials and literature, see Stevens 1991. Death masks: Drerup 1980. Note Pollini's comments about the unflattering and macabre aspect masks taken from bodies may have had, Pollini 2007. See also Noy forthcoming, which considers the production and uses for death masks in portrait production.

9   *Familia funesta*: Servius, *On Virgil's Aeneid* 6, 8 and 11, 2. For death pollution, see Lindsay 2000. Sulla's wife: Plutarch, *Sulla* 35. Tiberius and Drusus: Seneca the Younger, *Consolation to Marcia*, 15.3. Germanicus: Tacitus, *Annals* 1.62; Suetonius, *Caligula* 3.

10 Display of body, clothing and symbols of office: Polybius, *Histories* 6.53.7; Cicero, *On the Laws* 2.24.60; Livy, 5.41, 34.7; Juvenal, *Satire* 3, 171; Martial, *Epigrams* 9.57, 8; Persius, *Satire* 3, 1035; Suetonius, *Nero* 50; Pollux 8.1, Artemidorus, *The*

Interpretation of Dreams 1.13, Scriptores Historiae Augustae, *Antoninus Pius* 5.1; Tertullian, *De Corona* 10. Feet towards the door and being carried feet first: Pliny the Elder, *Natural History* 7.46; Persius, *Satire* 3, 105. Appearance and gestures of the bereaved: Virgil, *Aeneid* 10, 844 (soiling hair with dust), 12, 608–11 (tearing hair and cheeks and soiling hair with dirt and ashes); Tibullus 1.1, 67–8 (tearing hair and cheeks); Catullus 64, 349–61 (dishevelled hair and beating breasts); Propertius, *Elegies* 1.17, 21 (cutting hair); Pseudo Ovid, *Consolation to Livia* 40 (loosening hair), 98 (cutting hair); Seneca the Younger, *Letters* 99, 16–17 (beating breasts and falling to floor); Lucan, *Civil War* 2, 21–8 (dishevelled hair and beating breasts); Statius, *Silvae* 2.1, 170–3 (falling to the ground, tearing clothes and breast), 2.6, 82–3 (bruising arms), 3.3, 181 (torn cheeks), Statius, *Thebaid* 3, 138–40 (loosened dirty hair and scratched cheeks); Lucian, *On Funerals* 12 (beating breasts, tearing hair, bloody cheeks, soiling hair, falling to the floor, dashing head against the ground). For the dishevelled appearance of the bereaved and the significance of hair cutting, wailing and beating of the body, see Richlin 2001. For oppositional contrasts between the corpse and the living (for example, the corpse is clean but the living dirty, the corpse is still but the living agitated, the corpse is silent but the living noisy), see Ochs 1993: 48. For hired mourners and the singing or chanting of laments, see Dutsch 2008. For lament in the Greek context, see Alexiou 1974; Derderian 2001: 15–62.

11 Lucian, *On Funerals* 11.

12 Toynbee 1971: 44–5; Sinn and Freyberger 1996: n.5; Bodel 1999b: 267.

13 Heralds: Varro, *On the Latin Language* 7.42, 5.160; Festus 304.2. Death notice: *CIL* 4, 9116. Length of display: Servius, *On Virgil's Aeneid* 6, 218 (servabantur cadavera septem diebus). Lucian suggests three days between death and funeral: Lucian, *On Funerals* 24. For embalming, see Counts 1996. Poppaea: Tacitus, *Annals* 16.6; and compare Statius, *Silvae* 5.1, 225–31. Perfumes and incense: Pliny the Elder, *Natural History* 12.41.83.

14 For funeral processions, see, for example, Polybius, *Histories* 6.53–4; Propertius, *Elegies* 2.13b, 1–8; Appian, *Civil Wars* 1.105–6; Seneca, *Apocolocyntosis* 12; Pliny the Elder, *Natural History* 10.121; Suetonius, *Julius Caesar* 84. For the *imagines*, see Flower 1996; Pollini 2007.

15 Toynbee 1971: 46–7; Bodel 1999b: 264–5; Hughes 2005.

16 For biers, see Noy 2000a: 39–40. Marcus Aemilius Lepidus: Livy, *Summaries* 48. Quintus Metellus Macedonicus: Valerius Maximus, *Memorable Deeds and Sayings* 7.1; Pliny the Elder, *Natural History* 7.44. See also Pliny the Elder, *Natural History* 18.16 (bier carried on shoulders of the populace); Plutarch, *Aemilius* 39 (people took turns to carry the bier).

17 Petronius, *Satyricon* 42.

18 For hired mourners and lament singers, see Dutsch 2008. Note the suggestion that blood from the mourners' scratches and wounds and milk from their breasts

might be viewed as an offering to the dead, and that the noise from mourners and musicians may have enticed the dead to abandon the living: 'The mourners may have acted as macabre wet nurses of sorts, guiding their charges in the direction of the tomb' (Dutsch 2008: 263); see also Corbeill 2004: 67–106. Freed slaves as mourners: Dionysius of Halicarnassus, *Roman Antiquities* 4.24.6; Persius, *Satire* 3, 106.

19   Torches: Servius, *On Virgil's Aeneid* 6, 224; Tacitus, *Annals* 3.4. For discussion, see Rose 1923. Note also the presence of torches in Figure 5 and note Persius, *Satires* 3, 103; Eusebius, *Life of Constantine* 4.66. For the role of candles and lamps at the tomb and the 'lying-in-state', see Rushforth 1915. Funeral of Britannicus: Tacitus, *Annals* 13.17. For night-time and rapid disposal of infants, see: Servius, *On Virgil's Aeneid* 11, 143; Seneca the Younger, *On the Shortness of Life* 20.5; Seneca the Younger, *On Tranquillity* 11.7; Cicero, *In Defence of Cluentius* 27.

20   Paying mourners: *CIL* 14, 2112 (*ILS* 7212; Friggeri 2001: 175–6). *Sandapila*: Suetonius, *Domitian* 17; Martial, *Epigrams* 8.75; see also Martial, *Epigrams* 2.81.

21   Propertius, *Elegies* 2.13b, 1–8.

22   At the pyre: Valerius Maximus, *Memorable Deeds and Sayings* 4.6.3 (anointing and kissing of the body, lighting pyre); Lucan, *Civil War* 8, 739–41 (embracing body and lighting pyre); Statius, *Silvae* 3.3, 176–7 (kissing body on pyre). Opening of the eyes: Pliny the Elder, *Natural History* 11.55.150. Circling of the pyre (*decursio*): Livy 25.17.5; Virgil, *Aeneid* 11, 188–90; Statius, *Thebaid* 6, 213–6; Cassius Dio 56.42; Suetonius, *Claudius* 1; Herodian 4.2.9. Compare Plutarch's report that visitors to tombs would turn around before the graves: Plutarch, *Roman Questions* 14, compare Plutarch, *Numa* 14.

23   Speeches for Drusus: Cassius Dio, *Histories* 55.52. For funeral speeches, see Kierdorf 1980; Ochs 1993: 104–11. For funeral speeches in the Greek context, see Loraux 1986, Derderain 2001: 161–88.

24   Satirical lament: Lucian, *On Funerals* 13. Republican speeches: Polybius, *Histories* 6.54. Imperial speeches: Quintilian 3.7.2. Funeral of Verginius Rufus: Pliny the Younger, *Letters* 2.1. The fact that a speech was made is often recorded in historical sources (for example, Plutarch, *Julius Caesar* 5; Tacitus, *Annals* 5.1), but the precise nature of its content is rarely noted. For exceptions, see Appian, *Civil Wars* 144–6; Pliny the Elder, *Natural History* 7.139–40; Suetonius, *Julius Caesar* 6.1. For a list of ancient references to funeral speeches, see Kierdorf 1980: 137–49.

25   Murdia: *CIL* 6, 10230 (*ILS* 8394). 'Turia': *CIL* 6 1527, 31570 (*ILS* 8393; Wistrand 1976; Ramage 1994; Friggeri 2001: 64–6; Hemelrijik 2004). Note as well the emperor Hadrian's eulogy to his mother-in-law, Matidia: *CIL* 14, 3579. For the significance of praising women at death, especially during the late Republic, see Tylawsky 2001.

26   Pliny the Younger, *Letters* 3.10.

27 Cicero, *Tusculan Disputations* 1.45.108; Lucian, *On Funerals* 21. See also Silius Italicus, *Punica* 13, 458–87.

28 Lucretius, *On the Nature of the Universe* 3, 870–93. Compare Petronius, *Satyricon* 115. For suicide to save honour, see Chapter Two.

29 Tacitus, *Annals* 6.29.1.

30 Three handfuls of earth: Horace, *Odes* 1.28 (2), 10–6. *Os resectum*: Cicero, *On the Laws* 2.22.55; Varro, *On the Latin Language* 5.23. For discussion of *os resectum*: Graham forthcoming.

31 For changes in burial rite between cremation and inhumation, see Nock 1932; Morris 1992. Inhumation as oldest rite and fears of corpse abuse: Cicero, *On the Laws* 2.22.55–7; Pliny the Elder, *Natural History* 7.54.187. Poppaea: Tacitus, *Annals* 16.6. Inhumation as Greek custom: Petronius, *Satyricon* 111.

32 For funeral pyres, see Noy 2000a. Pyre construction: Vitruvius, *On Architecture* 2.19.5. Painted pyres: Pliny the Elder, *Natural History* 35.49. Pyre of Pertinax: Cassius Dio, *Histories* 75.5.3. For monuments at cremation sites, see Boatwright 1985. For ustrina and bustum: Servius, *On Virgil's Aeneid* 11, 201; and discussion in Noy 2000a; Polfer 2000; Weekes 2005: 22–5.

33 Julius Caesar, *Gallic Wars* 6.19.4

34 Papyrus, incense and perfumes in pyre: Statius, *Silvae* 2.1, 159–62, 2.6, 84–93, 5.1, 209–15; Martial *Epigrams* 10.97, 11.54. Cinnamon and cassia: Pliny the Elder, *Natural History* 12.41.83. Cypresses: Virgil, *Aeneid* 6, 214–17; Servius, *On Virgil's Aeneid* 6, 216; Horace, *Epode* 5, 15; Ovid, *Tristia* 3.13.21. For a summary of types of offerings, see Noy 2000a. For disposal of jewellery for the unmarried, see Oliver 2000; and note also Martin-Kilcher 2000. Pyre built by Atedius Melior: Statius, *Silvae* 2.1, 157–65. Testator from Langres: *CIL* 13, 5708. Mockery of excessive offerings: Lucian, *On Funerals* 19, *Nigrinus* 30. Legal control: *Digest* (Ulpian) 11.7.14.5. Regulus' son's pyre: Pliny the Younger, *Letters* 4.2.4.

35 For tending of pyres, see Noy 2000a; Weekes 2005: 16–22. For half-burned corpses, see Noy 2000b. Clodius' corpse: Cicero, *For Milo* 33; see also Cicero, *Philippic* 2.91. Threats to Tiberius' corpse: Suetonius, *Tiberius* 75.

36 Collection of ashes: Virgil, *Aeneid* 6, 226–8; Tibullus 1.3, 5–8; Pseudo Tibullus, 3.2, 9–25; Statius, *Silvae* 2.6, 90–2; Suetonius, *Augustus* 100. For examples of ash containers, see Sinn 1987.

37 *Novissima verba*: Virgil, *Aeneid* 6, 213; Servius, *On Virgil's Aeneid* 6, 213; see Feldherr 2000: 219. *Porca praesentanea*: Cicero, *On the Laws* 2.22.55. *Silicernium*: Festus 294 (Paulus 417). Fasting: Lucian, *On Funerals* 24. For an interpretation of sacrifices and the order and significance of consumption of the food at the grave, see Scheid 2005: 170–4.

38 Cleansing rituals (*suffitio*): Festus 3L. *Feriae denicales*: Cicero, *On the Laws* 2.22.55. For the types of food offered to the dead, see: Lindsay 1998: 74; Feldherr 2000: 217. Crassus' troops: Plutarch, *Crassus* 19. Insult to a banquet: Tacitus, *Annals* 6.5.

Meager portion: Juvenal, *Satires* 5.85. Stealing food from cemeteries: Catullus 59, Tibullus 1.5.53. One late commentator notes that women who had eaten meat consecrated to the gods of the underworld were said to have borne dead babies (Festus-Paulus 479L).

39 Trimalchio's guest: Petronius, *Satyricon* 65.

40 Distribution of food: Livy 8.22.34. Banquet of Arrius: Cicero, *Vatinius* 30–1; Horace, *Satires* 2.3.86. Banquet of Tubero: Valerius Maximus, *Memorable Deeds and Sayings* 7.5.1; Cicero, *Murena* 75. First gladiatorial contests: Valerius Maximus, *Memorable Deeds and Sayings* 2.4.7. Games in memory of Julia: Plutarch, *Caesar* 55.2. For commemorative origins of games and shows, see Wiedemann 1992; Futrell 2005.

41 Twelve Tables: Cicero, *On the Laws* 2.24.60. Augustine: *Letters* 22; see also Augustine, *Against Faustus* 20.21. Note that Artemidorus mentions that a funeral feast could take place at the house of the deceased but does not specify the exact timing: Artemidorus, *The Interpretation of Dreams* 5.82.

42 Grieving widows: Ovid, *Art of Love* 3, 429–32. Funeral put on with style: Horace, *Satire* 2.5, 105–6.

43 Grief for Drusus and Germanicus: Seneca, *Consolation to Marcia* 3.1; Tacitus, *Annals* 3.4. Élite Republican funerals: Polybius, *Histories* 6.53–4. *Imagines*: Diodorus Siculus 31.15.2; Suetonius, *Vespasian* 19.2. For discussion of élite funerals and *imagines*, see Flower 1996; Bodel 1999b; Sumi 2002; Bettini 2005; Pollini 2007.

44 Polybius, *Histories* 6.54.

45 Sulla's funeral: Appian, *Civil Wars* 1.205–6; Plutarch, *Sulla* 38. For public funerals, see Wesch-Klein 1993. For discussion of when public funerals may have first been introduced in Rome, see Hillard 2001: 59–62.

46 Twelve Tables: Cicero, *On the Laws* 2.23.59. Funeral of Julius Caesar: Appian, *Civil Wars* 2.146–7. For élite funerals as arenas for display, competition and unrest, see Flower 1996; Sumi 1997; Bodel 1999b.

47 For change in nature of funeral display, see Bodel 1999b. Tacitus claims that Tiberius issued an edict at Augustus' death urging the people not to repeat the disturbances of Julius Caesar's funeral. This edict is not mentioned by other sources: Tacitus, *Annals* 1.8.5.

48 Funeral of Augustus: Tacitus, *Annals* 1.8; Suetonius, *Augustus* 100; Cassius Dio, *Histories* 56.34–43. For funerals of emperors and *apotheosis*, see Price 1987; Davies 2000. For emperors whose bodies were mutilated, see Chapter Two, note 33.

49 Funeral of Pertinax: Cassius Dio, *Histories* 75.4.2–5.5.

Notes to Chapter 4: Heaven and Hell

1   *AE* 2004, 919 (Brioude, France) and *CIL* 6, 31977 (Rome).

2   Description of the *mundus*: Festus 156; Macrobius, *Saturnalia* 1.16.18. Romulus and *mundus*: Plutarch, *Romulus* 11. Mundus and fertility: Ovid, *Fasti* 4, 820–4. For discussion: Warde Fowler 1912; Spaeth 1996: 63–4; Felton 1999: 13–14.

3   For an overview of festivals for the dead, see Toynbee 1971: 61–4; Felton 1999: 12–14; Hope 2007: 231–6. For Ovid's *Fasti* in the Augustan context, see Littlewood 2001.

4   *Lemuria*: Ovid, *Fasti* 5, 429–44. *Caristia*: Ovid, *Fasti* 2, 617–38. For domestic cult, see Turcan 2001: 14–50.

5   *Parentalia*: Ovid, *Fasti* 2, 533–70. Compare Virgil, *Aeneid* 5, 42–93, where Aeneas offers wine, milk, blood, flowers and sacrificial victims at his father's grave. Iunia Libertas: *AE* 1940, 94 (Dixon 1992b). Quintus Cominius Abascantus: D'Arms 2000. Other epitaphs mentioning the *Parentalia*: *CIL* 5, 2072, 4016, 4440, 4871, 5272, 5907; *CIL* 6, 10248 (*ILS* 8366), 10239; *CIL* 11, 1436; *ILS* 7258; *AE* 1976, 144.

6   For house tombs, see Eck 1987; Hope 1997b. Trimalchio's tomb: Petronius, *Satyricon* 71. Priscilla's tomb: Statius, *Silvae* 5.1, 237 ('domus ista, domus!'). For the theme of eternal home in epitaphs, see Lattimore 1962: 165–7. Lucius Runnius Pollio: *CIL* 12, 5102. 'Eternal house': *CIL* 1, 1108. Publius Atilius: *CIL* 5, 5278. Six-year-old child: *CIL* 11, 207. For STTL, see Lattimore 1962: 67–72. Anna and Dido: Ovid, *Fasti* 3, 560–4. Garlands and offerings: *CIL* 6, 30102 (Courtney 1995: n.186). For the lighting of a lamp at the tomb several days a month, see *CIL* 6, 10248 (*ILS* 8366); see also *CIL* 2, 2102; *CIL* 10, 633; and note Ovid, *Fasti* 2, 562. For lights and lamps at the tomb and the 'lying-in-state', see Rushforth 1915.

7   Homer, *Odyssey* 11. Elysian Fields: Homer, *Odyssey* 4, 561–8. For discussion, Bernstein 1993: 23–33; Sourvinou-Inwood 1995; Albinus 2000.

8   See, for example, Ovid, *Metamorphoses* 4, 430–46; Virgil, *Aeneid* 6; Lucian, *On Funerals* 2–9; Apuleius, *Metamorphoses* 6.17–21.

9   Virgil, *Aeneid* 6. For discussion, see Solmsen 1972; Feeney 1986; Bernstein 1993: 61–73; Feldherr 1999.

10 Plato, *The Republic* 614b2–621d3. Plutarch, *Divine Vengeance*. See Bernstein 1993: 52–61, 73–83. For discussion of the relationship between Virgil's and Plato's 'underworlds', see Feeney 1986.

11 Lucian, *True Story* 2.14–5.

12 Cicero, *On the Republic* (Scipio's Dream) 6.13.

13 For *apotheosis* see Chapter Three and Price 1987; Davies 2000: 75–101.

14 Ovid, *Metamorphoses* 15, 840–2.

15 For humans in the guise of gods, see Wrede 1981. Claudia Semne: *CIL* 6, 15594 (*ILS* 8036b). See also Statius, *Silvae* 5.1, 230–5. For the myths of Endymion and Adonis, see Koortbojian 1995. For Persephone, see Wood 2000.

16 For a Christian perspective on the merging of Roman gods and people, see
    Tertullian, *On Nations* 1, 10.26–9: 'You erect temples to your gods. You erect
    temples to your dead in equal measure. You build altars to your gods and the
    same for your dead. You confer the same titles on the gods as on the dead …
    Indeed your kings are accorded the same sacred rites as the gods: grand vehicles
    to transport their statutes, chariots, their images reclining on couches and chairs,
    wild beasts, and gladiatorial games.'

17 For mystery cults, see Cumont 1922; Burket 1987. Cult of Isis: Apuleius
    Metamorphoses 11.23. Gold tablets: Graf and Iles Johnston 2007.

18 Gate of false dreams: Virgil, *Aeneid* 6, 893–6. Cicero: Cicero, *Tusculan Disputations*
    1.6.11. For other dismissals of Hades, see: Lucretius, *On the Nature of the
    Universe* 3, 629–32, 966, 979–1022; Cicero, *Tusculan Disputations* 1.5.10; Seneca
    the Younger, *Consolation to Marcia* 19.4–5; Epictetus, *Discourses* 3.13.14–5;
    Juvenal, *Satire* 2, 149–52. For retelling of myths of the underworld as a means of
    communicating messages about (Greek) society, see Edmonds 2004.

19 Human vanity: Pliny the Elder, *Natural History* 7.55.188. Fear: Seneca the Younger,
    Letters 82.16. Cicero's different perspectives: Cicero, *Tusculan Disputations* 1.5.10
    and 1.6.11, *On the Republic* (Scipio's Dream) 6.13, *Philippics* 14.12.32.

20 The plebs believe everything: Lucian, *On Funerals* 2. Superstition as state control:
    Polybius, *Histories* 6.56.12. Antigenides: *CIL* 11, 6435. Iulius Gallanius: *CIL* 8,
    11597. 6-year-old child: *CIL* 6, 30552. Lucius Aviancus Didymus: *CIL* 6, 12877.
    Tiberius Claudius Tiberianus: *CIL* 6, 10097. Epitaphs promoting reunion: *CIL* 6,
    12649, 1779 (*ILS* 1259; Courtney 1995: n.32); and compare Propertius, *Elegies*
    4.7, 93–4; Pseudo Ovid, *Consolation to Livia* 163.

21 Dismissal of Hades: *CIL* 1, 6298; *CIL* 11, 856 (Modena). Flavius Agricola: *CIL* 6,
    17985a. Prima Pompeia: *CIL* 6, 24653. For epitaphs with statements on the variant
    of 'I was not, I was, I am not, I don't care', see Lattimore 1962: 84–5; and examples
    in Hope 2007: 230–1.

22 Pliny the Younger, *Letters* 7.27.

23 Verginia: Livy 3.58.11. Apuleius: *Metamorphoses* 9.31. Pliny's ghost story: Pliny
    the Younger, *Letters* 7.27. Cynthia: Propertius, *Elegies* 4.7. Spanish epitaph: *CIL*
    2, 4427. Compare also the common consolatory device of the dead speaking to
    comfort the bereaved (see Chapter Five). For ghost stories in general, see Felton
    1999; Ogden 2002.

24 For curse tablets, see Gager 1992; Graf 1997: 118–74; Ogden 2002: 210–36 and
    2008: 115–145. Rhodine tablet: *CIL* 12, 1012 (*ILS* 8749). For Egyptian pots and
    tablets, see Gager 1992: n.28; Beard, North and Price 1998: 266–7.

25 For necromancy, see Ogden 2001 and sources in Ogden 2002: 184–7, 193–205.
    Pliny's ghost story: Pliny the Younger, *Letters* 7.27. Apollonius of Tyana: Philostratus,
    Life of Apollonius, especially 3.38–3.39, 4.25. Vatinius: Cicero, *On Vatinius* 14. Nero:
    Suetonius, *Nero* 34.4; Pliny the Elder, *Natural History* 30.14–18. Galba's ghost:

Suetonius, *Otho* 7.2. Caracalla: Cassius Dio, *Histories* 78.15.3–4.

26 Erictho: Lucan, *Civil War* 6, 450–830. For discussion, Masters 1992: 179–215; Graf
    1997: 190–204; Ogden 2001: 202–8 and 2008: 51–6. Canidia: Horace, *Satires* 1.8
    and *Epode* 5.

27 Horace, *Epode* 5, 86–102.

Notes to Chapter 5: Mourning the Dead

1 For studies of contemporary grief, mourning and grief counselling, see, for
   example, Gorer 1965; Walter 1999; Hockey, Katz and Small 2001; Worden 2003.

2 For the appearance and dress of the bereaved, see Chapter Three, note 10. For
   cypress branches, see Pliny the Elder, *Natural History* 16.60.139; Servius, *On
   Virgil's Aeneid* 3, 64; 4, 507. For sense of pollution, see Chapter Three, note 9.

3 Legislation for mourning: Plutarch, *Numa* 12; Paulus, *Opinions* 1.21.2–5. Note
   that Numa was alleged to have lived in the seventh century BC, but his biographer,
   Plutarch, was writing in the second century AD.

4 Paulus, *Opinions* 1.21.3–5.

5 Remarriage of Octavia: Plutarch, *Antony* 31.3; Cassius Dio, *Histories* 48.31.3.
   Secular Games: *CIL* 6, 32323, lines 110–14 (*ILS* 5050). Suspension of mourning
   under Gaius: Cassius Dio, *Histories* 59.7.5. *Digest* on mourning: *Digest* 3.2.10
   (Paul), 3.2.9 (Paul).

6 Mourning defined by learning, culture and gender: Seneca the Younger, *Consolation
   to Marcia* 7.3; Plutarch, *Letter to Apollonius* 22 (note that there is some uncertainty
   about the identity of the author of the latter work). Seneca on gender distinctions:
   Seneca the Younger, *Letters* 63.13. For grieving as 'womanly' (*muliebris*), see, for
   example, Cicero, *Letters to his Friends* 9.20.3, *Tusculan Disputations* 3.62; Seneca
   the Younger, *Consolation to Marcia* 2.3.4; Plutarch, *Consolation to his Wife* 4.

7 For women's role in funerary ritual, see Chapter Three and Richlin 2001; Corbeill
   2004: 67–106; Mustakallio 2005; Suter 2008. For women's role as empowering in
   the Greek context, see Stears 1998. Twelve Tables: Cicero, *On the Laws* 2.23.59.
   Aftermath of Cannae: Livy 22.53.3, 22.56.4–5; Valerius Maximus, *Memorable
   Deeds and Sayings* 1.1.15. Senatorial decree concerning Piso: Eck, Caballos
   and Fernández 1996 (Potter and Damon 1999). Male control over mourning:
   Mustakallio 2005.

8 Fathers who mourned their sons admirably: Seneca the Younger, *Consolation
   to Marcia* 13–14; Valerius Maximus, *Memorable Deeds and Sayings* 5.10.2.
   For discussion of men's response to the loss of their sons, see Prescendi 1995.
   Despising human concerns: Cicero, *Tusculan Disputations* 3.7.15. For Cicero's
   grief at the death of his daughter, see this chapter – 'Philosophy and Consolation'.
   Death of Pliny's wife: Pliny the Younger, *Letters* 9.13.4–5.

9   For changing female role in mourning, see Mustakallio 2005. For blurring of male and female virtues, see Wilcox 2006. Cleopatra's grief: Plutarch, *Antony* 77, 82. Livia's mourning for Drusus: Seneca the Younger, *Consolation to Marcia* 2–6; Pseudo Ovid, *Consolation to Livia*.

10 Agricola's grief: Tacitus, *Agricola* 29.1. Gaius (Caligula) and Drusilla: Seneca the Younger, *Consolation to Polybius* 17.4–6. Note that Gaius had his dead sister deified, and she was the first Roman woman to be so honoured. Compare also the assertion that the emperor Hadrian 'wept like a woman' at the death of his lover Antinous: *Lives of the Later Caesars, Hadrian* 14.5–6. Nero's daughter: Tacitus, *Annals* 15.23. Regulus' son: Pliny the Younger, *Letters* 4.1. Tiberius and Germanicus: Tacitus, *Annals* 3.1–6. Tacitus also noted that Tiberius continued to attend the Senate and 'derived comfort from his work' at the death of his own son, Drusus: Tacitus, *Annals* 4.5–12. Josephus, however, noted that Tiberius avoided contact with his son's friends, as he found it upsetting: Josephus, *Jewish Antiquities* 18.146. For displays of grief in the courtroom, see Seneca the Elder, *Controversia* 4, pr.6, 4.1, 10.19; and discussion in Richlin 2001.

11 For an overview of mourning figures in Roman art, see Corbeill 2004: 77–84.

12 For consolation literature, see Kassel 1958; Ochs 1993: 111–15. For detailed discussion of authors, see Wilson 1997; Erskine 1997; Wilcox 2005a, 2005b, 2006.

13 Cicero, *Letters to his Friends* 5.16.

14 Letter from Servius Sulpicius Rufus: Cicero, *Letters to his Friends* 4.6 (249). Letter from Lucius Lucceius: Cicero, *Letters to his Friends* 5.14 (251). For discussion, see Erskine 1997; Wilcox 2005a, 2005b.

15 Seneca the Younger, *Letters* 99. For discussion, see Wilson 1997.

16 Seneca the Younger, *Consolation to Marcia* and *To Polybius on Consolation*. Quotations in order: *Polybius* 18.5, *Marcia* 25.1, *Marcia* 6.1, *Polybius* 6.2. For discussion, see Wilcox 2006.

17 Pliny the Younger, *Letters* 8.1 and 5.6. For discussion of the letters as a male élite showcase, see in particular Wilcox 2005a, 2005b. Contrast informal consolation letters found on Egyptian papyri, which indicate that messages to the bereaved were commonplace and not always driven by philosophy: Chapa 1998.

18 Philosophical perspective: Plutarch, *Consolation to his Wife* 11. Treatment of bodies of babies: Cicero, *Tusculan Disputations* 1.39; Pliny the Elder, *Natural History* 7.16.72; Juvenal, *Satire* 15, 138–40; Fulgentius 7. Night-time burials: Chapter Three, note 19. For children's funerals, see: Néraudau 1987. Archaeological evidence for infant burial: Scott 1990, 1999: 109–23; Gowland 2001; Pearce 2001. Note that graves of older children, especially unmarried teenage girls, may have held distinctive grave goods: Martin-Kilcher 2000; Oliver 2000.

19 For discussions of childhood, infant death and the relationships between children, parents and other carers, see Golden 1988; Bradley 1991; Garnsey 1991; King

2000; Rawson 2003; and selected evidence in Hope 2007: 180–8. Exposure of infants: Harris 1994; Corbier 2001; Scott 2001.

20 Nero's daughter: Tacitus, *Annals* 15.23. Son of Marullus: Seneca the Younger, *Letters* 99. Fronto's grandson: Fronto, *Letters to his Friends* 1.12 and *Letters to Antoninus Augustus* 2.

21 Martial, *Epigrams* 7.96.

22 *CIL* 6, 1334; *CIL* 8, 1652 (Theveste – Tébessa, Numidia); *AE* 1982: 112; *CIL* 6, 15268; *CIL* 6, 8038; *CIL* 6, 4864.

23 *CIL* 5, 1198 (Aquileia, Italy); *AE* 1951: 266; *CIL* 3, 5618 (Eholfing, Germany); *CIL* 2, 748 (Norba – Brozas, Spain); *CIL* 3, 2875 (Nadin, Croatia); *AE* 1997: 927 (Rome).

24 Use of *pientissimus*: Sigismund Nielsen 1997: 197–8. For the study of infant and children's epitaphs, including analysis of age statements, see King 2000; McWilliam 2001; Laes 2007; Sigismund Nielsen 2007. Epitaph to 6-year-old: *CIL* 9, 5407. For idealized good deaths for children, see Chapter Two, including note 17. Néraudau argues that mourning for children may have become more acceptable under the emperors, with increased emphasis on private sentiment and reduced emphasis on public duty: Néraudau 1987.

25 Grief for dear ones: Seneca the Younger, *Consolation to Marcia* 7.1. For an overview of Roman marriage and associated ideals, see Treggiari 1991; Dixon 1991, 1992a: 61–95; Harlow and Laurence 2002: 79–91. Claudia: *CIL* 6, 15346 (*ILS* 8403). Postumia Matronilla: *CIL* 8, 11294 (*ILS* 8444 – Thelpte, Algeria).

26 Arria: Pliny the Younger, *Letters* 3.16; Martial, *Epigrams* 1.13. Pompeius Labeo and wife: Tacitus, *Annals* 6.29.7. Seneca and Paulina: Tacitus, *Annals* 15.63–4. Women starving themselves to death: Appian, *Civil War* 4.21–3. Servilia: Velleius Paterculus 2.88.3. Porcia: Plutarch, *Brutus* 54–5; Valerius Maximus, *Memorable Deeds and Sayings* 4.6.5; Martial, *Epigrams* 1.42.

27 'To love a wife is joy . . .': Statius, *Silvae* 5.1, prologue. Cornelia: Propertius, *Elegies* 4.11. Priscilla and Abascantus: Statius, *Silvae* 5.1, 200–8.

28 Quintilian's wife: Quintilian 6, prologue. Ausonius' wife: Ausonius, *Parentalia* 9, 7–14. Macrinus: Pliny the Younger, *Letters* 8.5. Turia: see Chapter Three, note 25. Claudia Homonoea: *CIL* 6, 12652 (Courtney 1995: n.180). Claudia Piste: *CIL* 6, 15546, 8–12. Marcus Annidius Ponticus and Sabina: *CIL* 11, 6249. Hermodorus and Euphroysne: *CIL* 6, 9693.

29 Propertius, *Elegies* 4.7, 93–4. See also Propertius, *Elegies* 1.19, 2.1, 2.8a; Tibullus 1.1, 1.3. For discussion of love and death in poetry, see Griffin 1985; Papanghelis 1987; Houghton forthcoming.

30 Marcus Servilius Rufus: *CIL* 6, 1906.

31 *CIL* 6, 15488.

32 Relationship between sadness and pleasure: Seneca the Younger, *Letters* 99.28–9. Note that Seneca contrasts Stoic arguments with those of Metrodorus, an

Epicurean philosopher. Grief as genius: Seneca the Elder, *Controversia* 4, pr.6.

33 Virgil, *Aeneid* 9, 477–83. The lament is spoken by the mother of the dead Trojan Euryalus.

34 For discussion of the anger in epic lament and its gender characteristics, see Fantham 1999; Markus 2004; Keith 2008. *Thebaid* references in order: Statius, *Thebaid* 6, 170; 9, 375–97; 12, 95–7.

35 Statius, *Thebaid* 9, 40–5. This is Polynices' reaction at hearing of the death of Tydeus.

36 Ovid, *Amores* 3.19.

37 Cornelia: Propertius, *Elegies* 4.11. Drusus: Pseudo Ovid, *Consolation to Livia*, and see Schoonhoven 1992. Quotation from Statius: Statius, *Silvae* 5.1, 1–2.

38 Statius, *Thebaid* 12, 44–5.

Notes to Chapter 6: Commemorating and Remembering the Dead

1 Allia Potestas: *CIL* 6, 37965 (Horsfall 1985; Friggeri 2001: 168–9).

2 Augustus and grandson: Suetonius, *Gaius* 7. Octavia, Livia and the memory of their sons: Seneca the Younger, *Consolation to Marcia* 2.1 and 3.2. Regulus and his son: Pliny the Younger, *Letters* 4.7. Finger rings and bracelets could be inscribed with names, but it is difficult to assert whether these were ownership labels or whether they performed a commemorative function. Excessive amounts of jewellery were not to be buried with the dead, and legal texts emphasize that precious items were expected to be handed down to the next generation: *Digest* 11.7.14.5 (Ulpian); *Digest* 34.2.16 (Scaevola); *Digest* 34.2.32.4 (Paul). Jewellery and other precious items may have then functioned as heirlooms and mementos, even if they were not inscribed with the name of the original owner. Vespasian and his grandmother's cup: Suetonius, *Vespasian* 2.

3 Twelve Tables: Cicero, *On the Laws* 2.23.58. See also Paulus, *Opinions* 1.21.2. For an example of a town charter from Spain, see *ILS* 6087 (Crawford 1996: 424). The emperor Hadrian enforced penalties for those who buried bodies within two miles of the city: *Digest* (Ulpian) 17.12.3.5.

4 For urban burial in the east see, for example, Cormack 2004: 37–49. Exceptional burials within Rome's walls: Cicero, *On the Laws* 2.23.58; Plutarch, *Publicola* 23 and *Roman Questions* 79. The exact significance of the term *pomerium* and whether it was an open space or simply a line is unclear from the ancient sources: Richardson 1992: 294–6; Patterson 2000b.

5 For the nature of Rome's suburbs, see Purcell 1987; Patterson 2000b; Goodman 2007.

6 Standardization in plot size: Eck 1987; Reusser 1987; Carroll 2006: 98–102. Trimalchio's tomb: Petronius, *Satyricon* 71. Aquilia's plot: *CIL* 14, 2139.

7   Isola Sacra tomb 78: Thylander 1952: A61.

8   Communal nature of tombs: Eck 1987; Sigismund Nielsen 1996; Hope 1997b. Tomb of Valeria Trophime: Thylander 1952: A96, A124, A251 (Hope 2007: 138). Marcus Valerius Polyclitus: *CIL* 6, 5039.

9   Horatius Balbus: *CIL* 11, 6528 (*ILS* 7846). Gaius Veienus Trophimus: *CIL* 9, 5570 (*ILS* 7847).

10 For undertaker regulations, see Chapter Three, note 6. Abandoned dead body: Suetonius, *Nero* 48; see also Suetonius, *Vespasian* 5 and *Domitian* 15; Martial *Epigrams* 10.5, 6–11. Estimates for rate of mortality and number of unwanted corpses: Bodel 2000: 129–30. *Puticuli*: Varro, *On the Latin Language* 5.25. Excavation of pits near the Esquiline Gate: Lanciani 1888; Hopkins 1983: 208–9; Bodel 1994: 40; Graham 2007. Conversion of Esquiline graveyard to garden: Horace, *Satires* 1.8, 7–16. Continuation of pits or introduction of mass crematoria: Bodel 1994b: 83; Kyle 1998: 169–70; Bodel 2000: 133.

11 Simple burials from Pompeii: *CIL* 10, 8349–61; Senatore 1999. For examples of simple memorials and burials, see Tranoy 2000; Graham 2007. For the Isola Sacra necropolis, see Calza 1940; Baldassere 1996. Nerva's burial grant: Chapter Three, note 4.

12 Epitaph stating location of remains: *CIL* 11, 5563. Stelae, funerary altars, sarcophagi and ash chests survive in large numbers and have been extensively catalogued, with emphasis often placed on the type or style of the sculptural décor; see, for example, Altmann 1905; Boschung 1987; Kleiner 1987; Sinn 1987.

13 Pompeian cemeteries: Kockel 1983; D'Ambrosio and De Caro 1983.

14 For chronological changes in the level and type of monumentalization in the Roman cemetery, see, in particular, von Hesberg 1992. For chronological patterning in the production of epitaphs, see note 24 below. For the location and development of Christian cemeteries, see Brown 1981.

15 For cyclical patterns in the production of funerary monuments, see Cannon 1989. Differences in opinion between Frontinus and Verginius Rufus: Pliny the Younger, *Letters* 6.10, 9.19.

16 Freed slaves and funerary portraiture: Zanker 1975; Kleiner 1977 and 1987; Kockel 1993; D'Ambra 2002. For freed slaves, preference for commemoration and status dissonance: Taylor 1961; Shaw 1991: 87–8; Whitehead 1993; Hope 2001; Mouritsen 2005. Note also words of caution about making generalized assumptions about the aspirations and expectations of freed slaves: Sigismund Nielsen 1997; Hackworth Petersen 2006.

17 Across the empire, the use of funerary monuments, or at least specific monument designs, may have appealed to certain social groups, such as freed slaves, new citizens, soldiers and auxiliary troops, who were eager to demonstrate acceptance (and sometimes difference) to the wider population. See, for example, Meyer 1990; Hope 1997a, 2000c, 2001. For an overview of different types of monuments

from across the empire, see Toynbee 1971; von Hesberg 1992. For North African tower tombs, see Lassère et al 1993; Hitchner 1995; Moore 2007. For North African cemeteries and monuments, pre-Roman and Roman, see: Stone and Stirling 2007.

18 Spanish barrel tombs: Tupman 2005; compare Stirling 2007. For paucity of inscribed monuments from Roman Britain, see Mann 1985; Hope 1997a.

19 For introductions to ancient epigraphy, see Keppie 1991; Bodel 2001. For selections of epitaphs, see, for example, Lattimore 1962; Courtney 1995; Carroll 2006. Cicero on epitaphs: *On Old Age* 7.21.

20 *CIL* 6, 5323.

21 Reading inscriptions: Petronius, *Satyricon* 58. For reading epitaphs 'quasi-pictographically', see Woolf 1996: 27–8. For levels of literacy, see Harris 1989; Humphrey 1991.

22 Estimates for number of inscriptions and epitaphs: Bodel 2001: 8 and 30. For relative densities of inscriptions and the urban nature of epigraphy, see Woolf 1998. The bibliography for studying the Roman family through epitaphs is extensive, and scholars are not always in agreement as to methodology. The most influential study is Saller and Shaw 1984. See also Hopkins 1964; Shaw 1984, 1987, 1991; Saller 1987, 1994; Martin 1996; Lelis, Percy and Verstraete 2003. For the Roman family in general and the implications of some of these epigraphic studies for our understanding of the family, see, for example, Bradley 1991; Dixon 1992a, Harlow and Laurence 2002.

23 For the use of epigraphic age statements in calculating age at death, see Hopkins 1966, 1987; Duncan-Jones 1977, 1990. For the study of Roman demography in general, see Parkin 1992; Frier 2000. For further discussion of life expectancy, see Chapter Two.

24 For chronological variations in the epigraphic habit, see in particular MacMullen 1982. For attempts at explaining the patterning, see Meyer 1990; Woolf 1996; and see also Cherry 1998: 111. Note that Christian epitaphs survive in large numbers from the city of Rome. Mainly dating to the fourth, fifth and sixth centuries AD, to some extent these Christian epitaphs represent a renaissance in the epigraphic habit following the decline of the second and third centuries AD: see Galvao-Sobrinho 1995, and for a useful regional study of the nature of Christian epitaphs, see Handley 2003.

25 For the importance of studying epitaphs in context, especially uniting image and text, see, for example, Koortbojian 1996; Hope 2001; Carroll 2006. For taking a contextual approach to funerary evidence in general, see Morris 1992.

26 Marcus Cocceius Daphnus: Thylander 1952: A83. Messia Candida: Thylander 1952: A180. There was a mismatch between the exact letter of the law, which said that as a burial place was religious it could not be sold, and how people actually managed, sold and gifted burial spaces: see Crook 1967: 133–8.

27 Trimalchio's tomb guard: Petronius, *Satyricon* 71. Propertius, with typical poetic irony, suggested that his tomb should be in a secluded spot rather than close to the street, 'where lovers' tombs are profaned after death'; he also imagined his lover standing guard at his tomb: Propertius *Elegy* 3.16, 25–30. Abascantus: D'Arms 2000. Testator from Langres: *CIL* 13, 5708 (*ILS* 8379; Le Bohec 1991). Claudia Semne: *CIL* 6, 15593 (*ILS* 8063); and see Chapter Four for the statues. For tomb gardens: Jashemski 1979: 141–53; Toynbee 1971: 94–100. Epitaphs that mention a *cepotaphium* or *hortus*: *AE* 1957: 185b; *CIL* 6, 2469, 3056, 3554, 8505, 10675, 13040, 13244, 19039, 25250, 29135, 33900a, 13823, 15593, 23090, 29770, 35450. Titus Vettius Hermes: *CIL* 5, 7454. Inscribed plans of gardens: Heulsen 1890; Toynbee 1971: 98–100.
28 For tomb cult, see Chapters One and Four. For people picnicking and dining at tombs, see Graham 2005a, 2005b.
29 Epitaph of Atilius Calatinus: Cicero, *On Old Age* 17.61. Tomb of Licinii Crassi: Kragelund 2002. Virgil's tomb: Pliny the Younger, *Letters* 3.7.8. Graffiti on Pompeian tombs: Jashemski 1979: 142. Wall at Chester: Wright and Richmond 1956: 5. Tombstone as a toilet seat: Meiggs 1973: 143. Sidonius Apollinaris' grandfather's grave: Sidonius Apollinaris, *Letters* 3.12.1.
30 For laws protecting graves: *Digest* (Paul) 47.12.11. Permission required to remove remains: *Digest* 11.7.7–8. Arrius Alphius: *CIL* 6, 2120 (*ILS* 8380; Beard, North and Price 1998: 201–2). *Sub ascia dedicavit*: Hatt 1951: 85–107. Threats against would-be violators: Strubbe 1991. Bereaved mother: *CIL* 6, 7308. Allia Potestas: see note 1. Quintus Iulius Hermes: *CIL* 14, 1153 (Thylander 1952: B88).
31 Prostitutes: Martial, *Epigrams* 3.93, 15, 1.34, 8. Homeless and displaced: *Digest* (Ulpian) 47.12.3; Suetonius, *Nero* 38.2. Stash for thieves: Apuleius, *Metamorphoses* 4.18. Werewolf story: Petronius, *Satyricon* 62. Witches: Horace, *Epode* 5, *Satires* 1.8; Tibullus 1.2, 41–5, 1.5, 51–2; Lucan, *Civil War* 6, 450–830, and see Chapter 4, note 26. Cures from the dead: Pliny the Elder, *Natural History* 28.2.4–5, 28.11.45–6. For exploitation and abuse of bodies, the dead and the cemetery in general, see Hope 2000a: 120–5; 2007: 165–71.
32 Location of the tombs of Claudii Marcelli, Servilii, Metelli and Scipios: Cicero, *Tusculan Disputations* 1.7.13. Tomb of the Scipios: Flower 1996: 160–6; Claridge 1998: 328–32. Campus Esquilinus: Cicero, *Philippics* 9.17. Sulla's grave: Plutarch, *Sulla* 38. Mausoleum of Augustus: Strabo, *Geography* 5.3.8. Discussion of relationship between tombs, villas (houses) and memory: Bodel 1997; Treggiari 1999; Patterson 2000a; Hales 2003.
33 For Horatius Balbus, see note 9. For gladiatorial tombstones and their grouping, see Hope 1998; Edmondson 1999, Hope 2000b: 99–100.
34 Gemonian Steps: Valerius Maximus, *Memorable Deeds and Sayings* 6.9.13. Sejanus: Cassius Dio, *Histories* 58.11.1–6. For a selection of relevant sources on controlling memory, see Hope 2007: 80–4. For discussions of *damnatio memoriae*:

Mustakallio 1994; Hedrick 2000; Varner 2001a, 2001b, 2004; Flower 2006. Decree against Piso: Eck, Caballos and Fernández 1996; Griffin 1997; Potter and Damon 1999; Bodel 1999a.

Bibliography

Albinus, L. (2000), *The House of Hades: Studies in Ancient Greek Eschatology.* Aarhus, Denmark, and Oxford: Aarhus University Press.

Alexiou, M. (1974), *The Ritual Lament in Greek Tradition.* Cambridge: Cambridge University Press.

Altmann, W. (1905), *Die Römische Grabaltäre der Kaiserzeit.* Berlin: Weidmann

Ariès, P. (1981), *The Hour of Our Death.* Translated by H. Weaver. New York: Alfred Knopf.

Atkins, M. and Osborne, R. (eds) (2006), *Poverty in the Roman World.* Cambridge: Cambridge University Press.

Baldassere, I. (1996), *Necropoli di Porto: Isola Sacra.* Rome: Istituto Poligrafico e Zecca dello Stato.

Barber, B. and Bowsher, D. (2000), *The Eastern Cemetery of Roman London: Excavations 1983–1990.* London: Museum of London Archaeological Service.

Bauman, R. (1996), *Crime and Punishment in Ancient Rome.* London: Routledge.

Beard, M., North, J. and Price, S. (1998), *Religions of Rome Volume 2: A Sourcebook.* Cambridge: Cambridge University Press.

Beck, R. (2007), *A Brief History of Ancient Astrology.* London: Blackwells.

Bernstein, A. (1993), *The Formation of Hell: Death and Retribution in the Ancient and Early Christian Worlds.* London: University College of London Press.

Bettini, M. (1991), *Anthropology and Roman Culture: Kinship, Time, Images of the Soul.* Translated by J. van Sickle. London and Baltimore, MD: Johns Hopkins University Press.

—— (2005), 'Death and its double: *imagines, ridiculum* and *honos* in the Roman aristocratic funeral', in K. Mustakallio, J. Hanska, H-L. Sainio, V. Vuolanto (eds), *Hoping for Continuity: Childhood, Education and Death in Antiquity and the Middle Ages* [Acta Instituti Romani Finlandiae 33]. Rome: Institutum Romanum Finlandiae, pp. 191–202.

Bisel, C. and Bisel, J. F. (2002), 'Health and nutrition at Herculaneum: an examination of skeletal remains', in W. F. Jashemski and F. G. Meyer (eds),

The Natural History of Pompeii. Cambridge: Cambridge University Press, pp. 451–75.

Boatwright, M. (1985), 'The *Ara Ditis-ustrinum* of Hadrian in the western Campus Martius, and other problematic Roman *ustrina*'. *American Journal of Archaeology*, 89, 485–97.

Bodel, J. (1994a), 'Trimalchio's underworld', in J. Tatum (ed.), *The Search for the Ancient Novel*. London and Baltimore, MD: Johns Hopkins University Press, pp. 237–59.

—— (1994b) [1986], 'Graveyards and groves: A study of the Lex Lucerina'. *American Journal of Ancient History*, 11, 1–133.

—— (1995), 'Minicia Marcella: taken before her time'. *American Journal of Philology*, 116, (3), 453–60.

—— (1997), 'Monumental villas and villa monuments'. *Journal of Roman Archaeology*, 10, 5–35.

—— (1999a), 'Punishing Piso'. *American Journal of Philology*, 120, (1), 43–63.

—— (1999b), 'Death on display: looking at Roman funerals', in B. Bergmann and C. Kondoleon (eds), *The Art of Ancient Spectacle*. London and New Haven, CT: Yale University Press, pp. 259–81.

—— (2000), 'Dealing with the dead: undertakers, executioners and potter's fields in ancient Rome', in V. Hope and E. Marshall (eds), *Death and Disease in the Ancient City*. London: Routledge, pp. 128–51.

—— (2004), 'The organisation of the funerary trade at Puteoli and Cumae', in S. Panciera (ed.), *Libitina e Dintorni: Atti dell' XI Rencontre franco-italienne sur l'épigraphie (Libitina, 3)*. Rome: Quasar, pp. 149–70.

Bodel, J. (ed.) (2001), *Epigraphic Evidence: Ancient History from Inscriptions*. London and New York: Routledge.

Boschung, D. (1987), *Antike Grabaltäre aus den Nekropolen Roms*. Bern: Staempfli.

Bradley, K. (1991), *Discovering the Roman Family*. Oxford: Oxford University Press.

Bremmer, J. (2002), *The Rise and Fall of the Afterlife*. London and New York: Routledge.

Brown, P. (1981), *The Cult of the Saints: Its Rise and Function in Latin Christianity*. Chicago: University of Chicago Press.

Burkett, W. (1987), *Ancient Mystery Cults*. Cambridge, MA: Harvard University Press.

Calza, G. (1940), *La Necropoli del Porto di Roma nell'Isola Sacra*. Rome: Libreria dello Stato.

Cannon, A. (1989), 'The historical dimension in mortuary expressions of status and sentiment'. *Current Anthropology*, 30, 437–57.

Carroll, M. (2005), 'Portraying opulence at the table in Roman Gaul and

Germany', in M. Carroll, D. Hadley and H. Wilmott (eds), *Consuming Passions: Dining from Antiquity to the Eighteenth Century*. Stroud, UK: Tempus, pp. 23–38.

Carroll, M. (2006), *Spirits of the Dead: Roman Funerary Commemoration in Western Europe*. Oxford: Oxford University Press.

Champlin, E. (1991), *Final Judgments: Duty and Emotion in Roman Wills, 200 BC–AD 250*. Berkeley: University of California Press.

Chapa, J. (1998), *Letters of Condolence in Greek Papyri* [Papyrologica Florentina 29]. Firenze: Gonelli.

Cherry, D. (1998), *Frontier and Society in Roman North Africa*. Oxford: Clarendon Press.

Claridge, A. (1998), *Rome* [Oxford Archaeological Guides]. Oxford: Oxford University Press.

Coleman, K. M. (1990), 'Fatal charades: Roman executions staged as mythological enactments'. *Journal of Roman Studies*, 80, 44–73.

Collingwood, R. and Wright, R. (1995), *The Roman Inscriptions of Britain*, Volume I. Oxford: Oxford University Press. First published 1965.

Cooley, A. (forthcoming), 'Commemorating the war dead of the Roman world', in P. Low, G. Oliver and P. Rhodes (eds), *Cultures of Commemoration*. Oxford: Oxford University Press/British Academy.

Corbeill, A. (2004), *Nature Embodied: Gesture in Ancient Rome*. Princeton, NJ: Princeton University Press.

Corbier, M. (2001), 'Child exposure and abandonment', in S. Dixon (ed.), *Childhood, Class and Kin in the Roman World*. London and New York: Routledge, pp. 52–73.

Cormack, S. (2004), *The Space of Death in Roman Asia Minor*. Vienna: Phoibos.

Counts, D. B. (1996), '*Regum externorum consuetudine*: the nature and function of embalming in Rome'. *Classical Antiquity*, 15, 189–202.

Courtney, E. (1995), *Musa Lapidaria: A Selection of Latin Verse Inscriptions*. Oxford: Oxford University Press.

Cramer, F. H. (1954), *Astrology in Roman Law and Politics*. Philadelphia: American Philosophical Society.

Crawford, M. (1996), *Roman Statutes*, Volumes 1 and 2 [Bulletin of the Institute of Classical Studies Supplement 64]. London: Institute of Classical Studies.

Crook, J. A. (1967), *Law and Life of Rome*. London: Thames and Hudson.

Cumont, F. (1922), *After Life in Roman Paganism*. New Haven, CT: Yale University Press.

Curchin, L. A. (1997), 'Funerary customs in central Spain: the transition from pre-Roman to Roman practice'. *Hispania Antiqua*, 21, 7–34.

D'Ambra, E. (2002), 'Acquiring an ancestor: the importance of funerary statuary among the non-élite orders of Rome', in J.Munk Højte (ed.), *Images of Ancestors*. Aarhus: Aarhus University Press, pp. 223–46.

D'Ambrosio, A. and De Caro, S. (1983), *Un Impegno per Pompeii: Fotopiano e Documentazione della Necropoli di Porta Nocera*. Milan: Touring Club Italiano.

D'Arms, J. H. (2000), 'Memory, money and status at Misenum: Three new inscriptions from the *collegium* of the *Augustales*'. *Journal of Roman Studies*, 90, 126–44.

Davies, J. (1999), *Death, Burial and Rebirth in the Religions of Antiquity*. London: Routledge.

Davies, P. (2000), *Death and the Emperor: Roman Imperial Funerary Monuments from Augustus to Marcus Aurelius*. Austin and Cambridge: University of Texas Press.

Derderian, K. (2001), *Leaving Words to Remember: Greek Mourning and the Advent of Literacy*. Leiden and Boston: Brill.

Dixon, S. (1991), 'The sentimental ideal of the Roman family', in B. Rawson (ed.), *Marriage, Divorce and Children in Ancient Rome*. Oxford and Canberra: Oxford University Press, pp. 99–113.

—— (1992a), *The Roman Family*. Baltimore, MD: Johns Hopkins University Press.

—— (1992b), 'A woman of substance: Iunia Libertas of Ostia'. *Helios*, 19, 162–73.

Drerup, H. (1980), 'Totenmaske und Ahnenbild bei den Römern'. *Mitteilungen des Deutschen Archäologischen Instituts, Römische Abteilung*, 87, 81–129.

Dunbabin, K. (1986), '*Sic erimus cuncti . . . .* the skeleton in Greco-Roman art' *Jahrbuch des Deutschen Archäologischen Instituts* 101, 185–225.

—— (2003), *The Roman Banquet: Images of Conviviality*. Cambridge: Cambridge University Press.

Duncan-Jones, R. (1977), 'Age-rounding, illiteracy and social differentiation'. *Chiron*, 7, 333–53.

—— (1982), *The Economy of the Roman Empire: Quantitative Studies*. Cambridge: Cambridge University Press.

—— (1990), *Structure and Scale in the Roman Economy*. Cambridge: Cambridge University Press.

Dutsch, D. (2008), '*Nenia*: gender, genre and lament in ancient Rome', in A. Suter (ed.), *Lament: Studies in the Ancient Mediterranean and Beyond*. Oxford: Oxford University Press, pp. 258–79.

Eck, W. (1987), 'Römische Grabinschriften: Aussageabsicht und Aussagefähigkeit im funerären Kontext', in Von Hesberg, H. and Zanker, P. (eds), *Römische Gräbertrassen: Selbstdarstellung, Status, Standard*. Munich: C. H. Beck, pp. 61–83.

Eck, W., Caballos, A. and Fernández, F. (1996), *Das Senatus Consultum de Cn. Pisone Patre*. Munich: C. H. Beck.

Edmonds, R. G. (2004), *Myths of the Underworld Journey: Plato, Aristophanes and the 'Orphic' Gold Tablets*. Cambridge: Cambridge University Press.

Edmondson, J. (1999), 'Epigraphy and history of Roman Hispania: the new edition of *CIL* II'. *Journal of Roman Archaeology*, 12, 649–66.

Edwards, C. (2007), *Death in Ancient Rome*. London and New Haven, CT: Yale University Press.

Erskine, A. (1997), 'Cicero and the expression of grief', in S. Morton Braund and C. Gill (eds), *The Passions in Roman Thought and Literature*. Cambridge: Cambridge University Press, pp. 36–47.

Fantham, E. (1999), 'The role of lament in the growth and eclipse of Roman epic', in M. Bessinger, J. Tylus and S. Wofford (eds), *Epic Traditions in the Contemporary World: The Poetics of Community*. Berkeley: University of California Press, pp. 221–35.

Feeney, D. (1986), 'History and revelation in Virgil's underworld'. *Proceedings of Cambridge Philological Society*, 32, 1–24.

Feldherr, A. (1999), 'Putting Dido on the map: genre and geography in Vergil's underworld'. *Arethusa*, 32, (1), 85–122.

—— (2000), '*Non inter nota sepulcra*: Catullus 101 and Roman funerary ritual'. *Classical Antiquity*, 19.2, 209–31.

Felton, D. (1999), *Haunted Greece and Rome: Ghost Stories from Classical Antiquity*. Austin: University of Texas Press.

Flower, H. I. (1996), *Ancestor Masks and Aristocratic Power in Roman Culture*. Oxford: Clarendon Press.

—— (2002), 'Were women ever "ancestors" in Republican Rome?', in J. Munk Højte (ed.), *Images of Ancestors*. Aarhus, Denmark: Aarhus University Press, pp. 159–84.

—— (2006), *The Art of Forgetting: Disgrace and Oblivion in Roman Political Culture*. Chapel Hill: University of North Carolina Press.

Fontana, S. (2001), 'Leptis Magna: the Romanization of a major African city through burial evidence', in S. Keay and N. Terrenato (eds) *Italy and the West: Comparative Issues in Romanization*. Oxford: Oxbow, pp. 161–72.

Frier, B. (2000), 'Demography', in A. K. Bowman, P. Garnsey and D. Rathbone (eds), *The Cambridge Ancient History 11* (second edn). Cambridge: Cambridge University Press, pp. 787–816.

Friggeri, R. (2001), *The Epigraphic Collection of the Museo Nazionale Romano at the Baths of Diocletian*. Translated by E. De Sena. Rome: Electa.

Futrell, A. (2006), *The Roman Games: A Sourcebook*. Oxford, UK: Blackwell.

Gager, J (1992), *Curse Tablets and Binding Spells from the Ancient World*. Oxford and New York: Oxford University Press.

Galvao-Sobrinho, C. (1995), 'Funerary epigraphy and the spread of
    Christianity in the West'. *Athenaeum*, 83, 431–62.
Gardner, J. F. and Wiedemann, T. (1991), *The Roman Household: A Sourcebook*.
    London: Routledge.
Garnsey, P. (1991), 'Child rearing in ancient Italy', in D. Kertzer and R. Saller
    (eds), *The Family in Italy: From Antiquity to the Present*. London and New
    Haven, CT: Yale University Press, pp. 48–65.
Golden, M. (1988), 'Did the ancients care when their children died?' *Greece and
    Rome*, 35, (2), 152–63.
Goodman, P. (2007), *The Roman City and its Periphery: from Rome to Gaul*.
    London and New York: Routledge.
Gorer, G. (1965), *Death, Grief and Mourning in Contemporary Britain*. London:
    Cresset Press.
Gowing, A. (2005), *Empire and Memory: The Representation of the Roman
    Republic in Imperial Culture*. Cambridge: Cambridge University Press.
Gowland, R. (2001), 'Playing dead: implications of mortuary evidence for the
    social construction of childhood in Roman Britain', in G. Davies, A. Garner,
    and K. Lockyear (eds), *Proceedings of the Theoretical Roman Archaeology
    Conference 2000*. Oxford: Oxbow, pp. 152–67.
Graf, F. (1997), *Magic in the Ancient World*. Translated by F. Philip. Cambridge,
    MA: Harvard University Press.
Graf, F. and Iles Johnston, S. (2007), *Ritual Texts for the Afterlife: Orpheus and
    Bacchic Gold Tablets*. London and New York: Routledge.
Graham, E-J. (2005a), 'Dining al fresco with the living and the dead in Roman
    Italy', in M. Carroll, D. Hadley and H. Wilmott (eds), *Consuming Passions:
    Dining from Antiquity to the Eighteenth Century*. Stroud, UK: Tempus,
    pp. 49–65.
—— (2005b), 'The quick and the dead in the extra-urban landscape: the
    Roman cemetery at Ostia/Portus as a lived environment', in J. Bruhn,
    B. Croxford and D. Grigoropoulos (eds), *TRAC 2004: Proceedings of the
    Fourteenth Roman Archaeology Conference, Durham 2004*. Oxford: Oxbow
    Books, pp. 133–43.
—— (2007), *Death, Disposal and the Destitute: The Burial of the Urban Poor
    in Italy in the Late Roman Republic and Early Empire* [British Archaeological
    Reports International Series 1565]. Oxford: Archaeopress.
—— (forthcoming). 'From fragments to ancestors: re-defining *os resectum* and
    its role in rituals of purification and commemoration in Republican Rome',
    in M. Carroll and D. Hadley (eds), *Living through the Dead: The Material
    Culture and Social Context of Commemoration of the Dead from Antiquity to
    the Eighteenth century*. Oxford: Oxbow.
Griffin, J. (1985), *Latin Poets and Roman Life*. London: Duckworth.

Griffin, M. (1976), *Seneca: A Philosopher in Politics*. Oxford: Clarendon Press.

—— (1997), 'The Senate's story'. *Journal of Roman Studies*, 87, 249–63.

Grottanelli, C. (1995), 'Wine and death – East and West', in O. Murray and M. Tecuşan (eds), *In Vino Veritas*. Oxford: Alden Press, pp. 62–87.

Hackworth Petersen, L. (2006), *The Freedman in Roman Art and Art History*. Cambridge and New York: Cambridge University Press.

Hales, S. (2003), *The Roman House and Social Identity*. Cambridge: Cambridge University Press.

Handley, M. (2003), *Death, Society and Culture: Inscriptions and Epitaphs in Gaul and Spain, AD 300–750* [British Archaeological Reports, International Series 1135]. Oxford: Archaeopress.

Harlow, M. and Laurence, R. (2002), *Growing Up and Growing Old in Ancient Rome: A Life Course Approach*. London and New York: Routledge.

Harris, W. (1989), *Ancient Literacy*. London and Cambridge, MA: Harvard University Press.

—— (1994), 'Child-exposure in the Roman Empire'. *Journal of Roman Studies*, 54, 1–22.

Hatt, J. J. (1951), *La Tombe Gallo-Romaine*. Paris: Picard.

Hedrick, C. W. (2000), *History and Silence: Purge and Rehabilitation of Memory in Late Antiquity*. Austin: University of Texas Press.

Hemelrijik, E. A. (2004), 'Masculinity and femininity in the *Laudatio Turiae*'. *Classical Quarterly*, 54, 185–97.

Henneberg, M. and Henneberg, R. J. (1999), 'Human skeletal material from Pompeii', in A. Ciarallo and E. De Carolis (eds), *Pompeii: Life in a Roman Town*. Milan: Electa, pp. 51–3.

Hesberg, H. von (1992), *Römische Grabbauten*. Darmstadt: Wissenschaftliche Buchgesellschaft.

Hesberg, H. von and Zanker, P. (1987), *Römische Gräbertrassen: Selbstdarstellung, Status, Standard*. Munich: C. H. Beck.

Heulsen, C. (1890), 'Piante iconografiche incise in marmo'. *Mitteilungen des Deutschen Archäologischen Instituts: Römische Abteilung*, 5, 46–63.

Hill, T. D. (2004), *Ambitiosa Mors: Suicide and Self in Roman Thought and Literature*. New York and London: Routledge.

Hillard, T. W. (2001), 'Popilia and *laudationes funebres* for women'. *Antichthon*, 35, 45–63.

Hinard, F. (1987), *La Mort au Quotidien dans le Monde Romain*. Paris: De Boccard.

—— (1995), *La Mort, les Morts et l'au-delà dans le Monde Romain*. Caen: University of Caen Press.

Hinard, F. and J. C. Dumont (2004), *Libitina: Pompes Funèbres et Supplices en Campanie à l'Époque d'Auguste*. Paris: De Boccard.

Hitchner, R. B. (1995), 'The culture of death and the invention of culture in Roman Africa'. *Journal of Roman Archaeology*, 8, 493–8.

Hockey, J., Katz, J. and Small, N. (eds) (2001), *Grief, Mourning and Death Ritual*. Buckingham, UK and Philadelphia: Open University Press, pp. 185–211.

Hope, V. M. (1997a), 'Words and pictures: the interpretation of Romano-British tombstones'. *Britannia*, 28, 245–58.

—— (1997b), 'A roof over the dead: communal tombs and family structure', in R. Laurence and A. Wallace-Hadrill (eds), *Domestic Space in the Roman World: Pompeii and Beyond* [Journal of Roman Archaeology Supplementary Series 22]. Portsmouth: Journal of Roman Archaeology, pp. 69–88.

—— (1998), 'Negotiating identity and status: the gladiators of Roman Nîmes', in J. Berry and R. Laurence (eds), *Cultural Identity in the Roman Empire*. London: Routledge, pp. 179–95.

—— (2000a), 'Contempt and respect: the treatment of the corpse in ancient Rome', in V. M Hope and E. Marshall (eds), *Death and Disease in the Ancient City*. London: Routledge, pp. 104–27.

—— (2000b), 'Fighting for identity: the funerary commemoration of Italian gladiators', in A. Cooley (ed.), *The Epigraphic Landscape of Roman Italy*. *Bulletin of the Institute of Classical Studies*, Supplement 73. London: Institute of Classical Studies, 93–114.

—— (2000c), 'Inscription and sculpture: the construction of identity in the military tombstones of Roman Mainz', in G. Oliver (ed.), *The Epigraphy of Death: Studies in the History and Society of Greece and Rome*. Liverpool: Liverpool University Press, pp. 155–86.

—— (2000d), 'Status and identity in the Roman world', in J. Huskinson (ed.), *Experiencing Rome: Culture, Identity and Power*. London: Routledge, pp. 125–52.

—— (2001), *Constructing Identity: The Roman Funerary Monuments of Aquileia, Mainz and Nimes* [British Archaeological Report, International Series 960]. Oxford: Archaeopress.

—— (2003), 'Trophies and tombstones: commemorating the Roman soldier', in R. Gilchrist (ed.), *The Social Commemoration of Warfare* [issue title], *World Archaeology*, 35, (1), 79–97.

—— (2007), *Death in Ancient Rome: A Sourcebook*. London and New York: Routledge.

—— (2009), 'At home with the dead: Roman funeral traditions and Trimalchio's tomb', in J. Prag and I. Repath (eds), *Petronius: A Handbook*. London: Blackwells, pp. 140–60.

—— (forthcoming), 'Soldiers of death: the practical and symbolic treatment of the Roman war dead', in D. Burton (ed.), *Good Deaths and Bad Deaths in the*

Ancient World [Bulletin of the Institute of Classical Studies Supplementary Series. London: Institute of Classical Studies.

Hope, V. M. and Marshall, E. (eds) (2000), *Death and Disease in the Ancient City*. London: Routledge.

Hopkins, K. (1964), 'The age of Roman girls at marriage'. *Population Studies*, 18, 309–27.

—— (1966), 'On the probable age structure of the Roman population'. *Population Studies*, 20, 245–64.

—— (1983), *Death and Renewal*. Cambridge: Cambridge University Press.

—— (1987), 'Graveyards for historians', in F. Hinard (ed.), *La Mort, les Morts et l'au-delà dans le Monde Romain*. Caen: University of Caen Press, pp. 113–26.

Horsfall, N. (1985), '*CIL* VI 37965 = *CLE* 1988 (Epitaph of Allia Potestas): a commentary'. *Zeitschrift für Papyrologie und Epigraphik* 61, 251–72.

Houghton, L. (2007), 'The drowned and the saved: shipwrecks and the cursus of Latin love elegy'. *Cambridge Classical Journal*, 53, 161–79.

—— (forthcoming), 'Death ritual and burial practice in the Latin love elegists', in V. M. Hope and J. Huskinson (eds), *Memory and Mourning: Studies on Roman Death*. Oxford: Oxbow.

Hughes, L. A. (2005), 'Centurions at Amiternum: notes on the Apisius family'. *Phoenix*, 59, 77–91.

Humphrey, J. (1991), *Literacy in the Roman World* [Journal of Roman Archaeology Supplementary Series 3]. Portsmouth: Journal of Roman Archaeology.

Hunt, A. S. and Edgar, C. C. (1970), *Select Papyri I: Non-Literary Papyri and Private Affairs*. London and Cambridge, MA: Harvard University Press, Loeb Classical Library. First published 1932.

Huskinson, J. (1996), *Roman Children's Sarcophagi: Their Decoration and its Social Significance*. Oxford: Oxford University Press.

Inwood, B. (2005), *Reading Seneca: Stoic Philosophy at Rome*. Oxford: Oxford University Press.

Jaeger, M. (1997), *Livy's Written Rome*. Ann Arbor: University of Michigan Press.

Jashemski, W. F. (1979), *The Gardens of Pompeii, Herculaneum and the Villas Destroyed by Vesuvius*. New York and New Rochelle, NY: Caratzas Brothers.

Jones, R. F. J. (1991), 'Cultural change in Roman Britain' in R. F. J. Jones (ed.) *Britain in the Roman Period: Recent Trends*. Sheffield: J. R. Collis Publications, pp. 115–20.

Kassel, R. (1958), *Untersuchungen zur griechischen und römischen Konsolationsliteratur*. Munich: C. H. Beck.

Keith, A. (2008), 'Lament in Lucan's Bellum Civile', in A. Suter (ed.), *Lament in the Ancient World and Beyond*. Oxford: Oxford University Press, pp. 233–57.

Keppie, L. (1991), *Understanding Roman Inscriptions*. London: Batsford.

Kierdorf, W. (1980), *Laudatio Funebris: Interpretationem und Untersuchungen zur Entwicklung der Römischen Leichenrede*. Meisenheim am Glam, Germany: Anton Hain.

King, H. (2002), 'De dokter aan het sterfbed'. *Raster*, 99, Special Issue, *Ars Moriendi*, 90–106.

King, M. (2000), 'Commemoration of infants on Roman funerary inscriptions', in G. Oliver (ed.), *The Epigraphy of Death: Studies in the History and Society of Greece and Rome*. Liverpool: Liverpool University Press, pp. 117–54.

Kleiner, D. E. E. (1977), *Roman Group Portraiture: The Funerary Reliefs of the Late Republic and Early Empire*. New York: Garland.

—— (1987), *Roman Imperial Funerary Altars with Portraits*. Rome: G. Bretschneider.

Kockel, V. (1983), *Die Grabbauten vor dem Herkulaner Tor in Pompeji*. Mainz: Zabern.

—— (1993), *Porträtreliefs Stadtrömischer Grabbauten*. Mainz: Zabern.

Koortbojian, M. (1995), *Myth, Meaning and Memory on Roman Sarcophagi*. Berkeley and London: University of California Press.

—— (1996), '*In commemorationem mortuorum*: text and image along the "street of tombs"', in J. Elsner (ed.), *Art and Text in Roman Culture*. Cambridge: Cambridge University Press, pp. 210–33.

Kragelund, P. (2002), 'The emperors, the Licinii Crassi and the Carlsberg Pompey, in in J.Munk Højte ed., *Images of Ancestors*. Aarhus, Denmark: Aarhus University Press, pp. 185–222.

Kyle, D. (1998), *Spectacles of Death in Ancient Rome*. London and New York: Routledge.

Laes, C. (2007), 'Inscriptions from Rome and the history of childhood', in M. Harlow and R. Laurence (eds), *Age and Ageing in the Roman Empire* [Journal of Roman Archaeology Supplementary Series 65]. Portsmouth: Journal of Roman Archaeology, pp. 25–37.

Lanciani, R. (1888), *Ancient Rome in the Light of Recent Discoveries*. Urbana: University of Illinois.

Lassère, J. M. (ed.). (1993), *Les Flavii de Cillium: Étude du Mausolée de Kasserine*. Paris: de Boccard.

Lattimore, R. (1962), *Themes in Greek and Latin Epitaphs*. Urbana, IL: University of Illinois Press.

Le Bohec, Y. (1991), *Le Testament du Lingon: Actes de la Journée d'Études du 16 Mai 1990*. Lyon: de Boccard.

Lelis, A., Percy, W. and Verstraete, B. (2003), *The Age of Marriage in Ancient Rome*. New York: Lewiston.

Lindsay, H. (1998), 'Eating with the dead: the Roman funerary banquet', in

I. Nielsen and H. Sigismund Nielsen (eds), *Meals in a Social Context*. Aarhus, Denmark: Aarhus University Press, pp. 67–80.

—— (2000), 'Death-pollution and funerals in the city of Rome', in V. M. Hope and E. Marshall (eds), *Death and Disease in the Ancient City*. London: Routledge, pp. 152–73.

Littlewood, R. J. (2001), 'Ovid among the family dead: the Roman founder legend and Augustan iconography in Ovid's *Feralia* and *Lemuria*'. *Latomus*, 60, 916–35.

Loraux, N. (1986), *The Invention of Athens: The Funeral Oration in the Classical Greek City*. Cambridge, MA: Harvard University Press.

MacMullen, R. (1982), 'The epigraphic habit in the Roman Empire'. *American Journal of Philology*, 103, 234–46.

Mann, J. C. (1985), 'Epigraphic consciousness'. *Journal of Roman Studies*, 75, 204–6.

Markus, D. D. (2004), 'Grim pleasures: Statius's Poetic *Consolationes*'. *Arethusa*, 37, (1), 105–36.

Martin, D. (1996), 'The construction of the ancient family: methodological considerations'. *Journal of Roman Studies*, 86, 40–60.

Martin-Kilcher, S. (2000), '*Mors immature* in the Roman world – a mirror of society and tradition', in J. Pearce, M. Millet, M. Struck (eds), *Burial, Society and Context in the Roman World*. Oxford: Oxbow: 63–77.

Masters, J. (1992), *Poetry and Civil War in Lucan's Bellum Civile*. Cambridge: Cambridge University Press.

McWilliam, J. (2001), 'Children among the dead: the influence of urban life on the commemoration of children on tombstone inscriptions', in S. Dixon (ed.), *Childhood, Class and Kin in the Roman World*. London and New York: Routledge, pp. 74–98.

Meiggs, R. (1973), *Roman Ostia*. Oxford: Clarendon Press.

Meyer, E. (1990), 'Explaining the epigraphic habit in the Roman Empire: the evidence of epitaphs'. *Journal of Roman Studies*, 80, 74–96.

Miles, G. (1995), *Livy: Reconstructing Early Rome*. New York: Cornell University Press.

Moore, J.P. (2007), 'The mausoleum culture of Africa Proconsularis' in D. Stone and L. Stirling eds., *Mortuary Landscapes of North Africa*. Toronto and London: University of Toronto Press, pp. 75–109.

Morris, I. (1987), *Burial and Ancient Society: The Rise of the Greek City-State*. Cambridge: Cambridge University Press.

—— (1992), *Death-Ritual and Social Structure in Classical Antiquity*. Cambridge: Cambridge University Press.

Mouritsen, H. (2005), 'Freedmen and decurions: epitaphs and social history in Imperial Italy'. *Journal of Roman Studies*, 95, 38–63.

Murdoch, A. (2006), *Rome's Greatest Defeat: Massacre in the Teutoburg Forest.*
Stroud, UK: Sutton Publishing.
Mustakallio, K. (1994), *Death and Disgrace: Capital Penalties with Post Mortem
Sanctions in Early Roman Historiography* [Annales Academiae Scientiarum
Fennica Dissertationes Humanarum Litterarum 72]. Helsinki: Suomalainen
Tiedeakatemia.
—— (2005), 'Roman funerals: identity, gender and participation', in
K. Mustakallio, J. Hansks, H-L. Sanio, V. Vuolanto (eds), *Hoping for
Continuity: Childhood, Education and Death in Antiquity and the Middle
Ages* [Acta Instituti Romani Finlandiae 33]. Rome: Institutum Romanum
Finlandiae, pp. 179–90.
Néraudau, J-P. (1987), 'La loi, la coutume et le chagrin: réflexions sur la mort
des enfants', in F. Hinard (ed.), *La Mort, les Morts et l'au-delà dans le Monde
Romain.* Caen, France: University of Caen Press, pp. 195–208.
Nock, A. D. (1932), 'Cremation and burial in the Roman Empire'. *Harvard
Theological Review* 25, 321–59. Reprinted in *Essays on Religion and the
Ancient World* (1972: two volumes). Oxford: Clarendon Press.
Noelke, P. (1998), 'Grabreliefs mit Mahldarstellung in den germanisch-
gallischen Provinzen – soziale und religiöse Aspekte', in *Bestattungssitte und
Kulturelle Identität. Grabanlagen und Grabbeigaben der Frühen Römischen
Kaiserzeit und den Nordwest Provinzen.* Cologne, pp. 399–418.
Noy, D. (2000a), 'Building a Roman funeral pyre'. *Antichthon*, 34, 30–45.
—— (2000b), 'Half-burnt on an emergency pyre: Roman cremations which
went wrong'. *Greece & Rome*, 47, 186–96.
—— (forthcoming), '"Goodbye Livia": dying in the Roman home', in
V. M. Hope and J. Huskinson (eds), *Memory and Mourning: Studies on
Roman Death.* Oxford: Oxbow.
Ochs, D. J. (1993), *Consolatory Rhetoric: Grief, Symbol and Ritual in the Greco-
Roman Era.* Columbia: University of South Carolina Press.
Ogden, D. (2001), *Greek and Roman Necromancy.* Princeton, NJ, and Oxford,
UK: Princeton University Press.
—— (2002), *Magic, Witchcraft and Ghosts in the Greek and Roman Worlds:
A Sourcebook.* Oxford and New York: Oxford University Press.
—— (2008), *Night's Black Agents: Witches, Wizards and the Dead in the Ancient
World.* London: Hambledon Continuum.
Oliver, A. (2000), 'Jewelry for the unmarried', in D. E. E. Kleiner and
S. B. Matheson (eds), *I Claudia II: Women in Roman Art and Society.* Austin:
University of Texas Press, pp. 115–24.
Papanghelis, T. (1987), *Propertius: A Hellenistic Poet on Love and Death.*
Cambridge: Cambridge University Press.
Parkin, T. (1992), *Demography and Roman Society.* London and Baltimore,

MD: Johns Hopkins University Press.

Patterson, J. R. (1992), 'Patronage, *collegia* and burial in imperial Rome', in S. Bassett (ed.), *Death in Towns*. Leicester: Leicester University Press, pp. 15–27.

—— (2000a), 'Living and dying in the city of Rome: houses and tombs', in J. Coulston and H. Dodge (eds), *Ancient Rome: The Archaeology of the Eternal City* [Oxford University School of Archaeology Monograph 54]. Oxford: Oxford University School of Archaeology, pp. 259–89.

—— (2000b), 'On the margins of the city of Rome', in V. M. Hope and E. Marshall (eds), *Death and Disease in the Ancient City*. London: Routledge, pp. 85–103.

Pearce, J. (2001), 'Infants, cemeteries and communities in the Roman provinces', in G. Davies, A. Garner, and K. Lockyear (eds), *Proceedings of the Theoretical Roman Archaeology Conference 2000*. Oxford: Oxbow, pp. 125–42.

Pearce, J., Millet, M. and Struck, M. (2000), *Burial, Society and Context in the Roman World*. Oxford: Oxbow.

Plass, P. (1995), *The Game of Death in Ancient Rome: Arena Sport and Political Suicide*. Wisconsin: University of Wisconsin Press.

Polfer, M. (2000), 'Reconstructing funerary rituals: the evidence of *ustrina* and related archaeological structures', in J. Pearce, M. Millet and M. Struck (eds), *Burial, Society and Context in the Roman World*. Oxford: Oxbow, pp. 30–7.

Pollini, J. (2007), 'Ritualizing death in Republican Rome: memory, religion, class struggle and the wax ancestral mask tradition's origins and influence on veristic portraiture', in N. Laneri (ed.), *Performing Death: Social Analyses of Funerary Traditions in the Ancient Near East and Mediterranean*. Chicago: University of Chicago Press, pp. 237–85.

Poortman, B. (1994), 'Death and immortality in Greek philosophy, from the Presocratics to the Hellenistic era', in J. M. Bremer, Th. P. J. van den Hout and R. Peters (eds), *Hidden Futures: Death and Immortality in Ancient Egypt, Anatolia, the Classical, Biblical and Arabic-Islamic World*. Amsterdam: Amsterdam University Press, pp. 197–220.

Potter, D. (1994), *Prophets and Emperors: Human and Divine Authority from Augustus to Theodosius*. Cambridge, MA: Harvard University Press.

Potter, D. and Damon, C. (1999), 'The Senatus consultum de Cn. Pisone Patre'. *American Journal of Philology*, 120, (1), 13–40.

Prescendi, F. (1995), 'Il lutto dei padri nella cultura Romana', in F. Hinard (ed.), *La Mort au Quotidien dans le Monde Romain*. Paris: De Boccard, pp. 147–54.

Price, S. (1987), 'From noble funerals to divine cult: the consecration of Roman emperors', in D. Cannadine and S. Price (eds), *Rituals of Royalty: Power and Ceremonial in Traditional Societies*. Cambridge: Cambridge University Press, pp. 56–105.

Purcell, N. (1987), 'Tomb and suburb', in H. von Hesberg and P. Zanker (eds), *Römische Gräbertrassen: Selbstdarstellung, Status, Standard*. Munich: C. H. Beck, pp. 25–42.

Ramage, E. S. (1994), 'The so-called Laudatio Turiae as panegyric'. *Athenaeum*, 82, 341–70.

Rawson, B. (2003), *Children and Childhood in Roman Italy*. Oxford: Oxford University Press.

Reusser, C. (1987), 'Gräberstrassen in Aquileia', in H. von Hesberg and P. Zanker, (eds), *Römische Gräbertrassen: Selbstdarstellung, Status, Standard*. Munich: C. H. Beck, pp. 239–49.

Revell, L. (2005), 'The Roman life course: a view from the inscriptions'. *European Journal of Archaeology*, 8, 43–63.

Richardson, L. (1992), *A New Topographical Dictionary of Ancient Rome*. London and Baltimore, MD: Johns Hopkins University Press.

Richlin, A. (1999), 'Cicero's head', in J. Porter (ed.), *Constructions of the Classical Body*. Ann Arbor: University of Michigan Press, pp. 190–211.

—— (2001), 'Emotional work: Lamenting the Roman Dead', in E. Tylawsky and C. Weiss (eds), *Essays in Honor of Gordon Williams: Twenty-five years at Yale*. New Haven, CT: Schwab, pp. 229–48.

Roller, M. (2006), *Dining Posture in Ancient Rome: Bodies, Values and Status*. Princeton, NJ: Princeton University Press.

Rose, H. J. (1923), 'Nocturnal funerals in Rome'. *Classical Quarterly*, 17, 191–4.

Rushforth, G. (1915), 'Funeral lights in Roman sepulchral monuments'. *Journal of Roman Studies*, 5, 149–64.

Sallares, R. (2002), *Malaria and Rome: A History of Malaria in Ancient Italy*. Oxford: Oxford University Press.

Saller, R. (1987), 'Men's age at marriage and its consequences in the Roman family'. *Classical Philology*, 82, 21–34.

—— (1994), *Patriarchy, Property and Death in the Roman Family*. Cambridge: Cambridge University Press.

Saller, R. and Shaw, B. (1984), 'Tombstones and Roman family relations in the Principate: civilians, soldiers and slaves'. *Journal of Roman Studies*, 74, 124–56.

Scheid, J. (2005), *Quand Faire, c'est Croire : Les Rites Sacrificiels des Romains*. Paris: Aubier.

Scheidel, W. (2001a), 'Roman age structure: evidence and models'. *Journal of Roman Studies*, 91, 1–26.

—— (2001b), 'Progress and problems in Roman demography', in W. Scheidel (ed.), *Debating Roman Demography*. Leiden, Boston, Cologne: Brill, pp. 1–81.

—— (2003), 'Germs for Rome', in C. Edwards and G. Woolf (eds), *Rome the Cosmopolis*. Cambridge: Cambridge University Press, pp. 158–76.

Schoonhoven, H. (1992), *The Pseudo-Ovidian Ad Liviam de Morte Drusi.* Groningen, Netherlands: E. Forsten.

Scobie, A. (1986), 'Slums, sanitation and mortality in the Roman world'. *Klio*, 68, 399–433.

Scott, E. (1990), 'A critical review of the interpretation of infant burials with a particular reference to Roman Britain'. *Journal of Theoretical Archaeology*, 1, 30–46.

—— (1999), *The Archaeology of Infancy and Infant Death* [British Archaeological Reports, International Series 819]. Oxford: Archaeopress.

—— (2001), 'Unpicking a myth: the infanticide of female and disabled infants in antiquity', in G. Davies, A. Garner, and K. Lockyear (eds), *Proceedings of the Theoretical Roman Archaeology Conference 2000.* Oxford: Oxbow, pp. 143–151.

Segal, C. (1990), *Lucretius on Death and Anxiety: Poetry and Philosophy in the De Rerum Natura.* Princeton, NJ: Princeton University Press.

Senatore, F. (1999), 'Necropoli e societa nell'antica Pompei: considerazioni su un sepolcreto di poveri', in F. Senatore (ed.), *Pompei, il Vesuvio e la Penisola Sorrentina.* Rome: Bardi, pp. 91–111.

Shaw, B. (1984), 'Latin funerary epigraphy and family life in the later Roman Empire'. *Historia*, 33, 457–99.

—— (1987), 'The age of Roman girls at marriage: some reconsiderations'. *Journal of Roman Studies*, 77, 30–46.

—— (1991), 'The cultural meaning of death: age and gender in the Roman family', in D. Kertzer and R. Saller (eds), *The Family in Italy: From Antiquity to Present.* London: Routledge, pp. 66–90.

—— (1996), 'Seasons of death: aspects of mortality in Imperial Rome'. *Journal of Roman Studies*, 86, 100–38.

Sigismund Nielsen, H. (1996), 'The physical context of Roman epitaphs and the structure of the "Roman family"'. *Analecta Romana Instituti Danici*, 23, 35–60.

—— (1997), 'Interpreting epithets in Roman epitaphs', in B. Rawson and P. Weaver (eds), *The Roman Family in Italy: Status, Sentiment, Space.* Oxford and Canberra: Clarendon Press, pp. 169–204.

—— (2007), 'Children for profit and pleasure', in M. Harlow and R. Laurence (eds), *Age and Ageing in the Roman Empire* [Journal of Roman Archaeology Supplementary Series 65]. Portsmouth: Journal of Roman Archaeology, pp. 39–54.

Sinn, F. (1987), *Stadtrömische Marmorurnen.* Mainz: Zabern.

Sinn, F. and Freyberger, K. (1996), *Vatikanische Museen: Museo Gregorio Profano ex Lateranense: Die Grabdenkmäler 2: Die Ausstattung des Hateriergrabes.* Mainz: Zabern.

Solmsen, F. (1972), 'The world of the dead in Book 6 of the *Aeneid*'. *Classical Philology*, 67, 31–41.

Sourvinou-Inwood, C. (1995), *'Reading' Greek Death: To the End of the Classical Period*. Oxford: Clarendon Press.

Spaeth, B. S. (1996), *The Roman Goddess Ceres*. Austin: University of Texas.

Stears, K. (1998), 'Death becomes her: gender and Athenian death ritual', in S. Blundell and M. Williamson (eds), *The Sacred and the Feminine in Ancient Greece*. London and New York: Routledge, pp. 89–100.

Stevens, S. (1991), 'Charon's obol and other coins in ancient funerary practice'. *Phoenix*, 45, 215–29.

Stone, D. and Stirling, L. (eds.), *Mortuary Landscapes of North Africa*. Toronto and London: University of Toronto Press.

Stirling, L. (2007), 'The *koine* of *cupula* in Roman North Africa and the transition from cremation to inhumation' in D. Stone and L. Stirling, (eds), *Mortuary Landscapes of North Africa*. Toronto and London: University of Toronto Press, pp. 110–37.

Strubbe, J. H. M. (1991), 'Cursed be he that moves my bones', in C. Faraone and D. Obbink (eds), *Magika Hiera*. New York: Oxford University Press, pp. 33–59.

Sumi, G. S. (1997), 'Power and ritual: the crowd at Clodius' funeral'. *Historia*, 46, 80–102.

—— (2002), 'Impersonating the dead: mimes at Roman funerals'. *American Journal of Philology*, 123, 559–85.

Suter, A. (2008), *Lament: Studies in the Ancient Mediterranean and Beyond*. Oxford: Oxford University Press.

Taylor, L. R. (1961), 'Freedmen and freeborn in the epitaphs of Imperial Rome'. *American Journal of Philology*, 82, 113–32.

Thylander H. (1952), *Inscriptions du Port d'Ostie*. Lund: C. W. K. Gleerup.

Toynbee, J. M. C. (1971), *Death and Burial in the Roman World*. London: Thames and Hudson.

Tranoy, L. (2000), 'The living and the dead: approaches to landscape around Lyons', in J. Pearce, M. Millet and M. Struck (eds), *Burial, Society and Context in the Roman World*. Oxford: Oxbow, pp. 162–8.

Treggiari, S. (1991), *Roman Marriage: Iusti Coniuges from the time of Cicero to the time of Ulpian*. Oxford: Clarendon Press.

—— (1999), 'The upper-class house as a symbol and focus of emotion in Cicero'. *Journal of Roman Archaeology*, 12, 33–56.

Tupman, C. (2005), 'The *cupae* of Iberia in their monumental contexts: a study of the relationship between social status and commemoration with barrel-shaped and semi-cylindrical tombstones', in J. Bruhn, B. Croxford and D. Grigoropoulos (eds), *TRAC 2004: Proceedings of the Fourteenth Roman Archaeology Conference, Durham 2004*. Oxford: Oxbow Books, pp. 119–32.

Turcan, R. (2001), *The Gods of Ancient Rome: Religion in Everyday Life from the Archaic to Imperial Times*. Edinburgh: Edinburgh University Press.

Tylawsky, E. (2001), 'Supplying a genealogy: self promotion and praising dead women' in E. Tylawsky and C. Weiss (eds), *Essays in Honor of Gordon Williams: Twenty-five years at Yale*. New Haven, CT: Schwab, pp. 249–60.

Van Hooff, A. J. L. (1990), *From Autothanasia to Suicide: Self-killing in Classical Antiquity*. London and New York: Routledge.

—— (2003), 'The imperial art of dying', in L. de Blois, P. Erkamp, O. Hesker, G. de Kleijn and S. Mols (eds)., *The Representation and Perception of Roman Imperial Power*. Amsterdam: Gieben, pp. 99–116.

—— (2004), 'Ancient euthanasia: "good death" and the doctor in the Graeco-Roman world'. *Social Science and Medicine*, 58, (5), 975–85.

Van Nijf, O. (1997), *The Civic World of Professional Associations in the Roman East*. Amsterdam: Gieben.

Varner, E. R. (2001a), 'Portraits, plots and politics: *damnatio memoriae* and the images of Imperial women'. *Memoirs of the American Academy at Rome*, 46, 41–93.

—— (2001b), 'Punishment after death: mutilation of images and corpse abuse in ancient Rome'. *Mortality*, 6, 45–76.

—— (2004), *Mutilation and Transformation: Damnatio Memoriae and Roman Imperial Portraiture*. Leiden, Boston and Cologne: Brill.

Vermeule, E. (1979), *Aspects of Death in Early Greek Art and Poetry*. Berkeley and Los Angeles: University of California Press.

Voisin, J. L. (1984), 'Les Romains, chasseurs de têtes', in *Du Châtiment dans la Cité: Supplices Corporels et Peine de Mort dans le Monde Antique* [Collection de l'École Française de Rome 79]. Rome: l'École Française de Rome, pp. 241–93.

Walker, S. (1985), *Memorials to the Roman Dead*. London: British Museum Press.

—— (1990), *Catalogue of Roman Sarcophagi in the British Museum: Corpus Signorum Imperii Romani, Great Britain* II.2. London:British Museum Press.

Walter, T. (1999), *On Bereavement: The Culture of Grief*. Buckingham, UK: Open University Press.

Warde Fowler, W. (1912), 'Mundus Patet: 24th August, 5th October, 8th November'. *Journal of Roman Studies*, 2, 25–33.

Warren, J. (2004), *Facing Death: Epicurus and his Critics*. Oxford: Oxford University Press.

Weekes, J. (2005), 'Reconstructing syntheses in Romano-British cremation', in J. Bruhn, B. Croxford and D. Grigoropoulos (eds), *TRAC 2004: Proceedings of the Fourteenth Roman Archaeology Conference, Durham 2004*. Oxford: Oxbow Books, pp. 16–26.

Wesch-Klein, G. (1993), *Funus Publicum: Eine Studie zur öffentlichen Beisetzung und Gewährung von Ehrengräbern in Rom und den Westprovinzen*. Stuttgart: F. Steiner.

Whitehead, J. (1993), 'The "Cena Trimalchionis" and biographical narration in Roman middle-class art', in P. Holliday (ed.), *Narrative and Event in Ancient Art*. Cambridge: Cambridge University Press, pp. 299–325.

Wiedemann, T. (1992), *Emperors and Gladiators*. London: Routledge.

Wilcox, A. (2005a), 'Sympathetic rivals: consolation in Cicero's letters'. *American Journal of Philology*, 126, (2), 237–55.

—— (2005b), 'Paternal grief and the public eye: Cicero *ad Familiares* 4.6'. *Phoenix*, 59, (3–4), 267–87.

—— (2006), 'Exemplary grief: gender and virtue in Seneca's Consolations to Women'. *Helios*, 33, (1), 73–100.

Williams, J. (2001), *Beyond the Rubicon: Romans and Gauls in Republican Italy*. Oxford: Oxford University Press.

Wilson, M. (1997), 'The subjugation of grief in Seneca's Epistles', in S. Morton Braund and C. Gill (eds), *The Passions in Roman Thought and Literature*. Cambridge: Cambridge University Press, pp. 48–67.

Wistrand, E. (1976), *The So-called Laudatio Turiae: Introduction, Text, Translation, Commentary*. Lund: Acta Universitatis Gothoburgensia.

Wood, S. (2000), 'Mortals, empresses, and earth goddesses: Demeter and Persephone in public and private apotheosis', in D. E. E. Kleiner and S. B. Matheson (eds), *I Claudia II: Women in Roman Art and Society*. Austin: University of Texas Press, pp. 77–99.

Woolf, G. (1996), 'Monumental writing and the expansion of Roman society in the early Roman Empire'. *Journal of Roman Studies*, 86, 22–39.

—— (1998), *Becoming Roman: The Origins of Provincial Civilization in Gaul*. Cambridge: Cambridge University Press.

Worden, J. W. (2003), *Grief Counselling and Grief Therapy: A Handbook for the Mental Health Practitioner*. New York and Hove, England, and New York: Psychology Press.

Wrede, H. (1981), *Consecratio in Formam Deorum: Vergöttlichte Privatpersonen in der Römischen Kaiserzeit*. Mainz: Zabern.

Wright, R. and Richmond, I. (1956), *Catalogue of Roman Inscribed and Sculpted Stones in the Grosvenor Museum Chester*. Chester: Chester and North Wales Archaeological Society.

Zanker, P. (1975), 'Grabreliefs Römischer Freigelassener'. *Jahrbuch des Deutschen Archäologischen Instituts*, 90, 267–315.

Index